D1552576

MOLOTOV

ALSO BY GEOFFREY ROBERTS

The History and Narrative Reader (2001) (editor)
Ireland and the Second World War (2000) (coedited with Brian Girvin)
The Soviet Union and the Origins of the Second World War (1995)
The Soviet Union in World Politics: Coexistence, Revolution, and Cold War, 1945–1991 (1998)
Stalin: His Times and Ours (2005) (editor)
Stalin's Wars: From World War to Cold War, 1939–1953 (2006)
The Unholy Alliance: Stalin's Pact with Hitler (1989)
Victory at Stalingrad: The Battle That Changed History (2002)

ALSO IN THE SHAPERS OF INTERNATIONAL HISTORY SERIES

Edited by Melvyn P. Leffler, University of Virginia

Dean Acheson and the Creation of an American World Order
—Robert J. McMahon (2009)

Vladimir Putin and Russian Statecraft
—Allen C. Lynch (2011)

ADDITIONAL FORTHCOMING TITLES IN THE SHAPERS OF INTERNATIONAL HISTORY SERIES

Deng Xiaoping–Warren Cohen
Fidel Castro–Piero Gleijeses
George Kennan–Frank Costigliola
Henry Kissinger–Jeremi Suri
Ho Chi Minh–Robert K. Brigham
Jimmy Carter–Nancy Mitchell
Konrad Adenauer–Ronald Granieri
Madeleine Albright–Peter Ronayne
Mikhail Gorbachev–Robert English
Robert McNamara–Fredrik Logevall
Ronald Reagan–Nancy Tucker
Yasser Arafat–Omar Dajani
Zhou Enlai–Chen Jian

MOLOTOV
STALIN'S COLD WARRIOR

GEOFFREY ROBERTS

Sʜᴀᴘᴇʀs ᴏғ Iɴᴛᴇʀɴᴀᴛɪᴏɴᴀʟ
Hɪsᴛᴏʀʏ Sᴇʀɪᴇs

Edited by Melvyn P. Leffler, University of Virginia

Potomac Books
Washington, D.C.

Library of Congress Cataloging-in-Publication Data
Roberts, Geoffrey, 1952–
 Molotov : Stalin's cold warrior / Geoffrey Roberts.–1st ed.
 p. cm.
 Includes bibliographical references and index.
 ISBN 978-1-57488-945-1 (hardcover: alk. paper)
 ISBN 978-1-61234-429-4 (electronic edition)
 1. Molotov, Vyacheslav Mikhaylovich, 1890–1986. 2. Statesmen–Soviet Union–Biography. 3. Soviet Union–Politics and government. I. Title.
 DK268.M64R63 2011
 947.084'2092–dc23
 [B]
 2011023384

Printed in the United States of America on acid-free paper that meets the American National Standards Institute Z39-48 Standard.

Potomac Books
22841 Quicksilver Drive
Dulles, Virginia 20166

First Edition

In memory of Eduard Mark (1943–2009)

CONTENTS

ILLUSTRATIONS

SERIES EDITOR'S FOREWORD

by Melvin P. Leffler

As human beings, we are interested in our leaders. What they say and do has a profound impact on our lives. They can lead us into war or help to shape the peace; they can help promote trade and prosperity or sink us into poverty; they can focus on fighting terror or combating disease, or do both, or neither.

We also know that they are not as strong and powerful as they pretend to be. They, too, are enveloped by circumstances that they cannot control. They are the products of their time, buffeted by technological innovations, economic cycles, social change, cultural traditions, and demographic trends that are beyond their reach. But how they react to matters they cannot control matters a great deal. Their decisions accrue and make a difference.

This series focuses on leaders who have shaped international relations during the modern era. It will consider those who were elected to high office and those who were not, and those who led revolutionary movements as well as those who sought to preserve the status quo. It will include leaders of powerful states and those of weak nations who nevertheless had the capacity to influence international events extending well beyond the power of the country they led. This series will deal with presidents and dictators, foreign secretaries and defense ministers, diplomats and soldiers.

The books in the series are designed to be short, evocative, and provocative. They seek to place leaders in the context of their times. How were they influenced by their families, their friends, their class, their status, their religion, and their traditions? What values did they inculcate and seek to disseminate? How did their education and careers influence their perception of national interests and their understanding of threats? What did they hope to achieve as leaders, and how did they seek to accomplish their goals? In what ways and to what extent were they able to overcome constraints and shape the evolution of international history? What made them effective leaders? And to what extent were they truly agents of change?

The authors are experts in their field writing for the general reader. They have been asked to look at the forest, not the trees, to extrapolate important insights from complex circumstances, and to make bold generalizations. The aim here is to make readers think about big issues and important developments, to make readers wrestle with the perplexing and enduring question of human agency in history.

In this book Geoffrey Roberts provides a provocative reassessment of Vyacheslav Mikhailovich Molotov, the foreign minister of the Soviet Union for much of the time from 1939 to 1955. We see Molotov as a deeply committed communist, eager to overthrow the tsar and eradicate an unjust capitalist order, as he perceived it. Molotov aligned himself with Joseph Stalin in the early days of the revolution and became a loyal, efficient, and dedicated assistant. He supported collectivization and rapid industrialization, and willingly engaged in the purges of the mid- and late 1930s. Molotov believed there were enemies who sought to overthrow the new order and they had to be killed. This was the regrettable price that had to be paid in pursuit of a utopian revolution that, in Molotov's view, would ameliorate the human condition. Roberts forces us to ponder such contradictions, contradictions that bedevil the human experience.

He also argues that Molotov mattered. Using new archival materials, Roberts shows that Molotov was an independent thinker, that he often viewed things differently than Stalin, and that he was confident enough of his relationship with the dictator that he could express his views. Of course, once Stalin decided what he wanted to be done diplomatically, Molotov not only went along but also could be relied upon to implement Stalin's will with a tenacity and skill that exasperated negotiators and interlocutors.

But Molotov also mattered because after Stalin's death in 1953, he championed important changes in Soviet foreign policy. Radically reassessing Molotov, Roberts claims that Molotov never welcomed the Cold War and sought to alter its trajectory as soon as he could. Fearing Germany and hating NATO, Molotov worked tirelessly to shape a pan-European system of collective security, end the Cold War, and unite Europe. He championed what later became known as détente and launched initiatives that would eventually culminate in the Helsinki Accords of 1975 and the Conference on Security and Cooperation in Europe (CSCE) process.

By this time, of course, Molotov had long since been purged from a leadership position in the party. After Nikita Khrushchev outmaneuvered him, Molotov lived for almost three decades in quiet retirement. But during his four decades as a revolutionary leader and Soviet official, he helped shape the history of the twentieth century.

PREFACE AND ACKNOWLEDGMENTS

When Melvyn Leffler asked me to contribute a volume on Molotov to this series, I was finishing up some research in the Russian archives on Soviet foreign policy in the post-Stalin era. I had been trying to figure out who was responsible for important changes in Soviet foreign policy after Stalin's death, not least of which were Moscow's efforts to end the Cold War and reverse the postwar polarization of Europe into competing military-political blocs. The conventional view was that Georgii Malenkov, the new Soviet prime minister, was responsible, or Nikita Khrushchev, Stalin's successor as leader of the Communist Party of the Soviet Union (CPSU). There were even those who argued that Lavrentii Beria, the security chief, was the most enlightened and liberal foreign policy advocate in the post-Stalin leadership.

But these interpretations did not make sense in light of the evidence I had found in the archives, which showed clearly how the initiative for change had come from the Foreign Ministry. Since Molotov himself had a reputation as a conservative hardliner, my first thought was that mid-level officials in the Foreign Ministry—the people who wrote the policy documents I was reading—were responsible for the innovations in foreign policy. However, when a Russian colleague, Alexei Filitov, pointed out the officials could only be acting in accordance with Molotov's wishes, the scales fell from my eyes. It was Molotov who drove the changes in post-Stalin Soviet foreign policy. So Mel's proposal that I conduct a wide-ranging reappraisal of Molotov's career as Soviet foreign minister could not have come at a better time. The result is a book that challenges the traditional stereotype of Molotov as simply Stalin's acquiescent sidekick and asserts the importance of his independent role as a shaper of mid-twentieth-century international history.

My study of Molotov is based primarily on my own archival research (all excerpts of original documents are my own translations, unless otherwise noted). Over the years I have been fortunate to access hundreds of Molotov files in the archives of the Russian Foreign Ministry, and I would like to acknowledge the help of archive staff in this regard. Another important source was the documents contained in Molotov's *lichnyi fond* (personal file series) in the Russian State Archive of Social-Political History (Russian abbreviation: RGASPI)– the archive that houses the pre-1953 files of the Soviet Communist Party. The post-1953 party files are held by the Russian State Archive of Recent History (RGANI). A substantial microfilm collection of the RGANI files for the mid-1950s is held by Mark Kramer's Cold War Studies Program at Harvard University. Accessing these collections would have been impossible without the support of various funding bodies: University College Cork's College of Arts, Celtic Studies and Social Sciences; the Irish Research Council for Humanities and Social Sciences; and the Fulbright Commission, Ireland. Grants from the Kennan Institute for Advanced Russian Studies and the Eisenhower Presidential Library enabled me to do invaluable research in American archives.

I am not the first scholar to study Molotov, and I have benefited greatly from the research of other historians. Of particular importance was the late Derek Watson's 2005 biography of Molotov, a work that no serious scholar of Soviet history can afford to be without. I would also like to acknowledge Albert Resis's translation of Molotov's unofficial memoir compiled from conversations with Felix Chuev, a source quoted frequently in the pages that follow. When I first read that book, I was skeptical of its value, wondering what words Molotov had actually said and what the journalist had attributed to him. But since I have had the opportunity to read Molotov's *lichnyi fond* files dating from the time of those conversations, I am now convinced the book is a fairly accurate reflection of Molotov's thinking.

An opportunity to present an outline of my revisionist account of Molotov to a highly informed seminar audience was provided by the Norwegian Nobel Institute when I was a senior research fellow there in 2008. The institute has an outstanding library, and I am grateful to director Geir Lundestad and his staff for all the help they gave me. I was particularly intrigued to learn that Molotov had been nominated for the Nobel Peace Prize in 1948.

Professor Jay Calvitt Clarke was kind enough to read the whole manuscript, and I am immensely grateful to him for his detailed comments and corrections, which have helped to improve the text enormously. Thanks also to Mel Leffler and the publisher's anonymous referee for their incisive comments and advice, which prompted a major revision of the book's first draft. Among the many colleagues with whom I have discussed Molotov over the years are the late Lev Bezymensky, Michael Carley, Gabriel Gorodetsky, Warren Kimble, David Painter, Caroline Kennedy-Pipe, Mark Kramer, Jochen Laufer, Sergei Listikov, Victor Mal'kov, Mikhail Myagkov, Vladimir Pechatnov, Silvio Pons, Oleg Rzheshevsky, Geoffrey Warner, Deborah Welch Larson, and Natalia Yegorova. I would also like to thank the Potomac editorial team, Hilary Claggett and Julie Gutin, and Don McKeon for doing such a thorough copyediting job. If there are any more mistakes, they are my own.

I had many conversations and exchanges about Molotov with Eduard Mark, the person to whom this book is dedicated. Eduard and I met through H-Diplo, the H-Net Internet discussion list for historians of international relations. We came together through our overlapping interpretations of Stalin's postwar foreign policy in that we both identified his agenda as being driven by ideology, but an ideology more sophisticated, flexible, and contingent than the crude oversimplifications posited by Western cold warriors. Eduard, an outstanding American historian of the early Cold War, died in 2009. He hated to be labeled, but I'd like to think our shared view was a dynamic synthesis of his posttraditionalism and my postrevisionism. We also agreed that scholars must go wherever the evidence takes us, even if that means ruffling colleagues' feathers and being unpopular in some quarters.

The publisher's anonymous reviewer, who praised and criticized the manuscript in equal measure, wondered if in the book there was "a 'politics' at work, meaning a general worldview–or epistemological understanding of history–that influenced [its] judgments." My philosophy of history is quite simple: individuals matter, and it is people's choices that make the difference in history. Within that perspective I do not see the Cold War as inevitable, and neither do I believe it had to go on as long as it did. The history of the Cold War is littered with missed opportunities to bring it to an end, including Molotov's own abortive efforts after Stalin's death. As for my politics, the story is a little more complicated, but I consider myself to be a liberal social democrat capable of discerning both the good and the bad in the history of the Soviet experiment in socialism. I was not sorry when the Soviet system collapsed in 1991, although I do think the transition to capitalism in Russia could have been better managed and more gradual. As a citizen I take an ethical stance on many issues—which I will gladly share—but as a historian I do not see it as my job to pass moral judgment on Soviet communism and its leaders. That would be too easy. I hope this book contributes toward a greater understanding of the complexities and paradoxes of Soviet history. Molotov's life and career was an embodiment of those contradictions.

In an earlier book I wrote that I was running out of superlatives to describe the importance of the editorial and intellectual input of my partner, Celia Weston. Well, I have now run out, so I can only add another heartfelt thank-you.

TIME LINE OF MAJOR EVENTS
IN MOLOTOV'S LIFE AND CAREER

1890	March 9: Birth of Vyacheslav Mikhailovich Molotov (né Skryabin) in Kukarka, Vyatka Province, central Russia
1905	Revolution in Russia
1906	Molotov joins the Russian Social Democratic and Labor Party
1909	Molotov arrested and sentenced to two years' exile in Vologda Province
1912	Molotov meets Stalin in St. Petersburg
1914	July: Outbreak of World War I
1915	Molotov arrested and exiled to Siberia
1916	Molotov escapes from exile and returns to St. Petersburg (now Petrograd); becomes member of the Russian Buro of the Bolshevik Central Committee
1917	March: Tsar Nicholas II resigns; provisional government formed
	April: Lenin returns to Russia from exile abroad
	November: Bolshevik coup overthrows the provisional government
1918	Beginning of Russian Civil War
1919	March: Establishment of the Communist International (Comintern)
1920	March: Molotov elected candidate member of the Communist Party Central Committee
1921	March: Molotov elected full member of the Central Committee and candidate member of the Politburo
	Summer: Molotov marries Polina Zhemchuzhina
1922	April: Stalin becomes general secretary of the Communist Party
1924	January: Death of Lenin

1926	January: Molotov elected full member of the Politburo; becomes member of the Executive Committee of the Comintern
1928	Molotov becomes secretary of the Moscow party organization
1930	December: Molotov becomes chairman of the Council of People's Commissars
1934	January: Seventeenth Party Congress
	December: Assassination of Sergei Kirov in Leningrad
1936	August: First Stalinist show trial of Old Bolsheviks
1937	January: Second Stalinist show trial of Old Bolsheviks
1938	March: Third Stalinist show trial of Old Bolsheviks
1939	May: Molotov appointed people's commissar for foreign affairs
	August: Molotov signs the Nazi-Soviet Pact
	September: Outbreak of World War II; Soviet invasion of Eastern Poland; signature of Soviet-German Boundary and Friendship Treaty
	December: Soviet attack on Finland
1940	March: Soviet-Finnish peace treaty; celebrations of Molotov's fiftieth birthday
	June: Fall of France
	July: Incorporation of Baltic states into the USSR
	November: Molotov-Hitler-Ribbentrop talks in Berlin
1941	May: Stalin becomes chairman of the Council of People's Commissars, with Molotov as his deputy
	June: German invasion of the USSR; Molotov radio-broadcasts the news to the Soviet people; establishment of the State Defense Committee with Stalin as chair and Molotov his deputy
	July: Soviet-British agreement on joint action against Germany
	December: Molotov-Stalin-Eden negotiations in Moscow; United States enters the war; Red Army counteroffensive at Moscow
1942	May–June: Molotov travels to London and Washington; signature of British-Soviet Treaty of Alliance
	August: Churchill-Stalin conference in Moscow
	November: Stalingrad counteroffensive
1943	April: German announcement of discovery of mass graves at Katyn; breakdown of Soviet-Polish relations
	May: Dissolution of Comintern
	October: Molotov chairs Moscow Conference of Foreign Ministers
	November–December: Tehran summit

1944   August: Warsaw Uprising

August–September: Dumbarton Oaks Conference

October: Churchill-Stalin conference in Moscow

1945   February: Yalta Conference

April: Death of Roosevelt; Truman becomes president

April: Molotov meets Truman in Washington and travels to San Francisco for the founding conference of the United Nations

May: Germany surrenders

July–August: Potsdam Conference

August: Atom bombs dropped on Hiroshima and Nagasaki; Japan surrenders

September: First meeting of the Council of Foreign Ministers in London

November: Molotov speech on the anniversary of the Russian Revolution

December: Moscow meeting of the American, British, and Soviet foreign ministers

1946   March: Churchill's Iron Curtain speech; "commissars" become "ministers"

July–October: Paris Peace Conference

1947   February: Signing of peace treaties with Bulgaria, Finland, Hungary, Italy, and Romania

March: Truman Doctrine speech

March–April: Moscow meeting of the Council of Foreign Ministers

June: Marshall Plan speech

September: Zhdanov's two-camps speech; founding of the Cominform

1948   January: Molotov nominated for the Nobel Peace Prize

June: Soviet blockade of Berlin (ends May 1949)

June: Yugoslavia expelled from the Cominform

August: World Congress of Intellectuals for Peace in Wroclaw

December: Arrest of Molotov's wife

1949   March: Molotov removed as foreign minister

April: Establishment of NATO

May: Establishment of West German state

August: Soviet A-bomb test

October: Establishment of East German state; People's Republic of China proclaimed in Beijing

1950   February: Sino-Soviet Treaty signed
        March: Launch of the Stockholm Petition to ban nuclear weapons
        June: North Korea invades South Korea
        October: Prague Declaration on German remilitarization
1951   January: Kremlin conference on the rearmament of the Eastern bloc
        March–June: Paris conference of the deputy foreign ministers of
        the USSR, France, Britain, and the United States
1952   March: "Molotov Note" proposing a German peace treaty
        October: Nineteenth Party Congress
1953   March: Stalin's death; Molotov reinstated as foreign minister and
        reunited with his wife
        June: Uprising in East Germany
        July: Beria plenum of the Central Committee; end of the Korean War
1954   January–February: Berlin Conference of Foreign Ministers
        March: Molotov proposes that the Soviet Union join NATO
        April–July: Geneva Conference on Korea and Indochina
        October: West Germany joins NATO
1955   May: Signatures of the Warsaw Pact and the Austrian State Treaty
        July: Plenum of the Central Committee; Geneva Summit
        October–November: Geneva Conference of Foreign Ministers
1956   February: Twentieth Party Congress
        June: Removal of Molotov as foreign minister
        October–November: Polish and Hungarian crises
1957   June: Plenum of the Central Committee; Molotov and members
        of the anti-party group expelled from the leadership
        August: Molotov appointed ambassador to Mongolia
1960   April: Beginning of the Sino-Soviet split
        July: Molotov posted to Vienna
1961   October: Molotov and anti-party group denounced at Twenty-
        second Party Congress
1962   March: Molotov expelled from the Communist Party
        June: Molotov recalled from Vienna
1963   September: Molotov retired
1964   October: Khrushchev ousted from power
1970   April: Death of Molotov's wife
1984   July: Molotov's membership of the Communist Party restored
1986   November 8: Molotov dies

1

INTRODUCTION:
"THE KREMLIN'S BRILLIANT MEDIOCRITY"

Not often, but sometimes I dream of Stalin. In extraordinary situations. In a destroyed city. I can't find a way out. Then I meet him. In a word, strange dreams, very confused.

— V. M. Molotov (ca. 1976)[1]

The orthodox view of Vyacheslav Mikhailovich Molotov is that he was no more than Stalin's faithful servant, a dogmatic communist and a conservative hardliner of little or no imagination. Ruthless and efficient in the service of his master and the authoritarian Soviet regime, Molotov had little else to offer the world apart from these dubious qualities. Winston Churchill famously described him as "the agent and instrument of the policy of an incalculable machine" and claimed he had "never seen a human being who more perfectly represented the modern conception of a robot." Yet Churchill thought highly of Molotov's skills as a diplomat, comparing him to the great realpolitik statesmen of the nineteenth century: "in the conduct of foreign affairs, Mazarin, Talleyrand, and Metternich would welcome him to their company," Churchill said. Such grudging admiration was typical of Western reactions to Molotov. "The Kremlin's Brilliant Mediocrity" was the oxymoronic headline on a *New York Times* profile of Molotov in 1954.

From the 1920s right through to the 1950s, Molotov was Soviet dictator Joseph Stalin's right-hand man. In 1930 Stalin appointed Molotov his prime minister, and together the two men presided over a maelstrom of mass violence and political terror that resulted in the deaths of several million Soviet citizens. In 1939, on the eve of World War II, Stalin made Molotov his people's commissar for foreign affairs, a post he held until 1949 when a dispute over the expulsion of Molotov's wife from the Communist Party prompted a temporary falling out with the Soviet dictator. As foreign affairs commissar Molotov signed the Nazi-Soviet Pact of 1939, played a central role in maintaining the Grand Alliance of Britain, the United States, and the USSR during the war, and in the aftermath helped to forge the communist bloc that fought the West in the long Cold War that began in 1947.

This book proposes a radical reappraisal of Molotov as Soviet foreign minister and challenges the orthodox view of him as an unthinking, brutal servant. His life and career were more complex and more contradictory than is suggested by that crude stereotype or by his self-presentations when an old man. Most important, Molotov was not the foreign policy hawk he was reputed to be, but a strategic dove. Stalin was by far the more enthusiastic cold warrior, and Molotov did his job by representing Stalin's hardline stance in public. When the Grand Alliance broke up after World War II, it fell to Molotov to defend Soviet interests in the global struggle to wield power and to influence the postwar world. He was identified as the public face of Soviet intransigence in the often-acrimonious negotiations with the Western powers about the details of a postwar peace settlement. James F. Byrnes, President Truman's secretary of state, dubbed Molotov "Mr. Nyet"–the man who persistently vetoed Western proposals for the peace settlement. Thus Molotov's role during the Cold War became the main source of the caricature that depicts him as an inveterate foreign policy hardliner.

In reality, Molotov strove to end the Cold War almost as soon as it began, and he continued these efforts with renewed vigor when he was reappointed Soviet foreign minister after Stalin's death in 1953. During the post-Stalin period, Molotov sought a radical détente with the West in the form of an all-embracing system of European collective security that would have ended the Cold War and halted the division of Europe into competing military-political blocs. Among the many obstacles to the realization of Molotov's vision was the opposition of Nikita Khrushchev, Stalin's successor as head of the Communist Party. In 1957 Molotov tried and failed to oust Khrushchev from power and, outmaneuvered by his rival, was expelled from the party leadership and then from the party itself in 1962. Molotov ended his political career serving in lowly diplomatic posts in Mongolia and Austria, and was not readmitted to the Communist Party until 1984. When Molotov died in 1986 at the age of ninety-six, there was no public fanfare to mark his passing. The reform-minded Mikhail Gorbachev was now the Soviet leader, and he had no interest in rehabilitating an unrepentant old Stalinist like Molotov.

It had suited Khrushchev and his followers to steal Molotov's foreign policy clothes and to bolster the stereotype of him as a militant cold warrior, as an opponent of détente with the West, and as a devotee of outmoded, fundamentalist political and ideological views––not least his continued loyalty to the memory of Stalin. Ironically, in his old age Molotov reinforced this caricature of himself. He wrote no memoirs, but from the late 1960s to the early 1980s he regularly reminisced in conversations with the Soviet journalist and poet Felix Chuev. When Chuev published a Russian-language edition of his *One Hundred and Forty Conversations with Molotov* in 1991 (later published in English as *Molotov Remembers*), it was not clear to what extent the journalist had attributed words to Molotov that were not his own. However, subsequent research into Molotov's personal files in the Russian archives has revealed that what Chuev reported was broadly in line with Molotov's views as expressed in numerous articles written, but unpublished, during his retirement years.

Like his rambling talks with Chuev, the main theme of Molotov's unpublished articles was a staunch defense of his old boss. Stalin was not a political genius like Vladimir Lenin, Molotov told Chuev, but he was a great man who had played an indispensable role in safeguarding and building the Soviet communist system. Molotov also defended strongly his and Stalin's acts of repression against millions of people in the 1930s as a necessary purging of an internal enemy, or "fifth column," in Soviet society. There had been mistakes and excesses, admitted Molotov, but the policy of terror to secure the socialist system was basically correct and "the principal responsibility rested with Stalin and those of us who approved it and were active in and stood for adopting those measures. And I had always been active and stood for adopting these measures. I never regretted and will never regret that we acted very harshly. But mistakes did occur."[2]

Yet this was the politician of whom John Foster Dulles, Eisenhower's secretary of state, wrote that "observing in action all the great world statesmen of our century, I never came across diplomatic skills at as high a level as those of

Molotov."[3] And a frustrated Byrnes may have called Molotov "Mr. Nyet," but he penned this almost affectionate portrait of him "in action" during postwar peace treaty negotiations:

> If we are correctly informed about the patience exercised by Job, I am certain Mr. Molotov is one of his lineal descendants. He has unlimited patience as well as a fine mind and tremendous energy. Any exhibition of impatience or bad temper by others gives him amusement. At such times it is interesting to watch his serious, solemn expression as he protests his innocence of any provocation. . . . Mr. Molotov likes to discuss questions of procedure. In such discussions he has no equal. He will argue for hours about what subjects should be placed on an agenda. . . . In any conference . . . he will win your reluctant admiration for the resourcefulness he exhibits in his delaying tactics. He will sit through it all imperturbably, stroking his mustache or spinning his pince-nez glasses as he waits for a translation and smoking Russian cigarettes in what seems to be an endless chain.[4]

COMMITTED COMMUNIST

One respect in which the crudely drawn caricature of Molotov was accurate is that he was indeed a hardline, doctrinaire communist, a true believer in the tenets of the Marxist theory that constituted the official ideology of the Soviet state. As a conventional Marxist, Molotov believed history was a series of struggles between oppressed classes and their ruling-class exploiters. The culmination of these bitter class struggles would be the overthrow of capitalism, the creation of a world socialist system, and eventually the advent of a communist utopia characterized by social harmony, personal fulfillment, and material prosperity for all—from each according to his ability, to each according to his needs. He viewed such an outcome of human development as both historically inevitable and politically desirable.

As with many politicians, Molotov's expression of youthful idealism became embedded in his way of life, helping to create his personal as well as his political identity. Then, as a member of the Soviet government, the exercise of power for Molotov became an end in itself, as well as a means to the achievement of communism. In the context of the brutal history of the authoritarian Soviet regime, this allowed him to justify the system's perpetration of human suffering and sorrow on a truly vast scale in the name of ending working class oppression. As unpalatable as his rationale might be, Molotov's authentic and deep commitment to pursuing the socialist ideal is key to understanding his life and career as a loyal Soviet politician.

Molotov's commitment to communism began at an early age.[5] He was only sixteen and still at school when in 1906 he joined the Russian Social Democratic and Labor Party (RSDLP). Like many disaffected youths of his generation, he opposed the autocratic rule of the tsars over Russia and was appalled by what he knew of the miserable living conditions of the country's lower classes. The alternative to tsarism was a democratic and socialist Russia—a goal to be achieved, Molotov thought, not by gradual reform as moderate socialists believed, but through a radical revolution to rapidly overturn the injustice of the capitalist order.

Important to galvanizing the teenage Molotov into political activity was the 1905 Russian Revolution, a series of disturbances and popular uprisings throughout the country following the brutal suppression in St. Petersburg (then the capital) of a peaceful demonstration to petition the tsar about working conditions. At first Tsar Nicholas II tried to head off the popular revolt by promising political reform, but he quickly resorted to mass repression instead. Among the tsarist authorities' targets were members of such revolutionary socialist groups as the RSDLP, which had been greatly involved in the 1905 upheavals.

Molotov was active in the student movement in Kazan in central Russia, not far from his birthplace in Vyatka Province. In 1909 he was arrested, imprisoned, and then sentenced to two years' internal exile to Vologda Province in northern Russia. By this time Molotov had aligned himself with the Bolshevik (i.e., "majority") faction of the RSDLP led by Lenin. Its members believed the coming revolution in Russia would be brought about by the struggles of the industrial working class in alliance with poorer sections of the peasantry. This was why Molotov—whose real name was Skryabin—derived his revolutionary pseudonym from *molot*, the Russian word for hammer. He thought the name had an industrial and proletarian ring to it. Molotov also had a slight stammer, and his new name, adopted in 1914, had the additional benefit of being easier for him to pronounce.

The Bolsheviks' opponents in the RSDLP, the so-called Mensheviks (i.e., "minority"), envisioned the achievement of socialism in Russia through an incremental rather than a revolutionary process. The first stage was to be a democratic revolution to overthrow the tsar. They also disputed Lenin's contention that the RSDLP should be a highly disciplined and centralized party whose activities and policies must be directed by an enlightened elite of party activists and intellectuals. These and other doctrinal disputes led to a formal split between the two RSDLP factions by 1912.

Both the Bolsheviks and Mensheviks emphasized the power of ideas and the role of Marxist theory in informing their strategies for gaining power in Russia. Both also claimed to be internationalists who saw Russia's coming revolution in the context of a worldwide struggle by the working classes to achieve power. They were also cosmopolitan in their outlook and in sourcing their ideas. Karl Marx, after all, was a German of Jewish heritage. When the British writer Rachel Polonsky discovered the remnants of Molotov's personal library in the 1990s, she was surprised at the breadth of literary and cultural interests the books revealed. But like many "Old Bolsheviks" (defined as those who joined the party before the 1917 revolution), Molotov was as urbane and sophisticated culturally as he was simplistic in his politics and ideology.[6]

One of Molotov's comrades from the prerevolution days was Joseph Vissarionovich Dzhugashvili, better known as Stalin ("Man of Steel"). Molotov first met Stalin in St. Petersburg in 1912 when they were both involved in working to create a new party newspaper, *Pravda*. Stalin was a decade older than Molotov, and socially and culturally the two men had little in common. Stalin was the son of a Georgian cobbler, while Molotov's father was a lower-middle-class salesman from central Russia and a distant relative of the classical composer Aleksandr Skryabin.[7] But both men were committed Bolsheviks and shared a common experience of illegal political activity followed by imprisonment and internal exile. Their first encounter was fleeting, however, and not until later did they develop a close personal and political relationship.

Molotov worked as a Bolshevik journalist and agitator for the next few years, moving to Moscow following the outbreak of World War I in August 1914. In 1915 he was arrested again and exiled to Siberia, but a year later he escaped and returned to St. Petersburg (renamed Petrograd because the original sounded too Germanic, and Germany was Russia's main enemy in the war).

It was in Petrograd in March 1917 that Molotov again met Stalin. Tsar Nicholas had resigned following a popular revolt and a military mutiny in the Russian capital. A liberal and democratic provisional government now ruled Russia. Molotov's response to this upheaval was initially more militant and leftist than Stalin's. He did not support the provisional government, while Stalin favored collaboration with moderate socialist elements of the new regime. But Stalin changed his stance after Lenin returned to Russia in April 1917 and announced his opposition to the provisional government. Thereafter Stalin and Molotov were among Lenin's most stalwart supporters in the run-up to the Bolshevik coup in November 1917 that overthrew the provisional government and established a socialist regime based on the "soviets"—the councils of workers, peasants, and soldiers who had toppled the tsar. Molotov took part in Lenin's coup against the provisional government in Petrograd—indeed he was a member of the military revolutionary committee that staged the coup—but he was a propagandist, not one of the Bolshevik soldiers who seized control of public buildings and arrested government ministers.

THE BOLSHEVIKS IN POWER

After the Bolsheviks seized power, Molotov was appointed chairman of an economic council for the Petrograd area, a role that allowed him to show his talents as an administrator as well as a political agitator. This assignment was followed in summer 1919 by command of the *Krasnaya Zvezda* (*Red Star*), an agitprop steamship used to promote revolution as it cruised up and down the Volga. By now the Russian Civil War had broken out as the Bolsheviks' opponents attempted to overthrow the new Soviet regime by armed force. Molotov's job was to buttress the Bolsheviks' political hold in regions adjacent to the Volga.

At the end of 1919 the Bolshevik leadership sent Molotov to take control of the party's organization in Nizhny Novgorod, to the east of Moscow. However, the imposition of his leadership was resisted by some local party members, and in July 1920 he was forced to resign. Surprisingly this setback did not damage his burgeoning political career. In September he was dispatched to help consolidate Soviet rule in the Ukraine, and at the tenth congress of the Bolshevik Party in March 1921, he was elected a full member of the Central Committee. (He had been a candidate, or probationary, member since the ninth party congress a year earlier.)

The Russian Civil War—during which millions of people were killed or starved to death—was a defining, formative experience for Molotov, as it was for all Bolsheviks of his generation, including Stalin. During the war the Bolsheviks learned to be ruthless in pursuit of victory and to use whatever level of violence was required to defend their regime. Coercion became commonplace, replacing persuasion as a method of political mobilization. The Bolshevik Party (it changed its name to the Communist Party in 1918) became even more rigidly hierarchical and authoritarian in its administration. At the height of the civil war in 1919–1920, the Bolsheviks came close to defeat as their stronghold in central and northern Russia came under siege from all sides by counter-revolutionary "White" armies. Adding to the strain on Lenin's government and its forces were military interventions supporting the White armies made by a number of foreign governments–Britain, France, Japan, and the United States–that feared the contagion of a successful Bolshevik revolution could spread to their own countries.

The Bolsheviks characterized the civil war as a life-and-death struggle not only with their internal foes, but with the whole capitalist world. The Bolsheviks hoped revolutionary socialist movements in other countries would come to their aid. When this did not happen, they accepted the Soviet socialist state had to coexist with capitalism, at least for a while, but feared the revival of an imperialist coalition dedicated to the forcible overthrow of the Bolshevik regime. This siege mentality still gripped Soviet minds twenty years later when Molotov became foreign affairs commissar–an attitude given added piquancy by Stalin's belief that the stronger the Soviet Union became, the more desperate its capitalist enemies (and their internal allies) would be to overthrow the socialist system. This theory that the class struggle would intensify under socialism led Stalin and Molotov in the 1930s to believe in the existence of a "fifth column"–internal enemies who had to be purged from Soviet society through a process of mass terror.

The Bolsheviks won the civil war, but at a high cost. The Communist Party was the only civil institution to survive the conflict intact and functioning more or less effectively, although many of its most committed and active members had been killed. So the party and its surviving members took over running the whole of Soviet society–its government and economy as well as its social and cultural life. The Communist Party did not simply control the Soviet state–it totally dominated it. The existence of such a "party state" placed a high premium on the administrative talents of devoted party members such as Molotov.

The tenth party congress in 1921 marked the end of the civil war, but the Bolsheviks continued their authoritarian rule, including banning any and all factions within their own party. After the congress Molotov was appointed head of the Central Committee Secretariat, a member of the Organization Buro (Orgburo), and a candidate member of the Political Buro (Politburo)–the party's three top committees. In effect, Molotov became Lenin's administrative deputy within the party. Lenin reputedly described Molotov as the "best filing clerk in Russia," while Trotsky disparaged him as "mediocrity incarnate." Neither comment was particularly apposite. Molotov was certainly, as he admitted himself, a painstaking administrator. When he was foreign minister, he drove his aides to distraction with demands for draft after draft of diplomatic documents. But Molotov was no mere paper-shuffling bureaucrat. The Politburo was the most important political decision-making body of the new Communist Party–controlled Soviet state, and Molotov was responsible for preparing its agenda, resolutions, and minutes. He may not have been a top political player in Lenin's Politburo, but his new role brought him into direct contact with high-level economic and political decision making of all kinds, including on foreign affairs.

The year 1921 was momentous for Molotov personally as well politically. At the International Congress of Women in Moscow that summer, he met fellow party member Polina Zhemchuzhina and married her soon after. In Russian her name means "Little Pearl"–an appellation derived from her original name, Perl Karpovskaya. Born in 1897, she was the daughter of a Jewish tailor from southern Russia. Her brother Sam Carp had emigrated to the United States before World War I and became a successful businessman. The two siblings kept in touch, and in the 1930s Sam emerged as a go-between in Soviet-American trade negotiations. During trips to the Soviet Union he lodged with his sister and brother-in-law in their Kremlin flat.

Molotov's grandson, Vyacheslav Nikonov–a well-known political commentator in contemporary Russia–described the relationship between his grandfather and grandmother as

> love at first sight for life. This was a union of two hearts, filled with a depth of romantic feeling that was preserved until death. . . . Grandfather did not just love her. He respected her, admired her, was proud of her and helped her with her career. Between them there was complete mutual understanding: they were a single entity who saved each other and helped one another, and their daughter, to survive repression.[8]

Like many Bolshevik leaders Molotov could be severe with his staff and he generally presented a hard face to the outside world, but within his family (his daughter, Svetlana, was born in 1929) he was caring, considerate, and affectionate.

AT STALIN'S SIDE

In April 1922 Stalin was appointed general secretary of the Communist Party, and Molotov became his deputy. Like Lenin before him, Stalin found Molotov to be a reliable, hardworking, and highly efficient assistant. By this time, too, Molotov had acquired a nickname within the party, *Kamenny Zad*, which means "Stony Bottom." (A less polite translation would be "Iron Ass.") It was a pejorative description derived from the chess world and dated from a time when there were no chess clocks, and games went on for as long as they lasted. In such competitions the ability to outsit an opponent was a distinct advantage. The nickname referred to Molotov's endless patience and stamina in political negotiations and bureaucratic matters, qualities that would later bring him much renown—and not a little hostility—in international diplomatic circles, too.[9]

Molotov's main value to Stalin was not as an efficient administrator, but as a loyal and reliable political lieutenant who supported him in the fierce succession struggle that erupted after Lenin's death in January 1924. Pitted against Stalin was the Left Opposition led by Leon Trotsky, the organizer of the Bolshevik coup in 1917 and the commissar for war who was credited with leading the Red Army to victory in the civil war. As Molotov later recalled, it was in succession battles against the Left Opposition, and later the Right Opposition, that he honed his political and polemical skills:

> Quite often I had to give speeches at big party meetings—against the Trotskyists, against right-wingers—in a situation when you were told at noon that you were to give a speech at 6.30. You couldn't read the speech. No one would rewrite or edit for you. This kind of experience was highly useful for diplomacy because you had to deal with such serious opponents, politically sophisticated, like the Trotskyists and the right-wingers.[10]

While the struggle between Stalin and Trotsky was driven by personal rivalry and power-seeking, it was also a dispute about how high a priority should be given to building the socialist system in the Soviet Union, the alternative being to support and pursue opportunities for spreading revolution abroad. Molotov supported Stalin's policy of building socialism in a single country—the

USSR—as did the great majority of communists, and this was the primary reason for Trotsky's defeat in the inner-party struggle. By end of the 1920s, Trotsky had been driven out of the country as well as the party. In exile in Mexico in 1940, he met his death at the hands of a Stalin-commissioned assassin.

Molotov's reward for supporting Stalin was his elevation to full membership of the Politburo in 1926 and a seat on the Executive Committee of the Communist International (Comintern)—the organization established by the Bolsheviks in 1919 to foster world revolution. Stalin and Molotov may have prioritized building socialism at home, but they remained committed to the global spread of the communist movement and the struggle to achieve a world socialist system. The difference with Trotsky was their belief that defense of the Soviet Union should be the foremost task undertaken by revolutionaries everywhere. The USSR was presented as the mainstay of the historical process leading to world socialism and the Soviet system as a model of how socialism could work in practice. That this model was in many respects vastly inferior to its capitalist rivals did not trouble Molotov. He had faith that in the long run the Soviet system would prove to be economically superior to capitalism and victory in the class struggle—at home and abroad—would eventually secure communism the popularity it deserved.

Molotov remained Stalin's deputy within the party, and when Stalin went on vacation Molotov kept the "*bikbos*"—as Stalin sometimes liked to be called—informed of party affairs and was responsible for relaying the "big boss's" views and instructions back to the rest of the leadership. Communications were mainly by letter, and the extensive correspondence between the two men during the 1920s was important to consolidating their personal and political relationship.[11]

In 1928 Molotov was placed in charge of the Moscow Communist Party organization—a key position in the political struggle with the Right Opposition to Stalin led by Nikolai Bukharin. The Right Opposition preferred a more moderate pace of socialist industrialization in the USSR while maintaining good relations with the country's peasants, still the vast majority of the population. Stalin, supported by Molotov, identified a sea of class enemies residing in the countryside, notably among the "kulaks," or rich peasants. He also feared that if industrialization did not happen quickly enough, the Soviet Union's capitalist enemies would take advantage of its economic weakness and backwardness to yet again use military force in an attempt to crush the nascent socialist state. Stalin's message proved to be the more popular one within the party, and the

Right Opposition was defeated at the April 1929 plenum of the Central Committee. Among the political casualties was Bukharin's ally Alexei Rykov, who
subsequently lost his job as chairman of the Council of People's Commissars.
In December 1930 Stalin nominated Molotov for the position.

Molotov's new job was his first major nonparty post. Stalin's aim in appointing him was to ensure closer and deeper control by the party leadership
over the activities of government ministries, or commissariats, as they were still
called at this time (the terminology changed in 1946). As chairman, Molotov
was to supervise the implementation of party policy by the commissariats and
mediate relations between the commissars at their head, who were often, like
Molotov, powerful figures in the party as well. Molotov's position as head of
the government was second in importance to that of Stalin, leader of the party,
which meant Molotov was at the heart of the Soviet dictator's brutal program
for the modernization of the Soviet Union. This program had three main aspects.

First, the accelerated industrialization and urbanization of the USSR. In
1928 the Soviets adopted the first of a series of five-year plans to radically
raise industrial production and to transform the country from a largely peasant
society into an advanced, industrialized state. According to official statistics,
industrial production increased by 850 percent in the 1930s. The true figures
were probably somewhat lower, but there is no doubting the vast scale of industrialization, which resulted in the construction of thousands of factories;
the building of many new dams, canals, roads, and railways; and a 30 million
increase in the urban population. Much of the industrialization effort was directed at the defense industry, and there was a seventy-fold increase in muni-
tions production in the decade before the outbreak of World War II. Molotov's
job was to supervise the achievement of plan targets and to hold the ring between rival commissars competing for resources and political influence, a task
that, according to his British biographer Derek Watson, he handled in a quite
statesmanlike way.

Second, the forced collectivization of Soviet agriculture. The Bolsheviks
were ideologically committed to a state-controlled agricultural sector, but not
until the late 1920s did they begin to force peasants to give up their land and
become members of collective farms. By 1937 more than 90 percent of Soviet
agriculture had been collectivized. But there was considerable peasant resistance and severe disruption of agricultural production. Stalin's response to the

problems and crises caused by the collectivization drive was mass executions, arrests, and deportations. The result was the deaths of millions of peasants, particularly in 1932–1933 when the brutalities of collectivization combined with bad weather to produce a famine in the Ukraine and parts of Russia. Molotov was very active in the collectivization campaign, especially in relation to the forced procurement of food supplies to feed the growing urban population. As Watson notes, there is substance to the argument that Molotov's policies and actions contributed significantly to famine conditions in the Ukraine, although wilder accusations that he and Stalin were guilty of the attempted genocide of the Ukrainian peasantry can be safely discounted. Peasants perished as a byproduct of Stalin and Molotov's policy of mass political repression to secure their goals in the countryside, not genocidal design.

Third, the Stalinization and terrorization of Soviet society. In the 1930s Soviet society was hit by wave after wave of terror. Millions of citizens were arrested and several hundred thousand executed for political crimes. After the assassination in December 1934 of Sergei Kirov, the head of the Leningrad Communist Party, thousands of party members were arrested, suspected of involvement in a plot to kill Soviet leaders. In the mid-1930s there were a series of public political show trials of former leading members of the Bolshevik Party who were accused of being spies, saboteurs, and plotters against Stalin. Among the more prominent victims was Bukharin, who was executed in 1938, while Trotsky was accused in absentia of being at the center of various perceived conspiracies against the Soviet state. The "Great Terror," as it came to be called, climaxed in 1937–1938 with a hysterical hunt for internal enemies that resulted in mass arrests of party and state officials. There was also a significant purge of the military, including the arrest and execution of some of the Red Army and Soviet Navy's top generals and admirals.

The reasons for the Great Terror remain controversial. Some historians see the Terror as driven primarily by Stalin's ideology and political paranoia, his genuine belief the Soviet system was besieged by internal and external enemies. Other historians emphasize Stalin's manipulation of the Terror as a means of consolidating his personal dictatorship. Molotov's oft-repeated view was that there really were enemies who had to be eliminated and that most of those who suffered were guilty of something.

Molotov's personal role in authorizing and sponsoring the Terror was second only to that of Stalin. Indeed, in 1937–1938, when the practice developed of Politburo members authorizing arrests, executions, and imprisonments by the list, Molotov signed more lists than Stalin–373 compared to 362. On these lists were the names of approximately forty-four thousand people–thirty-nine thousand to be shot, five thousand to be imprisoned, and a hundred or so destined for short-term imprisonment and exile.

Whatever the reasons for the Terror, its effect was clear: by the end of the 1930s Stalin's leadership was unquestionable and unchallengeable. The Soviet system may not have been as totalitarian as some commentators have claimed, but it did exercise a high degree of political control over the lives of its citizens, and in that respect it was a thoroughly modern dictatorship.[12]

Molotov was little known outside party circles when, at the age of forty, he became Soviet premier. But he soon emerged as a national and international Soviet public figure. By the end of the 1930s, the concept of a Stalin-Molotov leadership was a commonplace of Soviet political discourse and alongside the cult of Stalin's personality there ran a minor Molotov cult. The first edition of the official *Great Soviet Encyclopedia*, in a volume published in 1938, devoted several pages to Molotov's biography and described him as "a true pupil of Lenin and a close comrade in arms of leader of the people–Stalin."[13]

Molotov's prewar celebrity peaked with the celebrations of his fiftieth birthday in 1940. The city of Perm, located on the western edge of the Urals in central Russia, was renamed after him, as was one of the USSR's highest mountains in Tajikistan. There were also numerous Molotov museums, art galleries, schools, colleges, factories, and hospitals. In March 1940 the women workers' journal *Rabotnitsa* celebrated Molotov's fiftieth with a special issue that featured a pinup picture of him on the front page and the text of a "Song about Molotov":

> For you,
> Comrade Molotov,
> This song we sing.
> Faithful friend
> Of the Great Leader,
> This is your 50th year
> Together with him
> You forge and shape
> The happiness of our land.[14]

Molotov always considered himself to be a politician rather than a diplomat, in part because he did not have full command of any foreign languages. Yet he could read English, French, and German. Sir William Seeds, who was British ambassador to Moscow in 1939, complained of Molotov that "it is my fate to deal with a man totally ignorant of foreign affairs and to whom the idea of negotiations—as distinct from imposing the will of his party leader—is utterly alien."[15] In truth, Seeds was frustrated by Molotov's effectiveness as a negotiating opponent, not by his ignorance. Schooled in Bolshevik internationalism, Molotov had always followed events abroad very closely, even more so after he became premier. In the 1920s and 1930s, he gave many wide-ranging speeches about international affairs, including some notable denunciations of Nazi Germany. As a member of the Politburo he had dealt with foreign policy issues since the Lenin era. Most importantly, he had the ear of Stalin and thus could act and speak with authority in his role as foreign minister.

Apart from his wife, Molotov's closest political and personal relationship was with Stalin. A crude but telling indicator of their relative intimacy is provided by the entries in Stalin's appointments diary, which reveal that Molotov attended more than two thousand meetings in the Soviet leader's private office between 1928 and 1953.[16] No one else in Stalin's inner circle came close to matching that. When Stalin died, Molotov was one of the main speakers at the funeral meeting in Red Square. Newsreel film of his speech shows him to be visibly moved during his oration:

> Today, we, his old and close friends, as well as millions of Soviet citizens and working people from every country, from the whole world, say goodbye to Comrade Stalin, whom we all loved and who will always live in our hearts. . . . The immortal name of Stalin will always live in our hearts, in the hearts of the Soviet people, and of all progressive humanity.[17]

Stalin dominated everyone who came into close personal contact with him, and Molotov was no exception. There was never any doubt that Stalin was the senior partner in their relationship or that Molotov's loyalty to the Soviet dictator was absolute—but it was a loyalty born out of conviction, not fear. Molotov retained his independence of mind. "I was not one to hang on Stalin's every word. I argued with him, told him the truth," Molotov said to Chuev. "That was why Stalin valued me. He saw that I had my own views and my own thinking on the issues. Of course, I can't say he would always agree with me, but I must say that he did frequently agree with me. Otherwise we wouldn't have worked closely together for thirty years."[18]

One close observer of Molotov's relationship with Stalin during the war years was Marshal Georgii Zhukov, Stalin's deputy supreme commander. He recalled Molotov's persistence in disputes with Stalin: "Molotov was a willful and stubborn person whom it was difficult to shift from the position he had adopted. He was able to exert a strong influence on Stalin, especially in relation to questions of foreign policy."[19] While Stalin always got his way and Molotov backed off when it became clear the dictator's mind was made up, Molotov's career as foreign minister is littered with examples of policy differences with Stalin.

Portrait of Vyacheslav Mikhailovich Molotov.
Society for Cooperation in Russian and Soviet Studies

But Molotov's most damaging dispute with Stalin was personal and concerned Molotov's wife. In 1949 Polina Zhemchuzhina was arrested because of her association with the Jewish Anti-Fascist Committee, whose members had been accused of Jewish nationalism–anathema to Stalin who viewed with suspicion any political ideology that challenged communism and his power–and of Zionist sympathies with the newly created state of Israel. The necessary and formal preliminary to her arrest was her expulsion from the Communist Party. However, when the matter came before the Politburo in December 1948, Molotov abstained in the vote on a resolution to expel her. No one else in Stalin's inner circle ever behaved in such a way.

And it was not the first time Molotov had rebelled. Comrade Zhemchuzhina had been in trouble before. Ten years earlier when she had been head of the People's Commissariat for Fishing, it was criticized for allegedly harboring enemy spies. She was relieved of her post and excluded from candidate membership of the party's Central Committee. When the matter came before the Politburo, Molotov abstained and nothing happened as a result of his abstention.

A decade on, however, Stalin was now overwhelmingly dominant in the party leadership and no scintilla of resistance to his rule was permitted. Molotov was forced to recant and on January 20, 1949, he wrote to Stalin:

> When I abstained from the CC vote on the exclusion of P. S. Zhemchuzhina from the party it was a political mistake. I declare that, having thought about this question, I vote for the decision of the CC, which meets the interests of the party and the state and teaches a true understanding of communist party-mindedness. In addition, I recognize that at the time I was seriously remiss in not preventing Zhemchuzhina, a person very close to me, from making false steps and from forming ties with anti-Soviet Jewish nationalists.[20]

Molotov's mea culpa was circulated to the other members of the leadership that same day, and six days later his wife was arrested. She spent the rest of the year being interrogated in prison before being exiled to Kazakhstan for five years. Molotov was forced to divorce her, and the two of them were not reunited until after Stalin's death.[21]

Years later, Molotov was asked by a leading Israeli communist how he could have allowed his wife to be arrested. Molotov replied: "Because I am a member of the Politburo and I must obey party discipline." In conversation with Chuev, Molotov speculated that Stalin "might have been influenced by anti-Semitic sentiments. Another of his extremes skillfully exploited by schemers." Even more remarkable, Zhemchuzhina did not blame Stalin for her misfortune and would not have a bad word said against him. In the 1960s she told Stalin's daughter, Svetlana: "Your father was a genius. He liquidated the fifth column in our country, and when the war broke out the Party and the people were one."[22]

Stalin's attitude toward Polina may have been colored by her close relationship with his wife, Nadezhda Alliluyeva, who committed suicide in 1932. There are many theories and much speculation about the circumstances of Nadezhda's suicide and Stalin's response to it, including that it provoked the rage that led to the Great Terror. Such speculation is at best farfetched, but Stalin does seem to have taken the suicide very hard, and it is possible that he harbored resentment about the intimacy of Polina with Nadezhda.[23]

More certain is that Polina was a victim of Stalin's political suspicions and of the fevered atmosphere of the Cold War in the late 1940s. Another victim of the paranoia of those times was her brother Sam Carp, who was called before the House Committee on Un-American Activities after the war and asked to account for his connections to the Kremlin. Carp, however, was neither arrested nor imprisoned and continued his career as a successful American businessman until his death in 1963.

AFTER STALIN

Events connected with his wife's arrest illustrated both Molotov's deep loyalty to Stalin and his ability to keep his own counsel. His independence of mind came to the fore again after the dictator's death in 1953. C. D. Jackson, President Eisenhower's adviser on politico-psychological warfare, captured the sense of personal liberation that Molotov must have felt, in a report on the 1954 Berlin Conference of Foreign Ministers:

> The Soviet delegation was unquestionably their first team. . . . The atmosphere between themselves seemed to be quite relaxed. The passing of notes and whispered advice during the conference was spontaneous and advisers volunteered information and advice to Molotov just as easily as he turned to consult them. . . . During the social gatherings . . . the Soviet

mood was one of great personal friendliness, sometimes verging on an al-most pathetic eagerness to be liked personally even though professionally the gap between us was as great as ever. Molotov . . . was by far the most entertaining member of the Soviet group. Compared to the others, his hu-mor was sharp, subtle and fast, and he seemed to derive genuine pleasure from being able to throw the switch and have verbal fun.[24]

Molotov had been Stalin's man, but he was not Khrushchev's. He had little or no respect for Stalin's successor as party leader, and there was a strong ele-ment of personal hostility in their power struggle. After being defeated in his attempt to oust Khrushchev in 1957, Molotov remained defiant, and in retire-ment devoted himself to criticizing Khrushchev's leadership, most especially the anti-Stalin campaign Khrushchev inaugurated in his "secret" speech at the twentieth party congress in 1956. Molotov continued to swim against the tide after Khrushchev's fall from power in 1964. His uncompromising defense of Stalin was an embarrassment to the party leaders, now headed by Leonid Bre-zhnev, who feared his critical gaze would be turned on them, too. But Molo-tov's loyalty and affection for the party remained undimmed. There were tears in his eyes when he received the news in 1984 that his party membership had been reinstated.[25]

When Molotov died in November 1986, the communist system he had done so much to help construct was on the brink of political upheavals that would lead to its collapse five years later. Only a year and a half earlier, Mikhail Gorbachev had become the leader of the Soviet Union. *Glasnost* (openness) and *perestroika* (reconstruction) were Gorbachev's watchwords as he introduced a program of political and economic reform intended to shake up and revive the communist regime. The result, however, was destabilization and disintegra-tion. By the end of 1991, Gorbachev had resigned, the Communist Party had lost power after more than seventy years of unbroken rule, and the multina-tional Union of Soviet Socialist Republics had split asunder into its constituent parts.

In 1986 few people had any inkling of the dramatic events that would shortly sweep into the dustbin of history the Soviet experiment in socialism–certainly not Molotov. After a lifetime of service to the Soviet system–as Polit-buro member, as premier, and above all as foreign minister–Molotov's faith in communism and its future remained as strong as ever.

When the Russian archives began to be made accessible to researchers in the 1990s, it quickly became apparent from the documents held there that Stalin had dominated Soviet decision making to an even greater extent than had hitherto been assumed. But it was equally apparent that without loyal and talented lieutenants like Molotov, Stalin's regime would barely have functioned, let alone survived and gone on to win World War II as well as fight the West to a standstill during the Cold War.

This book tells the story of Molotov's career as Soviet foreign minister. It shows that while Molotov was undoubtedly Stalin's cold warrior, he also stood for a radical alternative to the Cold War. His efforts to end it and unite a divided Europe were frustrated first by Stalin and then by Khrushchev. But Molotov's failure to realize his vision should not blind us to the importance of his efforts to end the Cold War, which helped shape and limit the nature of the conflict and provided a foundation for its stabilization and, eventually, its abolition.

2

NEGOTIATING WITH THE NAZIS
(1939–1941)

The art of politics in the sphere of foreign relations does not consist in increasing the number of enemies for one's country. On the contrary, the art of politics in this sphere is to reduce the number of such enemies and make the enemies of yesterday good neighbours, maintaining peaceable relations one with the other.

— V. M. Molotov (August 31, 1939)[1]

Molotov was appointed people's commissar for foreign affairs in May 1939 in controversial circumstances. Maxim Litvinov, his predecessor, was a popular figure internationally and the personification of the Soviet struggle for peace, collective security, and the containment of Fascist and Nazi aggression. A fortnight before his dismissal, Litvinov had launched the latest phase in the Soviet collective security campaign: a proposal for an Anglo-Soviet-French triple alliance to resist further German expansion in Europe following Adolf Hitler's takeover of Czechoslovakia in March 1939.

Why did Stalin choose to replace Litvinov at such a critical moment? A common interpretation is that it was a prelude to the pact with Nazi Germany signed in August 1939. The problem with this explanation is that far from abandoning the triple alliance negotiations with Britain and France, Molotov pursued them with even more vigor than Litvinov. The most likely explanation is that Molotov's appointment was connected to Litvinov's failure to make any headway in the negotiations.[2]

Litvinov presented the triple alliance proposal to Sir William Seeds, the British ambassador to Moscow, on April 17. The Soviets proposed a trilateral mutual assistance pact between Britain, France, and the USSR that would also guarantee the security of European states threatened by Nazi Germany. The Soviet proposal was prompted by a series of approaches from the British and French in March and April seeking to enlist the USSR in a collective security front against Hitler.[3] The Soviets were willing to participate in such a front but wanted guarantees the British and French would not renege on their commitments. After some hesitation Paris responded positively to the proposal, but from London there was silence. When Litvinov saw Seeds on May 3, the ambassador could only say the proposal was still being studied.

Later that day Litvinov reported to Stalin that the British were in no hurry to respond and were waiting for the Soviet reply to the French counterproposals. The French were prepared to join a triple alliance but wanted to extend security guarantees only to Poland, Romania, and Turkey. The Soviets, wary of the danger of a German thrust along the Baltic coast, wanted the Baltic states of Estonia, Latvia, and Finland included in any system of security guarantees. As a negotiating tactic, Litvinov suggested to Stalin that the Soviet Union could agree to guarantees for Holland, Belgium, and Switzerland in return for guarantees of the Baltic states.[4] Stalin decided to express his displeasure at the lack of progress in the negotiations in a more dramatic fashion: he dismissed Litvinov and appointed Molotov in his place, a move that meant Stalin was, in effect, taking direct charge of the triple alliance negotiations. No one was closer politically and personally to Stalin than Molotov and could be relied upon to do exactly what the Soviet dictator wanted.

THE TRIPLE ALLIANCE NEGOTIATIONS

As Molotov biographer Derek Watson has noted, the triple alliance negotiations were Molotov's apprenticeship in diplomacy, during which he displayed many of the qualities for which he was to become famous in diplomatic circles: intransigence, argumentativeness, obsession with detail, and, above all, persistence in pursuit of the Soviet position. William Strang, a Foreign Office official sent to Moscow to help Seeds with the negotiations, summed up their course as follows:

> The history of the negotiations for [the triple alliance] is the story of how the British government were driven step by step, under stress of Soviet

argument, under pressure from Parliament and the press and public opinion polls, under advice from the Ambassador at Moscow, and under persuasion from the French, to move towards the Soviet position. One by one
they yielded points to the Russians. In the end they gave the Russians the
main part of what they asked for. Everything in the essential structure of
the draft agreement represented a concession to the Russians.[5]

The key to Molotov's success was that the British and French needed the
military might of the Soviet Union to fulfill their guarantees to Poland and Romania. Geopolitics dictated that without the support of the Red Army, Poland
and Romania could not resist a German invasion.

Molotov's first meeting with the British ambassador was on May 8. Molotov told Seeds that the triple alliance remained Soviet policy as long as "there
were no changes in the international situation and in the positions of other
powers." Seeds had brought the British reply to the Soviet triple alliance proposal, and it was not welcome news. The British wanted a public declaration
from the Soviets that they would support Britain and France in the event of
hostilities arising from the Anglo-French guarantees to Poland and Romania.
This was completely unacceptable to Moscow: the whole point of the triple
alliance proposal would be to create a system of reciprocal security guarantees
under which Soviet obligations to the British and French would be balanced by
those to the USSR (e.g., Anglo-French support for Soviet action in defense of
the Baltic states against German aggression). "As you can see, the English and
French are demanding of us unilateral and gratuitous assistance with no intention of rendering us equivalent assistance," Molotov cabled his ambassadors in
London and Paris.[6]

On May 14 the Soviets responded to the British proposal with an aide-
mémoir reiterating their triple alliance proposal. On May 27 the British and
French responded to this démarche by submitting to Molotov the text of a
draft mutual assistance pact between the three states. The proposed pact was
limited in scope, its system of guarantees restricted to those states wanting to
be guaranteed (thus excluding the Baltic states). But London and Paris had
conceded Moscow's essential demands for a formal triple alliance and a system of reciprocal guarantees. To the amazement of Seeds and Jean Payart, the
French diplomatic representative, Molotov immediately and angrily rejected
the proposal. It did not contain, Molotov argued, any plan for the organization

of effective defense against aggression, offered no indication of serious intent on the part of Britain and France, and proposed consultation rather than immediate assistance in the event of hostilities. The problem was that the mutual assistance envisaged in the Anglo-French draft was tied to League of Nations procedures. That, said Molotov, would transform the pact into "a mere scrap of paper" because "in the event of aggression mutual assistance will not be rendered immediately . . . but only after deliberations in the League of Nations, with no one knowing what the results of such deliberations would be." Payart and Seeds assured Molotov that the reference to the League of Nations was just a matter of public relations, but he remained implacable.[7]

On May 31, 1939, Molotov reported on the international situation to the Supreme Soviet—his first such speech since becoming people's commissar for foreign affairs. Molotov's theme was familiar, not just from his own past speeches but from those of Litvinov as well: Anglo-French appeasement of aggressive states had encouraged their appetite for expansion, the prime example being the Munich Agreement of September 1938, which had forced Czechoslovakia to concede the Sudetenland to Germany in return for a guarantee of its remaining territory. Six months later Hitler occupied Prague, claiming that the Czechoslovak state had collapsed internally and required German protection. Molotov noted recent changes in British and French foreign policy but said that "at present it is impossible to say whether these countries have a sincere desire to abandon the policy of nonintervention, the policy of nonresistance to further aggression." Molotov also revealed details of the recent diplomatic exchanges with London and Paris, making it clear that any mutual assistance pact would have to be based on equal and reciprocal obligations.[8]

The Soviet response to the Anglo-French draft pact was formally set out in a counterdraft on June 2. The proposed mutual assistance treaty would give effect to League of Nations principles, but its operation would not be tied to League procedures, and Latvia, Estonia, and Finland were named as countries the Soviets wanted guaranteed. The catch, from the British and French point of view, was that those three Baltic states—fearing the Soviets as much as the Germans—did not want to be guaranteed by Moscow. But their rejection of a Soviet guarantee was of no importance to Molotov, who argued that the general interests of peace and the specific security needs of the USSR should override any Baltic objections. On June 10 Molotov instructed Ivan Maisky, Soviet ambassador to London:

To avoid misunderstandings we consider it necessary to make clear that the question of the three Baltic States is a question without whose satisfactory solution it would be impossible to bring the negotiations to a conclusion. We feel that without guaranteeing the security of the northwestern borders of the USSR by providing for decisive counteraction . . . against any direct or indirect attack by an aggressor on Estonia, Latvia, or Finland it will be impossible to satisfy public opinion in the Soviet Union. . . . This is not a question of technical formulas but one of agreeing on the substance of the question, after which it will not be difficult to find a suitable formula.[9]

On June 15 the British and French presented another document. It proposed that in the case of threats to states that did not want to be guaranteed, the triple alliance partners would consult with each other and decide if there was "a menace to security" that merited the implementation of mutual assistance obligations. This proposal was immediately rejected by the Soviets on grounds that the security guarantees were automatic in the case of states the British and French wanted guaranteed but subject to consultation in the case of states the USSR wanted guaranteed. If the British and French were unwilling to impose a guarantee on the Baltic states, said the Soviet aide-mémoir, then the whole issue of guarantees should be dropped, and the triple alliance would only operate in the event of direct attacks on the three signatories. That same day Molotov cabled Maisky and Yakov Suritz, Soviet ambassador to Paris:

The French and the English are putting the USSR in a humiliating and unequal position, something which under no circumstances would we accept. . . . We feel that the English and French want to conclude a treaty with us, which would be advantageous to them and disadvantageous to us, that is, they do not want a serious treaty based on the principle of reciprocity and equality of obligations. It is clear we shall not accept such a treaty.[10]

Molotov's threat to take the issue of security guarantees off the negotiating table was a very effective tactic, given that for the British and French the whole point of the triple alliance was to gain Soviet support for their guarantees to Romania and, especially, Poland, a state under immediate threat from Hitler because of the dispute over the so-called Polish Corridor, the strip of territory that gave Poland customs control of the port of Danzig and access to the Baltic but separated East Prussia from the rest of Germany.

By July 1 the British and French had agreed to the Soviet position on the question of guarantees, on condition that the list of countries guaranteed would not be published but contained in a secret protocol.[11] This was acceptable to the Soviets, but a much larger problem was now looming. Integral to the Soviet triple alliance proposal was agreement on a military convention detailing the terms of practical military cooperation among the three states. Stalin was expecting to fight a war with Hitler in the very near future, and he wanted clarity about what support he could expect from Britain and France. For this reason the Soviets insisted on the simultaneous signing of the military and political treaties that would constitute the triple alliance. London and Paris, on the other hand, thought that Hitler could be deterred from war by a political treaty followed by negotiations for a military convention. At a meeting with Seeds and Paul-Émile Naggier (the new French ambassador) on July 17, Molotov made it clear that this was unacceptable.[12] In a telegram to Maisky and Suritz later that day, Molotov's anger about the prolonged, tedious, and frustrating negotiations came to the fore:

> We are insisting that a military pact is an inseparable part of a military-political agreement . . . and categorically reject the Anglo-French proposal that we should first agree on the "political" part of the treaty and only then turn to the question of a military agreement. This dishonest Anglo-French proposal splits up what should be a single treaty into two separate treaties and contradicts our basic proposal to conclude the whole treaty simultaneously, including its military part, which is actually the most important and political part of the treaty. You understand that if the overall agreement does not include as an integral part an absolutely concrete military agreement, the treaty will be nothing but an empty declaration and this is something we cannot accept. Only crooks and cheats such as the negotiators on the Anglo-French side have shown themselves to be all this time could pretend that our demands for the conclusion of a political and military agreement are something new in the negotiations. . . . It seems nothing will come of the endless negotiations. Then they will have no one but themselves to blame.[13]

Bearing in mind that this telegram would likely have been read by Stalin, it is possible that Molotov's missive was aimed partly at covering up his own failure to make crystal clear to the British and French the importance of agreement on a military treaty. In any event, London and Paris soon gave way. On July 23 Seeds and Naggier told Molotov that the Soviet proposal had been accepted. Molotov seemed very pleased and suggested Moscow as the venue for military discussions, to start immediately: "The mere fact that the military conversations were starting would have a much greater effect in the world than any announcement about the political articles. It would be a powerful demonstration on the part of the three governments."[14]

The military talks opened in Moscow on August 12. Two days later the head of the Soviet delegation, Defense Commissar Marshal Kliment Voroshilov, posed the key question to the British and French delegation: would the Red Army be allowed to cross into Poland and Romania in the event of German aggression? The Anglo-French negotiators responded that when war came, the Poles and the Romanians would surely invite the Red Army in. This was not satisfactory to the Soviets, who wanted to know in advance whether that would be the case. When it was suggested they should ask the Poles and Romanians for advance consent, Voroshilov replied that Poland and Romania were the allies of Britain and France and were protected by Anglo-French security guarantees, so it was up to London and Paris to obtain the permission. Talks continued while the British and French delegates consulted their governments, but on August 17 Voroshilov proposed an adjournment until the receipt of an answer to his question. When the meeting resumed on August 21, the British and French had nothing definite to report, and the talks were adjourned sine die, never to resume.[15]

The military talks collapsed because the British and French failed to satisfy Moscow on the question of the Red Army's right of passage across Poland and Romania. This was no idle question but a vital strategic issue for the Soviets, not least because the Red Army's operational plans called for an advance into Poland and Romania in the event of war with Germany.[16] But that was only one side of the story of the failure of the triple alliance negotiations. The negotiations also failed because Stalin had an alternative. By the time the Anglo-French military delegation arrived in Moscow, Molotov was already engaged in negotiations with Germany. Doubting the triple alliance negotiations would produce a satisfactory outcome, the Soviets had decided at the end of July 1939 to hedge their bets by seeing what Berlin had to offer.

THE NAZI-SOVIET PACT

The Germans had been trying to woo the Soviets since the beginning of the triple alliance negotiations. Their motive—to avert the triple alliance—was self-evident, and the German overtures were not at first taken seriously in Moscow. When Friedrich-Werner Graf von der Schulenburg, the German ambassador to Moscow, made an approach on May 20 about reopening trade talks, Molotov told him that he had "the impression that the German government was playing some sort of game instead of conducting business-like economic negotiations; and that for such a game it should have looked for its partner in another country and not the government of the USSR. . . . We had come to the conclusion that for the success of the economic negotiations it was necessary to create a corresponding political basis." Molotov further noted in his report to Stalin that "throughout the whole conversation it was evident that for the ambassador my statement was most unexpected. . . . The ambassador strove for a more concrete explanation of the political basis that my statement had in mind but I avoided giving a concrete answer to this question."[17]

Schulenburg did not meet with Molotov again until June 28. The ambassador reminded Molotov of what had been said at their previous meeting about the political basis of Soviet-German relations. Germany, Schulenburg told Molotov, wanted not only to normalize relations with the Soviet Union, but to improve them. As proof of this he pointed to the restrained tone of the German press in relation to the USSR and to Germany's recent nonaggression pacts with Latvia and Estonia. Schulenburg also reassured Molotov that Germany had no "Napoleonic" plans in relation to the USSR. Molotov responded that the Soviet Union was interested in the normalization and improvement in relations with all countries, including Germany, but he wanted to know how Berlin proposed to improve relations with the USSR. Since Schulenburg had nothing specific to propose, the conversation ended on an indeterminate note.[18]

The next major development came at the end of July when Georgii Astakhov, the Soviet diplomatic representative in Berlin, reported to Molotov on two conversations with Karl Schnurre, a German diplomat who specialized in economics and who had been involved in past discussions about Soviet-German trade:

Germany is prepared to discuss and come to an understanding with us on the questions that both sides are interested in, and to give all the security guarantees we would require. . . . To my question about how confident he was that his words reflected the mood and intention of higher circles, Schnurre said that he spoke on the direct instructions of [German foreign minister Joachim von Ribbentrop]. . . . Naturally, we didn't give Schnurre any hopes, limiting ourselves to general noises and promising to bring the talks to your attention."[19]

Two days later, on July 29, Molotov sent Astakhov his reply:

Political relations between the USSR and Germany may improve, of course, with an improvement in economic relations. In this regard Schnurre is, generally speaking, right. But only the Germans can say concretely how political relations should improve. Until recently the Germans did nothing but curse the USSR, did not want any improvement in political relations, and refused to participate in any conferences with the USSR. If the Germans are now sincerely changing course and really want to improve political relations with the USSR, they are obliged to state what this improvement represents in concrete terms. . . . The matter depends entirely on the Germans. We would, of course, welcome any improvement in political relations between the two countries.[20]

On August 2 the Germans made yet another approach when Foreign Minister Ribbentrop told Astakhov that "there are no contradictions between our countries from the Black Sea to the Baltic. On all problems it is possible to reach agreement."[21] The next day, Schulenburg met with Molotov and proposed an improvement in Soviet-German relations in three stages: (1) the conclusion of an economic agreement, (2) better press relations, and (3) the development of cultural and scientific cooperation. Schulenburg stressed, too, that there were no contradictions between Germany and the USSR in the Baltic and that Berlin had no plans that ran counter to Soviet interests in Poland. Molotov's response was mixed. He welcomed the German desire for an improvement in relations but cast doubt on the sincerity and durability of the apparent change in German foreign policy. Schulenburg's conclusion from the meeting was that "my overall impression is that the Soviet Government is at present determined to sign with England and France if they fulfill all Soviet wishes. . . . It will . . . take a considerable effort on our part to cause the Soviet Government to swing about."[22]

By the time Schulenburg next met Molotov on August 15, the Anglo-Soviet-French military negotiations were already in progress. At the meeting Molotov asked the ambassador about the German government's attitude toward a nonaggression treaty between the two countries.[23] Two days later the two men met again, and Molotov handed Schulenburg a formal written proposal for a nonaggression pact, together with a "special protocol." The ambassador pressed for Ribbentrop to be invited to Moscow for face-to-face negotiations, but Molotov refused to set a date.[24] At a meeting on August 19 Molotov made it clear that before Ribbentrop came to Moscow, it had to be certain that an agreement would be reached, especially in relation to the special protocol. The meeting ended at 3:00 p.m., but at 4:30 p.m. Schulenburg was summoned back to the Kremlin and told by Molotov that Ribbentrop could come to Moscow on August 26–27.[25]

According to Stalin's appointments diary, Molotov saw Stalin just before his meeting with Schulenburg and again after the second meeting, so the authorization for Ribbentrop's visit must have been cleared by Stalin on the telephone. But the date set by the Soviets was not soon enough for the Germans, and on August 21 Schulenburg handed Molotov an urgent personal letter from Hitler to Stalin requesting that Ribbentrop be received on August 22. "The tension between Germany and Poland has become intolerable. Polish demeanor toward a great power is such that a crisis may arise any day," Hitler wrote to Stalin. Two hours later Molotov delivered Stalin's positive reply to Schulenburg.[26]

Ribbentrop arrived in Moscow on August 23. As might be expected Stalin did most of the talking in the negotiations for the Soviets, with Molotov playing a supporting role. This was a pattern to be repeated at countless diplomatic conversations in the future. The upshot was the signature of a Soviet-German nonaggression treaty, together with a "secret additional protocol" delineating future Soviet and German spheres of influence in Eastern Europe.[27] The text of the treaty was published in the Soviet press on August 24. The picture of Molotov signing the pact with a smiling Stalin standing behind him has become one of the iconic photographs of twentieth-century international relations.

The nonaggression pact with Nazi Germany signaled a new, neutralist course for Soviet foreign policy. What this meant was spelled out by Molotov in a speech to the Supreme Soviet on August 31 proposing formal ratification of the treaty. He began by explaining why the triple alliance negotiations had failed: Poland, encouraged by Britain, had rejected Soviet military assistance, which meant that it was not possible to arrive at a suitable military agreement. Following the failure of the military negotiations with Britain and France, said Molotov, the USSR had decided to conclude a nonaggression pact with Germany. Explaining how it was possible for the Soviet Union to sign a nonaggression treaty with the anticommunist Nazi state, Molotov told his audience that "the art of politics does not consist in increasing the number of one's country's enemies. On the contrary, the art of politics in this sphere is to reduce the number of such enemies and make the enemies of yesterday good neighbours, maintaining peaceable relations one with the other."[28]

SPHERES OF INFLUENCE

Germany invaded Poland on September 1, 1939. On September 17 the Red Army invaded Poland from the east. This dual invasion was presaged in the secret additional protocol to the Nazi-Soviet pact:

In the event of a territorial and political rearrangement of the areas belonging to the Polish state the spheres of influence of Germany and the USSR shall be bounded approximately by the line of the rivers Narew, Vistula, and San. The question of whether the interests of both parties make desirable the maintenance of an independent Polish state and how such a state should be bounded can only be definitely determined in the course of further political developments.[29]

This agreement was not the clear-cut advance decision to invade and partition Poland that it might appear in retrospect. Stalin was far too cautious to commit himself in advance to such a radical course of action. In the event, Poland collapsed surprisingly quickly, and the British and French, although declaring war on Germany, showed no inclination to become militarily involved in operations in the east. In such circumstances it was safe for the USSR to occupy by force its sphere of influence in eastern Poland.

The Soviet invasion was announced in a radio broadcast by Molotov:

> The Polish-German war has revealed the internal bankruptcy of the Pol-
> ish State . . . the Polish State and its Government have virtually ceased
> to exist. . . . Abandoned to its fate and left without leadership, Poland
> has become a fertile field for any accidental and unexpected contingency,
> which may create a menace to the USSR. . . . Nor can the Soviet Gov-
> ernment remain indifferent when its blood brothers, the Ukrainians and
> White Russian living on Polish territory, having been abandoned to their
> fate, are left without protection.[30]

Molotov's rationale was not as fanciful as it might seem. The Polish territories occupied by the Red Army consisted mainly of the western regions of
the Ukraine and Belorussia, which lay east of the so-called Curzon Line—the
ethnographic frontier between Russia and Poland drawn up by a commission
of the Paris Peace Conference in 1919. The actual border, however, had been
determined by Poland's victory in the Russo-Polish War of 1919–1920 and under the 1921 Treaty of Riga, by which the Soviets were forced to cede Western
Belorussia and Western Ukraine to Poland. But they were never reconciled to
the permanent loss of those territories. The Soviet invasion of Eastern Poland
embodied, therefore, patriotic-nationalist aspirations as well as the geopolitical
logic of keeping the Germans out of Western Belorussia and Western Ukraine.
Indeed, much of the non-Polish population (Jews as well as the Belorussians
and Ukrainians) welcomed the Red Army as liberators and as their protectors
from the Germans. Admittedly, that popular enthusiasm did not last long. In
the latter part of 1939, Western Belorussia and Western Ukraine were forcibly
and violently "sovietized" and incorporated into the USSR. Among the victims
of the Soviet reign of terror were four hundred thousand ethnic Poles, imprisoned and then deported to the Soviet interior. Among their number were more
than twenty thousand Polish officers and officials executed in the infamous
Katyn Massacre of March and April 1940 in a forest near Smolensk and other
execution sites.

On September 27 Ribbentrop flew to Moscow to negotiate the German-
Soviet Boundary and Friendship Treaty, which would settle the demarcation
line in Poland. Following talks between Ribbentrop, Stalin, and Molotov, the
Soviet Union and Germany published a joint declaration on September 28

calling for an end to the war and blaming the Western powers for continuing hostilities.[31]

The theme of Anglo-French culpability for the war was taken up by Molotov in his speech to the Supreme Soviet on October 31, 1939:

> In the past few months such concepts as "aggression" and "aggressor" have acquired new concrete connotation, new meaning. It is not hard to understand that we can no longer employ these concepts in the sense we did, say, three or four months ago. Today, as far as the European great powers are concerned, Germany is in the position of a State which is striving for the earliest termination of war and for peace, while Britain and France, which but yesterday were declaiming against aggression, are in favour of continuing the war and are opposed to the conclusion of peace."[32]

In his August speech Molotov had announced the Soviet Union's dealignment in European international politics. Now he specified the USSR's realignment alongside Germany, albeit as political collaborator, not military ally:

> Relations between Germany and other western European bourgeois states have in the past two decades been determined primarily by Germany's efforts to break the fetters of the Versailles treaty. . . . Relations between the Soviet Union and Germany were based on a different foundation, which had nothing whatever in common with perpetuating the post-war Versailles system. We have always held that a strong Germany is an indispensable condition for a durable peace in Europe.[33]

These were precisely the terms in which Soviet Russia had justified the so-called Rapallo relationship with Germany in the 1920s—named after the 1922 pact that had restored diplomatic relations between the two states after World War I. Stalin and Molotov proposed to revive the intensive political, economic, and military cooperation with Germany that had existed in the 1920s. That relationship had broken down when Hitler came to power in 1933, but the Nazi regime was never seen by Stalin and Molotov as an insurmountable obstacle to good relations with Germany. As the Soviets were fond of saying, the USSR stood for peaceful coexistence with all states, irrespective of their internal regimes. Relations with Hitler had broken down because of his anti-Soviet foreign policy, not his political ideology. Whether Hitler would revert to an anti-Soviet foreign policy was an open question. For the time being, however, Stalin and Molotov did not rule out the possibility of long-term coexistence, even an alliance, with Nazi Germany.

Stalin's top priority after the partition of Poland was to incorporate the Baltic states into the Soviet sphere of influence. The terms of the secret additional protocol to the Nazi-Soviet pact specified that Estonia, Finland, and Latvia now lay in the Soviet sphere of influence while Lithuania remained in Germany's:

> In the event of territorial and political arrangement in the areas belonging to the Baltic States (Finland, Estonia, Latvia and Lithuania), the northern boundary of Lithuania shall represent the boundary of the spheres of influence of Germany and the USSR.[34]

Fearing German penetration of Lithuania, Stalin arranged for its transfer to the Soviet sphere of influence in a secret protocol attached to the Soviet-German Boundary and Friendship Treaty. In return the Germans got more Polish territory.[35] In late September and early October, the Soviets conducted a series of "negotiations" with Baltic politicians. During these discussions Stalin and Molotov played "good cop/bad cop," a routine that became a standard part of their negotiating repertoire.

The Estonians were dealt with first. On September 24 Molotov presented Karl Selter, the Estonian foreign minister, with a demand for a mutual assistance pact, including provision for Soviet air and naval bases in Estonia. "If you don't want to conclude this pact with us you can be sure that we will find other ways to guarantee our security, perhaps more drastic and complicated ways," said Molotov. Later in the conversation Molotov told Selter that the German-Polish war had shown that a great power cannot rely on others for its security, hence the demand for military bases in Estonia. Speaking softly as well as wielding a big stick, Molotov reassured the foreign minister that the USSR did not intend to sovietize Estonia or to interfere in its domestic affairs.[36] The Soviet-Estonian Mutual Assistance Pact was signed on September 28.

It was the Latvians' turn next. On October 2 Molotov told Vilhelms Munters, the Latvian foreign minister, "We cannot permit small states to be used against the USSR. Neutral Baltic States—that is too insecure." Stalin added, "I tell you directly a division into spheres of influence has taken place. . . . As far

From Geoffrey Roberts, *Stalin's Wars: From World War to Cold War, 1939–1953*
(London: Yale University Press, 2006).

as the Germans are concerned we could occupy you, but we want no abuse." At the second meeting, on October 3, Stalin told Munters, "The Germans could attack. For six years the German fascists and the communists cursed one another. Now in spite of history an unexpected turn has taken place, but one can't rely upon it. Others, who were not ready, paid the price."[37] The Latvians signed their mutual assistance pact with the Soviets on October 5. Again, the key provision was the establishment of Soviet military bases.

The Lithuanian delegation, headed by Foreign Minister Juozas Urbsys, arrived in Moscow on October 3. Urbsys reacted strongly to Soviet demands for bases, although he was happy to accept the transfer of Vilnius—Lithuania's historic capital—from Poland. Urbsys counterproposed a mutual assistance pact without the Soviet bases. Molotov rejected the proposal, telling him on October 7:

> Lithuania should not forget under what conditions Europe is now living. The present war has not unfolded entirely; it is difficult to forecast its repercussions and, therefore, the Soviet Union considers its security. We do not know what can happen in the west. The Germans can turn against us, if they would win the war. The aims of England are not clear either, if Germany should lose.[38]

The Soviet-Lithuanian treaty was signed on October 10. The Soviets also had in mind a treaty with the fourth Baltic state—Finland—but as we shall see the negotiations with the Finns had a radically different outcome.

A few months later, after the German conquest of France, the Soviet Union occupied Estonia, Latvia, and Lithuania completely and, as in the case of Western Belorussia and Western Ukraine, forcibly sovietized and incorporated them into the USSR. Was that the intention all along? It would seem not. On October 25 Stalin told Georgi Dimitrov, the leader of the Communist International:

> We believe that in our pacts of mutual assistance we have found the right form to allow us to bring a number of countries into the Soviet Union's sphere of influence. But for that we will have to maintain a consistent posture, strictly observing their internal regimes and independence. We are not going to seek their sovietization. The time will come when they will do that themselves![39]

In line with this policy, on October 14 Molotov reminded Nikolai Pozd-nyakov, the Soviet diplomatic representative in Lithuania, that "any approach-es and contacts with left wing circles are to cease. Maintain contact only with government and official circles, remembering always that the ambassador is accredited by the government and not by anyone else."[40] On October 20 Mo-lotov angrily telegraphed his representative in Estonia, Kirill Nikitin:

> I have read the report "The Situation in Estonia" by TASS's Tallinn cor-respondent. From this report it is clear that the author is trying to play up harmful sentiments concerning the "sovietization" of Estonia. . . . The am-bassador must remember that the USSR will honestly and punctiliously implement the mutual assistance pact. . . . Thoughtless and provocative elements whose actions excite rumors about the "sovietization" of Estonia . . . must be immediately and firmly rebuffed.[41]

Similarly, on October 21 Molotov informed Pozdnyakov that "you and all the embassy staff . . . are categorically prohibited from interfering in interparty affairs in Lithuania. . . . The idle chatter about the 'sovietization' of Lithuania should be rejected as provocative and harmful."[42] On October 23 it was Niki-tin's turn to again suffer Molotov's invective:

> You do not understand our policy in Estonia, . . . you have been carried away by the mood favoring Estonia's "sovietization," which at root con-tradicts our policy. You must finally understand that any encouragement of this mood . . . or even mere nonresistance to this mood plays into the hands of our enemies.[43]

Molotov's harsh words and tone were typical of the rhetoric he deployed when his diplomats did not carry out their instructions to the letter.

Finland was the one Baltic state that refused to capitulate to Soviet de-mands. The Finns were offered the same basic deal as the other Baltic nations: a mutual assistance treaty and Soviet military bases on their territory. But the key Soviet demand was an adjustment of the Soviet-Finnish border to move it away from Leningrad, thereby enhancing the defensive position of the USSR's second city. As compensation the Finns were offered territory in the far north in Soviet Karelia. By early November, negotiations had broken down, and the

Soviets began preparations for an attack on Finland. On November 29 Molotov broadcast a statement that denounced the Soviet-Finnish nonaggression treaty of 1932 and severed diplomatic relations with Finland.[44] The Red Army invasion began the next day.

The Winter War, as it came to be called, involved Molotov in one of the more bizarre episodes in his diplomatic career. On December 1 the Soviet Union recognized as the government of Finland a "people's government" headed by Otto Kuusinen, a Finnish communist. On December 2 the USSR signed a mutual assistance treaty with the Kuusinen government. This enabled the Soviets to claim that the USSR was not at war with Finland but lending its assistance to the people's government. This strange diplomatic maneuver was based on the conviction that the war would be easy and the Red Army's invasion would be met by a popular revolt against the Helsinki government. Neither belief proved to be true. The Finnish people chose to fight against rather than cheer on the Red Army, and the military campaign proved to be much tougher for the Soviets than expected. During the fighting the Finns adopted a tactic that had been used during the Spanish Civil War. They attacked pockets of Soviet troops with improvised incendiary devices—glass bottles filled with gasoline—that they called "Molotov Cocktails."

After the first Soviet invasion of Finland failed, the Red Army regrouped and launched a stronger, and successful, attack. By March 1940 the Soviets were in a position to collapse the remnants of Finnish defenses, advance on Helsinki, and overrun the whole country. Stalin and Molotov chose, however, to negotiate a peace treaty. Signed on March 12, 1940, the treaty forced the Finns to accept Soviet territorial demands in exchange for Finland remaining independent and unoccupied.

The Winter War was a costly military exercise, but Soviet war losses were not the reason Stalin opted for a diplomatic end to the war. The spur was British and French preparations to send an expeditionary force to aid the Finns. The Anglo-French aim was to use their intervention as an excuse to stop German supplies of iron ore from Sweden, shipped via the northerly Norwegian port of Narvik—an aim that threatened to engulf the whole of Scandinavia, as well as the Soviets and the Finns, in the wider European war. Neither the Finns nor the Soviets, or the Swedes for that matter, wanted that to happen.

When Molotov reported to the Supreme Soviet on March 29, his speech was devoted to a blistering attack on Britain and France, accusing them of planning to use Finland as a platform for an attack on the USSR. The Soviet victory in the Winter War, claimed Molotov, was a victory not only over Finland but also over Britain and France: "What was going on in Finland was not merely our collision with Finnish troops. It was a collision with the combined forces of a number of imperialist states."[45]

THE FALL OF FRANCE

In spring 1940 the European war took an unexpected turn. In April and May the Germans invaded Denmark, Norway, and the Low Countries, and in June inflicted a stunning defeat on France. Britain, under a new government headed by Winston Churchill, decided to fight on, but when France surrendered on June 22, German dominance of continental Europe seemed assured. Stalin responded by bolting the Baltic door to further German expansion. In mid-June Molotov delivered ultimatums to Estonia, Latvia, and Lithuania demanding the formation of pro-Soviet governments and Red Army occupation of the three countries.[46]

Another area of Soviet military and diplomatic action was the Balkans. Since Italy's entry into the war on June 10, the Soviets had begun to explore the possibility of a spheres-of-influence deal in the Balkans with the Italians. On June 25 Molotov offered to recognize Italy's preeminence in the Mediterranean in return for Italian recognition of Soviet predominance in the Black Sea. Presenting the proposal to the Italian ambassador, Molotov said that "it could provide the basis for a durable agreement between Italy and the USSR. When in autumn 1939 the USSR and Germany began to speak in clear language, they quickly agreed on cooperation."[47]

An even more forthright move was the Soviet ultimatum to Romania on June 26 demanding Bessarabia and North Bukovina. Bessarabia was a disputed territory, dating back to the Romanian occupation of the tsarist province in 1918. The existence of that dispute had been recognized in the secret protocol of the Nazi-Soviet Pact. North Bukovina was not mentioned in the protocol but was added to Soviet demands for strategic reasons: it secured land links between Bessarabia and Ukraine. The Romanians, after taking advice from the Germans, complied with the Soviet ultimatum two days later. Like Western Belorussia, Western Ukraine, and the Baltic states, the two former Romanian territories were sovietized and incorporated into the USSR.

For Stalin these were defensive moves, and he still saw the future in terms of a long-term alliance with Germany. This was evident from a conversation between Stalin and Stafford Cripps, the new British ambassador to Moscow, on July 1, 1940. Cripps brought with him a message from Churchill warning of the threat posed by German hegemony in Europe. According to a Soviet translator's report, Stalin told Cripps that it was "premature to speak of German domination of Europe. The defeat of France did not signify such domination. Such domination over Europe by Germany would require German domination of the seas, and that was hardly possible. . . . In all his meetings with German representative he had noted no desire for German domination of the world. . . . He did not deny that among the national-socialists there were those who spoke of German domination of the world. But . . . in Germany there are intelligent people who understand that Germany does not have the power to dominate the world."[48]

Molotov said much the same as Stalin in his speech to the Supreme Soviet on August 1. He began by noting the significance of the defeat of France, which was due in part to the French underestimating the role of the Soviet Union in European affairs. But the war was not over, said Molotov. It was entering a new phase in which Germany and Italy would be pitted against Britain and the United States. Stressing the continuing importance of the Soviet-German nonaggression pact, Molotov refuted speculation about differences between Moscow and Berlin, asserting that "the good-neighborly and friendly relations established between the Soviet Union and Germany are not based on fortuitous considerations of a transient nature, but on the fundamental political interests of both countries."[49]

Hitler's view of recent developments in relations with the Soviets was somewhat different. He saw Soviet actions in the Baltic states and in the Balkans as threatening. There was nothing the Germans could do to stop the takeover in the Baltic states, but they quickly scotched Soviet efforts to negotiate a Balkan spheres-of-influence agreement with Italy. Crucially, under the so-called Vienna Award of August 31, 1940, the Germans and Italians arbitrated various territorial claims in relation to Romania and then guaranteed the country against further territorial encroachments, including a possible Soviet demand for South Bukovina. The Soviets felt they should have been consulted about the Vienna Award, and there began a long wrangle between Molotov and Ribbentrop about the interpretation of the mutual consultation clauses in the Nazi-Soviet pact.

Adding to Moscow's concerns was the arrival in September of a German military mission in Romania and reports of German troop transits across Finland to Norway. On September 27 Germany, Italy, and Japan signed a Tripartite Pact under which they pledged to assist one another should they be attacked by a power not at that time involved in the war. Romanian and Hungarian accession to the pact quickly followed. Then, on October 28, Italy invaded Greece, thus spreading the European war to the Balkans and the Eastern Mediterranean.

Against this background of rising tension, Ribbentrop wrote to Stalin on October 13, inviting him to send Molotov to Berlin for negotiations about the long-term future of Soviet-German relations. Stalin agreed. On November 9, on the eve of his trip to Berlin, Molotov wrote down his instructions from Stalin:

> Aim of the trip: to find out the real intentions of Germany [and Italy and Japan] in relation to plans for a "New Europe" and for a "Greater East Asia Sphere." . . . To prepare a basic outline of the spheres of interest of the USSR in Europe and in the Near and Middle East, seeking possible agreement on this with Germany (also Italy), but not concluding any agreement with Germany and Italy at any stage in the negotiations, with a view to continuing these negotiations in Moscow. . . . In the negotiations to secure the following regarding the sphere of interest of the USSR: Finland—in fulfillment of the Soviet-German agreement of 1939, Germany must remove all difficulties and ambiguities (the withdrawal of German troops, ending all political gestures in Finland and Germany) harmful to the interests of the USSR. . . . To speak also about our dissatisfaction that Germany did not consult with the USSR on the question of guarantees and the entry of [German] troops into Romania.
>
> Bulgaria—the most important question of the negotiations, which must, with the agreement of Germany and Italy, be regarded as in the sphere of interest of the USSR on the basis of a guarantee of Bulgaria by the USSR like Germany and Italy have in relation to Romania, and by the entry of Soviet forces into Bulgaria. The question of Turkey's future must not be decided without our participation. . . . The future fate of Romania and Hungary, which have borders with the USSR, we are very interested in. . . . The question of Iran, where we have important interests, must not

be decided without the participation of the USSR. . . . We would like to know what the Axis are thinking of doing in relation to Greece and Yugoslavia. On the question of Sweden the USSR sticks to the position that the preservation of the neutrality of this state is in the interests of both the USSR and Germany. Does Germany stick to that position?[50]

It is evident from these notes that Stalin wanted to negotiate a new Nazi-Soviet pact based on a spheres-of-influence agreement with Germany and Italy in the Balkans and the Near East. Equally, he was determined to clarify a number of important security issues.

MOLOTOV IN BERLIN

When Molotov arrived in Berlin on November 12, 1940, he was met at the railway station by Ribbentrop and by a guard of honor, and a band that struck up the Soviet national anthem, still at this time the "Internationale"–the revolutionary hymn of the Communist International, a tune rarely heard in the German capital since the Nazi takeover in 1933. This was Molotov's first trip abroad since 1921. During the intervening years he had barely been outside Moscow. But he was far from being overawed by the occasion.

The pattern for negotiations was established during Molotov's first discussion with Ribbentrop later that day. Germany had already won the war, Ribbentrop told Molotov, and it was time to look to the future. He proposed a spheres-of-influence agreement between Germany, Italy, Japan, and the USSR that would define the direction of the future expansion of the four states, which in the Soviet case would be south toward the Persian Gulf and, it transpired later, the Indian Ocean. As bait Ribbentrop offered to help the Soviets negotiate an agreement with Turkey that would give them control over the straits that guarded the entrance to the Black Sea. In response Molotov wanted to know more about the Tripartite Pact and about the intentions of its participants. A spheres-of-influence agreement, said Molotov, required precision, particularly in relation to the respective spheres of Germany and the Soviet Union. At this point the conversation broke off and the two men went to meet Hitler.

True to form the Fuhrer subjected Molotov to a tour d'horizon of the war that was long on rhetoric but short on substance. In his reply Molotov made some noises of general assent but then asked Hitler the questions contained in his brief from Stalin: What was the significance of the Tripartite Pact? What was the meaning in Europe and Asia of the New Order, Nazi Germany's plan for global geopolitical restructurization? What was the USSR's projected role? Hitler indicated that what he had in mind was Soviet participation in the Tripartite Pact, to which Molotov responded that this appeared to him entirely "acceptable in principle, provided that Russia was to cooperate as a partner and not merely an object." During the conversation Molotov also said that the German-Soviet agreements of 1939 had all been fulfilled except in relation to Finland, where there were some unresolved issues. After two and half hours of discussion, the meeting broke off because of possible air raids.[51] Paul Schmidt, Hitler's interpreter, later recalled of this meeting: "The questions hailed down upon Hitler. . . . Until now, no foreigner visitor had spoken to him in this manner in my presence."[52]

The next morning Molotov met Herman Goering for a discussion about Soviet-German economic relations. He also met Hitler's deputy, Rudolf Hess, for a discussion about nothing in particular. (According to Molotov's report of the meeting it had no political significance.) In the afternoon he had his second meeting with Hitler, which was dominated by a prolonged exchange on Finland. The 1939 spheres-of-influence agreement meant, said Molotov, there should be an end to the transit of German troops across Finland and no more anti-Soviet demonstrations in the country. Hitler conceded the point about Soviet rights under the spheres-of-influence agreement but said there was nothing he could do about demonstrations within Finland, and in any case the troop transits would soon stop. Hitler then turned to what he considered a more important issue: when England was defeated the British Empire would collapse, and its territories would be up for grabs by Germany, Italy, Japan, and the USSR. In response Molotov once again turned the conversation to a specific issue, this time Turkey. Here Molotov's point was that as a Black Sea power, the Soviet Union wanted not just an agreement with Turkey on the straits but a guarantee for Bulgaria that would bind it to the USSR. Molotov wanted to know how Germany would feel about a Soviet guarantee to Bulgaria—a question Hitler sidestepped by saying he would have to consult Mussolini first. Once again the meeting ended in view of possible air raids.[53]

That evening there was a reception for Molotov at the Soviet embassy, followed by another meeting with Ribbentrop. This time the RAF did indeed turn up for the party, and the meeting took place in Ribbentrop's air raid shelter. Ribbentrop had a specific proposal to make: the Soviet Union would join the Tripartite Pact, and there would be two secret protocols to the treaty—one setting out spheres of influence and the other about ending Turkey's control of the Black Sea Straits. Molotov again raised the question of a Soviet guarantee for Bulgaria. He was interested, too, in the fate of Romania and Hungary, about German and Italian intentions in relation to Greece and Yugoslavia, and whether the Germans still supported the preservation of Sweden's neutrality. Ribbentrop was evasive and returned to his pet theme; "he could only repeat again and again that the decisive question was whether the Soviet Union was prepared and is in a position to cooperate with them in the great liquidation of the British Empire." Molotov's reply was the same as before: the prerequisite for Soviet participation in any such grand scheme was the settlement of outstanding issues in Soviet-German relations.[54]

One of the more memorable exchanges between Molotov and Ribbentrop in the air raid shelter—a story that Stalin loved to tell—came when Molotov interrupted the German's diatribe about finishing off the British Empire to ask, "If England is finished, why are we sitting in this shelter? And who is dropping bombs so close that we can hear them even from here?"[55]

Throughout the Berlin discussions, Molotov stuck closely to his brief and sent Stalin detailed reports on his conversations. In one of his responding telegrams, Stalin questioned Molotov's statement to Ribbentrop at their first meeting that the Soviet-German agreement of 1939 had been exhausted by developments, except in relation to Finland. According to Stalin, Molotov should have specified that he was talking about the secret protocol and not the non-aggression treaty itself. This correction was typical of the tight control Stalin exercised over Molotov when he was sent on missions abroad.[56]

What Molotov reported to Stalin when he returned home is unclear. According to the memoirs of Yakov Chadaev, a senior administrator in the Council of People's Commissars, Molotov gave the Politburo a detailed report on his discussions with Hitler and concluded that Germany would attack the USSR in the near future, a prognosis endorsed by Stalin.[57] However, the formal Soviet response to the Berlin negotiations suggests that Molotov and Stalin had not yet given up on a deal with Hitler. On November 25 Molotov presented Schulenburg with a memorandum setting out the conditions of Soviet adherence to the Tripartite Pact: (1) withdrawal of German troops from Finland, (2) a Soviet-Bulgarian mutual assistance pact, including the establishment of Soviet military bases, (3) recognition of Soviet aspirations in the direction of the Persian Gulf, (4) an agreement with Turkey providing for Soviet military bases on the Black Sea Straits, and (5) Japanese renunciation of rights to coal and oil concessions in North Sakhalin.[58] Molotov also told Schulenburg that Vladimir G. Dekanozov would be the new Soviet ambassador to Germany. Dekanozov was one of Molotov's deputy commissars (the other was Andrei Vyshinsky). He was a former member of the security services who had transferred to the Foreign Commissariat the same time as Molotov and had been instrumental in purging the commissariat of officials appointed during the Litvinov era. When Dekanozov presented his credentials to Hitler on December 19, the Fuhrer told him that the Berlin negotiations would be continued through official channels.[59] Hitler, however, had already decided on war. Just the day before, he had issued the directive giving the go-ahead for Operation Barbarossa—the code name for the German invasion of the Soviet Union.

THE ROAD TO WAR

By this time the Soviets were also actively preparing for war, too. Molotov's task on the diplomatic front was to contest German influence in the Balkans, and the diplomatic battle with Berlin centered on the alignment of Bulgaria. A year earlier the Bulgarians had politely declined the Soviet offer of a pact of mutual assistance. On November 25, 1940, that offer was revived, including a proposal for Soviet air and naval bases in Bulgaria. Again, the Bulgarians said no.[60] In early January 1941 there were reports that Bulgaria had agreed to sign the Tripartite Pact and German troops would be allowed into the country. In protest the Soviets issued a statement to the Germans saying that they considered Bulgaria within their security zone and would view the entry of foreign troops into the country a violation of the USSR's security interests. On March 1, however, Bulgaria joined the Tripartite Pact and allowed the entry of German troops. Molotov's response was the rather lame statement to Schulenburg that Germany "cannot count on support from the USSR for its acts in Bulgaria."[61]

With Bulgaria's adherence to the Axis, Moscow's attentions turned to Yugoslavia—the last remaining independent state in the Balkans apart from embattled Greece. The Soviets had been courting Belgrade, with little success, since the establishment of diplomatic relations with Yugoslavia in June 1940. At the end of March 1941, Soviet relations with Yugoslavia took a new turn

when a popular-backed coup in Belgrade overthrew the pro-German government and reversed its decision to join the Axis. On March 30 the new Yugoslavian government approached the Soviet embassy with proposals for a military
and political alliance, stressing, in particular, the need for arms to defend the
country's neutrality. The next day Molotov invited Belgrade to send a delegation to Moscow for urgent negotiations. The talks in Moscow were conducted
by Vyshinsky, who made it clear that the USSR wanted, above all, to avoid
antagonizing the Germans. In line with this priority, Molotov called in Schulenburg on April 4 and told him the Soviet Union was going to sign a nonaggression treaty with Yugoslavia. Schulenburg protested that relations between
Yugoslavia and Germany were tense at the moment because of the uncertainty
about Yugoslavia's membership in the Tripartite Pact. Molotov replied that
there was no contradiction between Yugoslavia's adherence to the Axis and a
friendship pact with the Soviet Union. The Soviet treaty with Yugoslavia, said
Molotov, was a contribution to peace in the Balkans.[62]

The Soviet-Yugoslavian pact of nonaggression was concluded on April
5, 1941. The next day Hitler, concerned about the Italians' faltering Greek
campaign, launched an invasion of Yugoslavia and Greece. Within a fortnight
Belgrade was suing for peace, and by early May mainland Greece was also under German occupation. The Yugoslavians received neither supplies nor much
sympathy from the Soviets.

The Soviet treaty with Yugoslavia in the face of German protests, like the
strong words in relation to Bulgaria, was a gesture of defiance by Moscow, but
that was all. It was also the last such gesture the Soviets would make. With the
fall of Yugoslavia to the Germans, Stalin and Molotov embarked upon a series
of appeasements designed to convince Hitler the Soviet Union posed no immediate threat to German hegemony in Europe.

The first of these moves was the signature of a neutrality pact with Japan on
April 13. Japan was one of Germany's partners in the Tripartite Pact, and the
Soviet-Japanese treaty was intended as a message to Hitler that Stalin was still
interested in developing the Soviet-German relationship. To reinforce the message, Stalin engaged in some extravagant gestures when the Japanese foreign
minister departed Moscow by train. At the railway station, Stalin sought out
and publicly embraced Schulenburg, saying to him, "We must remain friends
and you must do everything to that end." Later he turned to the German military attaché, Colonel Hans Krebs (who spoke Russian), and told him, "We will

remain friends with you—in any event."[63]

The pact with Japan was also a hedge against war with Germany, since it might keep the Japanese out of the war, at least for a while. A similar neutrality agreement had been signed with Turkey in March 1941.

The appeasement gestures continued on May 7 when it was announced that Stalin had been appointed chairman of the Council of People's Commissars, with Molotov becoming his deputy. Moscow had long cultivated Stalin's image as a peacemaker and conciliator, and, sure enough, Schulenburg cabled Berlin that he was "convinced that Stalin will use his new position in order to take part personally in the maintenance and development of good relations between the Soviets and Germany."[64] On May 8 the official Soviet news agency, TASS, issued a denial of rumors about troop concentrations along the Soviet border. The next day the Soviets withdrew diplomatic recognition from the governments-in-exile of German-occupied Belgium, Norway, and Yugoslavia. On May 12 the Soviet Union recognized an anti-British regime in Iraq. Around the same time the Soviets leaked to the Germans a sanitized version of a speech by Stalin to the graduates of the Red Army staff academies on May 5 in which he had supposedly talked about the need for a new compromise with Germany. In fact, Stalin had warned his officers to be prepared for war.[65]

Schulenburg evaluated these developments in a telegram to Berlin on May 12: "Stalin has set himself the goal of preserving the Soviet Union from a conflict with Germany."[66] Schulenburg was a German nationalist and an advocate of the Rapallo line in relation to the USSR—a position that still had some support within the German foreign office. Indeed, in the days preceding this telegram, Schulenburg had become engaged in a rather delicate personal diplomatic maneuver. In mid-April he had returned to Berlin for consultations, and at a meeting with Hitler on April 28 the Fuhrer complained bitterly about Soviet actions during the Yugoslavian crisis. Schulenburg returned to Moscow worried about the future of Soviet-German relations. In early May he had a series of meetings with Dekanozov, who was on leave from Berlin, in which he proposed that Stalin write to Hitler professing his peaceful intentions. In response Dekanozov suggested a joint Soviet-German communiqué as well. But when it was suggested Schulenburg negotiate the texts with Molotov, the ambassador backed away, saying he had no authority to conduct such negotiations.[67]

Schulenburg's personal overtures helped convince the Soviets that there were divided counsels in Berlin about the desirability of war with the USSR. The "split theory"[68] was reinforced by the dramatic flight of Rudolf Hess to Britain on May 10, 1941. Hess flew to Britain on a personal mission to broker a peace deal. In Moscow, however, Hess's defection was seen as evidence of the split between those who wanted war with the Soviet Union and those who prioritized the fight with Britain (with Ribbentrop numbering among the latter).

The Soviets decided to do everything possible to encourage the "peace party" in Berlin. While the Red Army's preparations for war continued apace, frontline units were ordered to avoid any provocative actions on the frontier. Vital raw materials, including oil, grain, and precious metals, continued to flow across the Soviet border into Germany. A big diplomatic gesture was a TASS statement on June 13 denying rumors of rifts between the Soviet Union and Germany. According to the statement, Germany had made no new demands of the Soviet Union, both countries were adhering to the nonaggression treaty, and stories to the contrary were lies and provocation.[69]

The Soviets evidently expected a German response to the TASS communiqué, but none was forthcoming. On the evening of June 21, Molotov called in Schulenburg. The ostensible purpose was to deliver a note protesting German violations of the Soviet frontier, but what Molotov really wanted to know was why there had been no response to the TASS statement and why Germany was displeased with the USSR. Schulenburg was unable to provide an answer, but he promised to communicate Molotov's questions to Berlin. A few hours later Schulenburg returned to Molotov's office, this time at his own request. Because of massive troop concentrations and Red Army maneuvers along Germany's eastern borders, stated Schulenburg, Germany had decided to take military countermeasures. When Molotov inquired what this meant, Schulenburg replied that, in his opinion, this was the beginning of war. When Schulenburg was leaving, Molotov asked him: "Why did Germany conclude a nonaggression treaty that it so easily broke?" Schulenburg had nothing to say except that for six years he had worked for "friendly relations between the USSR and Germany, but against fate nothing could be done."[70] Schulenburg was executed by the Nazis following the failed attempt on Hitler's life in July 1944.

Did Stalin and Molotov seriously believe their appeasement gestures would dissuade Hitler from attacking the USSR? Why did they disregard numerous sources of intelligence that showed the Germans were about to invade?

To what extent were the initial successes of Operation Barbarossa the result of political obstruction of a timely Red Army countermobilization and counterattack? Many years later, in conversation with Chuev, Molotov was unapologetic:

> We are blamed because we ignored our intelligence. Yes, they warned us. But if we had heeded them, had given Hitler the slightest excuse, he would have attacked us earlier. . . . On the whole, everyone expected the war would come and would be difficult, impossible for us to avoid it. We delayed it for a year, for a year and half. If Hitler had attacked us half a year earlier . . . it would have been very dangerous. So it was impossible to begin obvious preparations without revealing to German intelligence that we were planning serious measures. . . . Stalin trusted Hitler? He didn't trust his own people!"[71]

Missing from Molotov's explanation was a crucial piece of the puzzle: neither Stalin nor he, or the General Staff for that matter, believed that a sudden and unexpected German attack would be as devastating as it actually was. The Soviet military-political establishment was confident the USSR's defenses would hold. The Germans' concentration of their forces on the Eastern Front had been more than matched by the Soviet build-up. By June 1941 the Red Army had more than three hundred divisions, comprising 5.5 million personnel, of whom 2.7 million were stationed in the USSR's western border districts. As Molotov reportedly told Adm. Nikolai Kuznetsov, the head of the Soviet navy, in June 1941, "only a fool would attack us."[72] Stalin and Molotov's gamble on the preservation of peace was based on the calculation that even if they were surprised by a German attack, the cost would not be prohibitively high. Soviet defenses would absorb the shock of the initial attack, and there would be time to mobilize Soviet forces for both defensive and counteroffensive purposes. What neither they nor the General Staff expected was an initial German attack of such massive weight that it pulverized Soviet defenses and disrupted the Red Army's planned counteroffensive. It was a near-fatal miscalculation, one that the Soviet Union almost did not survive as Hitler's armies headed at breakneck speed toward Moscow and Leningrad.

3

FORGING THE GRAND ALLIANCE
(1941–1945)

Our cause is just. The enemy will be defeated. Victory will be ours.

—V. M. Molotov (June 22, 1941)[1]

The German invasion of the Soviet Union was launched just before dawn on Sunday, June 22, 1941, with an attack by 180 divisions across a thousand-mile front. Fearing such an attack, the Red Army had been put on alert the night before, and by the time Molotov met Schulenburg at 5:30 a.m., the first reports of the invasion were coming through from the front. At 5:45 a.m. Molotov arrived in Stalin's office with news of the German declaration of war. One of the first decisions taken was that Molotov should broadcast the news to the nation. Molotov's draft of his radio speech was heavily edited by Stalin, but its most memorable words, broadcast just after midday, were his own: "Our cause is just. The enemy will be defeated. Victory will be ours."

There is a story—dating from Khrushchev's secret speech to the twentieth party congress in 1956—that Stalin was so shocked by the German attack that he suffered a nervous collapse. In some versions of this story, it is Molotov who saves the day by leading a Politburo delegation to Stalin to bring the Soviet dictator back to his senses. There is no contemporary evidence to support these retrospective claims. On the contrary, the evidence is compelling that Stalin was highly active and very much in charge during the early days of the war. That is not to say he was unmoved by events. When questioned about Stalin's demeanor when the war broke out, Molotov recalled, "I wouldn't say he lost

51

his head. He suffered, but he didn't show any signs of this. Undoubtedly he had his rough moments. It's nonsense to say he didn't suffer."[2]

What shook Stalin was not so much the German invasion—hardly an unexpected event—but the catastrophic failure of Soviet defenses and the disastrous results of the Red Army's initial counterattacks. The most shocking development was the German destruction of the Red Army's western front and the fall, on June 30, of the Belorussian capital, Minsk. That same day Stalin established a state defense committee to run the Soviet war effort, with himself in the chair and Molotov as his deputy. Three days later Stalin made his first-ever radio broadcast to the nation. Like Molotov, he defined the struggle against Hitler as a patriotic, antifascist war of national and European liberation. He also defended the Nazi-Soviet pact as a tactic that had bought the country valuable time to prepare for war.[3]

On July 10 Stalin took direct charge of the armed forces, and on July 19 he was appointed people's commissar for defense. On August 8 he was named supreme commander. The effect of these reorganizations was to formally unify in the person of Stalin the control and direction of the entire Soviet war effort. In practice, however, Stalin concentrated on military affairs, and he devolved initiative and responsibility for most other aspects of the Soviet war effort to individual members of the Politburo. The one exception was foreign affairs, where his involvement in decision making was almost as continuous and detailed as in the military domain.

From the early days of the war, Stalin began an intensive personal correspondence with British prime minister Winston Churchill and Franklin D. Roosevelt, the American president. Before 1939 Stalin had received few foreigners, apart from fellow communists. During the period of the Nazi-Soviet Pact, he played a more active role in diplomacy, but it was only after June 1941 that Stalin became a familiar figure to visiting diplomats, politicians, and other dignitaries.

Stalin's enhanced role in foreign policy decision making was hardly surprising given the intimate connection between diplomacy and military strategy. From the outset Stalin and Molotov realized they were involved in a political and diplomatic contest with Hitler as well as a military struggle. The war—and the peace that followed—would be won or lost not only on the battlefield, but through the political alliances each side formed.

The Soviets' greatest fear was that the German invasion would catalyze a radical realignment internationally, and the Soviet Union would find itself in the nightmare scenario of fighting a grand capitalist coalition that had put aside its differences to destroy a common communist foe. From Stalin and Molotov's point of view this was not an unlikely turn of events given their experience of fighting the foreign anti-Bolshevik coalition during the Russian Civil War of 1918–1921. These fears had no foundation, but Molotov and Stalin's suspicions of their Western allies did not dissipate until the war turned in the Soviets' favor in 1943.

It is difficult to judge how proactive and important Molotov was in influencing and shaping Stalin's thinking and action in the foreign policy sphere. But it is probably fair to conclude that Soviet foreign policy during the war years was the result of a genuine partnership between the two men, albeit with Stalin in the dominant position. Molotov was Stalin's constant companion, and the dictator relied on him for briefings and for the drafting of documents, including his messages to Churchill and Roosevelt. There is no evidence that during the war Molotov held views radically at variance with Stalin's (later, during the Cold War, it was a different matter). The only known examples of significant discrepancies in their policy positions were the result of misunderstandings or changes in Stalin's views, to which Molotov quickly adapted.

As Stalin's deputy in the State Defense Committee, Molotov performed various duties in addition to those of foreign commissar. Molotov signed more than half the ten thousand decrees issued by the committee during the course of the war. Among his oversight responsibilities were the evacuation of Soviet industry from war zones, tank production, and the early research program on the development of atomic weapons—work for which he was made a Hero of Socialist Labor in 1943. In August 1941 Molotov led a high-powered Politburo delegation to Leningrad, sent to strengthen the city's defensive position in the face of imminent German encirclement. In October 1941, as the Germans approached Moscow, Molotov was tasked to organize the evacuation to Kuibyshev of both the Moscow diplomatic corps and his own commissariat. The strain of his multiple responsibilities seems to have taken its toll at this time. Stanislaw Kot, the Polish ambassador, recalled that when he saw Molotov in Kuibyshev he was "incredibly overworked, obsessed with the seriousness of the situation, but endeavouring nevertheless to master his exhaustion."[4]

However, Molotov's role within the State Defense Committee was strictly secondary to his work as foreign commissar. When Germany attacked, the immediate diplomatic task was to secure cooperation with Britain and with the United States. This proved easier than might have been expected, given the USSR's extensive collaboration with Nazi Germany during the previous eighteen months.

The day after the German attack, Churchill announced unconditional solidarity with the Soviets in their struggle against Hitler. At a press conference on June 24, Roosevelt announced that American lend-lease aid would be extended to the USSR. On July 12 Britain and the Soviet Union signed an agreement on joint action in the war against Germany. At the end of July Roosevelt sent his personal representative, Harry Hopkins, to Moscow to discuss American aid for the Soviet war effort. In early August the two states exchanged notes that formalized the American pledge to supply the USSR with war materials.

At the end of September Lord Beaverbrook, the British supplies minister, traveled to Moscow with Averell Harriman, Roosevelt's lend-lease administrator in London, to sign a detailed agreement on Anglo-American supplies to Russia. Molotov was the formal head of the Soviet delegation to the talks, but it was Stalin who took center stage in the negotiations. Most of the discussion was devoted to matériel issues, but at the second meeting with Beaverbrook and Harriman, on September 30, Stalin made a more general point: "I think that our agreement with England on cooperation against Germany and the non-conclusion of a separate peace should be transformed into a treaty of alliance which would cover not only the war but the postwar period."[5] Stalin followed up this idea in correspondence with Churchill. On November 8 he wrote to the British prime minister that there was a need for clarity on "war aims and the postwar organisation of the peace." Without such clarity there could be no mutual trust in Anglo-Soviet relations, said Stalin.[6] In response Churchill sent his foreign secretary, Anthony Eden, to Moscow to negotiate with the Soviets. The scene was set for Stalin and Molotov's first major diplomatic initiative of the war: an attempt to negotiate a postwar spheres-of-influence agreement with Britain.

EDEN IN MOSCOW

Eden arrived in Moscow on December 15 accompanied by Ivan Maisky, the Soviet ambassador to London. They were met by Molotov, and next day the three men saw Stalin. The Soviets proposed two Anglo-Soviet agreements, one on mutual military aid and another on the settlement of postwar problems. Crucially, to the second agreement would be attached a secret protocol dealing with the reorganization of European borders after the war. First, the USSR's borders would be those extant in June 1941 (i.e., including Estonia, Latvia, Lithuania, Western Belorussia, Western Ukraine, Bessarabia, and North Bukovina, as well as the territory ceded by Finland in March 1940). The Soviet-Polish border would run more or less along the Curzon Line, and Poland would be compensated by the acquisition of German territory. Second, Czechoslovakia, Greece, Albania, and Yugoslavia would be reestablished within their prewar boundaries, with the latter gaining Trieste at Italy's expense. Third, Turkey would get the Dodecanese Islands, some Bulgarian territory, and perhaps some Syrian territory in return for remaining neutral. Fourth, Germany would be weakened by various measures of disarmament and dismemberment. Fifth, Britain would have an alliance with Belgium and Holland, while the USSR would have alliances with Finland and Romania. In both cases there would be provision for the establishment of military bases. Sixth, overseeing the postwar order in Europe would be a military alliance of democratic states headed by some kind of central council or other body.[7]

In making this proposal, Stalin and Molotov were continuing the diplomatic practice they had developed in relations with the Nazi Germany in 1939–1941: wide-ranging discussions about borders and spheres of influence. However, compared to the grand schemes the Soviets discussed with the Germans, their proposal to the British was relatively modest. Moscow's sphere of influence was limited to Finland and Romania—two states that had joined in the German attack on the USSR—and the main content of the proposed secret protocol (the restoration of prewar European borders) was broadly in line with Stalin's public commitment to wage a war of liberation that would reestablish a Europe of independent sovereign states. Most important, the proposals on spheres of influence and postwar borders were secondary to Moscow's main goal in the negotiations: to gain advance British recognition of Soviet territorial gains during the period of the pact with Nazi Germany. As far as the Soviets were concerned, there could be no reasonable British objections to this proposal. Britain and the USSR were, after all, military allies, and the Soviets were bearing the brunt of the war. Eden was willing to sign general agreements on military cooperation and postwar collaboration, but any commitments on specific territorial issues, including Soviet borders, would require consultation not just with Churchill and the Cabinet, but with the United States and the British Dominions. Eden's stance was very frustrating for the Soviets, and at one point in the discussion Stalin protested that "Britain had had an alliance with Tsarist Russia when it comprised Finland, Bessarabia and more than half of Poland. Not a single British statesman in Britain had thought of protesting against that alliance then on the grounds that the said territories were part of the Russian Empire. Today, however, the question of the Finnish frontier and the Baltic Republics seems to be a stumbling-block."[8]

On the face of it Soviet insistence on an immediate agreement guaranteeing their 1941 frontiers was a little odd, given that most of European Russia remained under German occupation and the outcome of the war was still uncertain. However, Eden's visit to Moscow coincided with a successful counteroffensive in front of the Soviet capital–the first of the great turning points of the Eastern Front war–and the beginning of a strategic offensive by the Red Army to expel the Germans from the USSR. Stalin expected the war to be over sooner rather than later, and he wanted to secure his territorial gains in advance of any peace conference.

Another component of Soviet calculations concerned the United States. The Americans had formally entered the conflict after the Japanese attacked Pearl Harbor on December 7, 1941, and Hitler declared war on the United States on December 11. While very welcome militarily, direct U.S. involvement in the war complicated political negotiations about the postwar order. Washington was explicitly opposed to spheres-of-influence agreements and was likely to be even more recalcitrant than London in relation to recognition of the USSR's 1941 borders. The Soviet idea was to do a deal with the British that could then be presented to the Americans as a fait accompli. As Molotov put it to Stafford Cripps, "if the USSR and Great Britain could find a common language and achieve mutual understanding it would be easier to resolve these questions [about the postwar order] with American participation."[9]

Eden left Moscow on December 22 without any agreements being reached. Despite this setback Stalin and Molotov remained fixated on questions of the postwar order. On December 26 Deputy Foreign Commissar Solomon Lozovsky sent a memorandum to Stalin and Molotov on the postwar issue. The eventual outcome of the war was clear, said Lozovsky: the Axis Powers would be defeated, and there would be a peace conference at which the Soviet Union would be faced by a bloc of capitalist powers headed by Britain and the United States. There would be differences among the bourgeois states, but on the most important issues the USSR would find itself facing a united capitalist front. All the more reason, argued Lozovsky, to prepare plans for the peace. He highlighted three issues for special consideration: the payment of reparations from enemy states, the USSR's postwar borders, and the permanent weakening of Germany. He concluded by proposing the establishment of two commissions to consider postwar questions: an economic-financial commission to prepare proposals on reparations and a political commission to examine the issue of the Soviet, German, and other borders.

At the end of January 1942, the Politburo decided to establish a "Commission for the Preparation of Diplomatic Materials," chaired by Molotov. The commission's brief was to collect, examine, and summarize documentation relevant to the discussion of the postwar order in Europe, Asia, and other parts of the world. This research would then form the basis for planning the postwar world. Over the next two years the commission did some useful work, but its practical importance turned out to be far less than anticipated.[10] The reason was the deterioration in the military situation and the temporary fading of Stalin's interest in postwar questions.

By February 1942 the Soviet winter offensive was running out of steam. The Germans had been pushed back in a few places, but they still occupied vast swaths of Soviet territory. German armies remained entrenched only a hundred miles from Moscow. Leningrad remained surrounded, and most of the Ukraine was in German hands. In April Stalin finally called the counteroffensive off, and the Red Army went over to the defensive. He remained confident the Red Army's advance would resume in the summer, but the changed military outlook resulted in a new priority in Soviet relations with Britain and the United States: the opening of a second front in France that would draw a considerable body of German troops away from the Eastern Front.

On April 12, 1942, Roosevelt wrote to Stalin proposing that Molotov be sent to Washington to discuss "a very important proposal involving the utilization of our armed forces in a manner to relieve your . . . Front."[11] Subsequent inquiries revealed that what Roosevelt had in mind was a second front in France—something the Soviets had been pressing for since July 1941. Roosevelt's proposal was prompted, at least in part, by a series of conversations he held with the new Soviet ambassador to the United States, Maxim Litvinov, in early 1942.

When Molotov had replaced Litvinov in May 1939, the former foreign commissar was sent into retirement, but he was quickly reactivated after the German attack in June 1941. At the end of July he reemerged on the diplomatic scene when he reportedly served as Stalin's interpreter at a meeting with Harry Hopkins. Litvinov performed the same function in September at the Stalin-Beaverbrook-Harriman talks. On November 6 Moscow announced Litvinov's appointment as ambassador to the United States. The importance of this posting was signaled by a Politburo edict appointing Litvinov a deputy commissar for foreign affairs.[12]

Given Litvinov's credentials and expertise as a diplomat, his rehabilitation made practical and political sense. He was an antifascist campaigner renowned internationally and was well known in the United States for the negotiations that had led to the establishment of American-Soviet diplomatic relations in 1933. But the return of Litvinov would not have pleased Molotov. They had been personal rivals since the 1930s when Molotov, as Soviet premier, began to meddle in foreign affairs. Litvinov was not a member of the Politburo, and he was jealous of Molotov's greater access to Stalin. However, his posting to the United States made him privy to Stalin's secret correspondence with Roosevelt.

The main theme of Litvinov's ambassadorship—which lasted until mid-1943—was the need for a high degree of Allied cooperation, coordination, and unity during the war. This attitude informed his enthusiasm for opening a second front in France, which he saw as politically and militarily important. On January 20, 1942, Litvinov sent Molotov a long telegram asking for authorization to talk to Roosevelt about the question of an Anglo-American invasion of Europe. Since the second front was no longer an urgent matter, Molotov did not hurry to reply. Two weeks later he telegraphed Litvinov:

> We would welcome the creation of a second front in Europe by our allies. But, as you know, we have already received three refusals to our proposal for the creation of the second front and we don't want to run into a fourth refusal. Therefore, you must not raise the question of the second front with Roosevelt. We will wait for the time when our allies will, perhaps, raise this question with us.[13]

Litvinov adhered to his instructions, but in his subsequent conversations with Roosevelt he took every opportunity to nudge the president in the right direction.[14] The result was Roosevelt's invitation to Molotov, which Stalin accepted on April 20, announcing that his foreign commissar would also go to London.[15]

MOLOTOV'S TRIP TO BRITAIN AND THE USA

Molotov's mission to London and Washington in May and June 1942 was his first foreign assignment since the Berlin negotiations of November 1940. He flew first to Scotland, arriving on May 20, and then took the train to London. He stayed at Chequers, the British government's country retreat north of London. Molotov was not overly impressed by Chequers, complaining later about the lack of a shower and comparing the facilities unfavorably with those of the White House. Molotov brought his bodyguards with him and slept with a revolver beside his bed, at least according to Churchill—not always the most reliable of witnesses. Accompanying Molotov was Maj. Gen. Fedor Isaev of the General Staff, there to advise on military matters. Unfortunately, Isaev fell out of a car in London, injuring his knee, and had to be left behind to recuperate when Molotov continued his journey to the United States.

Molotov's brief from Stalin was twofold: to continue the Anglo-Soviet Treaty negotiations and to lobby for a second front. The sticking point in the treaty negotiations was the Polish-Soviet border, because the British were not ready to recognize the USSR's annexation of Western Belorussia and Western Ukraine. As a compromise Molotov suggested the matter be left open and subject to an agreement between Poland and the USSR. Eden was prepared to accept this, but he did not want to disavow Britain's existing commitment to the territorial integrity of Poland. Another disputed issue was Molotov's insistence on a secret protocol that would grant the USSR the right to mutual assistance pacts with Finland and Romania after the war—a device to draw the two enemy states into the Soviet sphere of influence.

On the second front, Churchill's view was that he would like to mount a cross-Channel invasion by the end of year but preferred to delay until 1943 when there would be more troops and resources available. On May 23, after two days of discussions, Molotov reported pessimistically to Stalin:

> While he is showing me particular personal attention—lunch, dinner, a long personal conversation till late at night at Chequers—Churchill is be-

having with obvious lack of sympathy toward us concerning the substance of the two main questions. . . . All the recent conversations give me the impression that Churchill is waiting for new events on our front and is not in a hurry to agree with us at the moment. . . . Most probably the prospects for my trip to the USA are not favorable either, but the promise to go has to be kept.[16]

Later that day Molotov met Eden again. The foreign secretary had a new proposal: Britain and the USSR should sign a twenty-year treaty of mutual assistance. On May 24 Molotov sent Stalin the British draft of the proposed treaty. Signed by Maisky as well as Molotov, the telegram concluded with a one-line sign-off comment: "We consider this treaty unacceptable, as it is an empty declaration which the USSR does not need."[17] The treaty was unacceptable because it contained no commitments on the USSR's borders or the organization of the postwar peace—the two issues Molotov had been sent to London to resolve. Stalin took a different view. "We have received the draft treaty Eden handed you," he cabled Molotov a few hours later. "We do not consider it an empty declaration but regard it as an important document. It lacks the question of the security of frontiers, but this is not too bad perhaps, for it gives us a free hand. The question of frontiers, or to be more exact, of guarantees for the security of our frontiers at one or another section of our country, will be decided by force."[18]

Behind Stalin's more positive evaluation of Eden's proposal were events on the battlefield. On May 12 the Red Army had launched a major operation to retake Kharkov, the Ukraine's second biggest city. This was the first in a series of projected offensives designed to roll the Germans back to the USSR's western borders by the end of the year. But the Kharkov operation was a disaster and called into question the rosy strategic scenario Stalin had expected to materialize. It made the solidification of the wartime alliance with Britain even more critical and enhanced the importance of a second front in France as a means of drawing German forces away from the Eastern Front.

Faced with Stalin's cable, Molotov beat a rapid retreat. "I shall act in accordance with the directive," he messaged Stalin on May 25. "I believe that the new draft treaty can also have positive value. I failed to appreciate this at once."[19] At his next meeting with Eden, Molotov—nowadays always the diplomat—dissembled, giving the impression that it was his own idea to proceed with discussions on the basis of the new British draft, rather than instructions from Moscow. Molotov's change in attitude was more than a little confusing for his British hosts, given his hostile reception of their new proposal the previous day.

The Anglo-Soviet Treaty of Alliance, signed by Molotov on May 26, 1942, provided for a twenty-year mutual assistance pact against Germany and contained a pledge of "close and friendly collaboration after the re-establishment of peace for the organization of security and economic prosperity in Europe."[20]

Molotov left London for the United States on May 27, but when his plane stopped to refuel in Iceland it was delayed by bad weather, and he did not arrive in Washington until May 29. He was met at the airport by Litvinov and Secretary of State Cordell Hull and driven straight to his first meeting with Roosevelt.

During the London talks Maisky had attended all of Molotov's meetings with Eden and Churchill. Litvinov, however, was mostly excluded from Molotov's conversations with Roosevelt and other American officials. In his memoirs Andrei Gromyko, at that time Litvinov's deputy in the Washington embassy, recalled a row between Molotov and Litvinov during a trip to the nearby Appalachian Mountains: "We were talking about the French and the British, and Molotov sharply criticised their prewar policy, which was aimed at pushing Hitler into war against the USSR. In other words, he voiced the official party line. Litvinov disagreed. This had been the prime reason for his removal from the post of Foreign Commissar in 1939, yet here he was, still stubbornly defending Britain and France's refusal to join the Soviet Union and give Hitler a firm rebuff before he could make his fateful attack upon the USSR."[21] While there is no official record of such a car trip, it is not difficult to envisage such an argument, but it is hard to believe that Litvinov would have defended British and French foreign policy in the terms suggested by Gromyko.

At his second meeting with Roosevelt, Molotov was told by the president that "in order to prevent a war in the next 25-30 years, it was necessary to establish an international police force of three or four states. . . . The four Powers [the USA, Britain, the USSR, and China] will have to maintain peace by force."[22] On being informed of Roosevelt's proposal, Stalin responded enthusiastically. However, most of Molotov's conversations with Roosevelt were devoted to the second front. Molotov always averred little interest in the details of military affairs, but he was able to give the Americans a very clear and astute exposition of the strategic situation on the Soviet-German front, including identifying the likely direction of Hitler's next offensive—toward Baku and the oilfields of the Caucasus. To emphasize the importance of the second front, Molotov stressed that Moscow could still fall and that further serious setbacks for the Red Army were not ruled out. His clinching argument in favor of an immediate second front was that while such an operation might be difficult and dangerous in 1942, it would be even more so in 1943 when Hitler would be that much stronger. The time to act, urged Molotov, was now when the launch of a second front would have its greatest value and impact.[23]

The American response to Molotov's pitch was very positive. Roosevelt, in particular, was keen on a second front. But the Americans could give no hard and fast commitment to opening a second front in 1942 until they had consulted the British and had found solutions to the logistical problems posed by such an operation, above all the availability of sufficient landing craft. Having heard their response, Molotov cabled Stalin on May 31: "My mission in Washington may be considered complete." The next day Molotov had another meeting with Roosevelt, but the discussion progressed no further than the previous conversations. Since his plane was not ready, Molotov decided to take the train to New York to see the sights and meet Soviet representatives based in the city. Shortly after his return on the evening of June 2, there was a message from Stalin containing an instruction to make sure that the joint communiqué on his visit to the United States stated that "full understanding" had been reached on the question of creating a second front in Europe. In the same message Stalin upbraided his foreign commissar for not reporting fully enough to him: "You convey to us from your talks with Roosevelt and Churchill only what you yourself consider important and omit all the rest. . . . [I] would like to know everything, what you consider unimportant and what you think important." Molotov, naturally, complied, saying that in the future he would provide complete information and would seek the necessary amendment to the draft communiqué.[24]

Among the accolades heaped upon Molotov as a result of his American trip was his election in June 1942 to the "Society of Red Tape Cutters" by the readers of *PM*, a left-wing New York daily newspaper. According to the citation, the honor was bestowed because of Molotov's efforts in "snipping through the red tape of diplomatic suspicion and protocol to work out sound agreements with the USA and Great Britain for united action against the Nazis."[25]

Molotov left Washington on June 5 and flew to London, where his main task was to secure British agreement to a joint communiqué that would state, as did its Soviet-American counterpart, that "full understanding was reached with regard to the urgent task of creating a Second Front in Europe in 1942." The British agreed, and the two communiqués were published simultaneously on June 12, the day after Molotov left for home.[26]

Churchill made it clear in this second round of conversations with Molotov that the British had in mind a small-scale landing in Europe of six to ten divisions, and he could not even guarantee that. Molotov's summary assessment to Stalin on June 10 was, "The British Government is not undertaking any obligation to open the second front this year, but is saying, and with reservation at that, that it is preparing a trial landing operation."[27]

It is doubtful Stalin held out any great hope for a second front in 1942; the point of the two communiqués was to signal the possibility of such an operation and to deter the Germans from transferring too many resources to the Eastern Front. In line with this tactic, Molotov's speech to the Supreme Soviet on June 13 hailed the results of his trip to Britain and the United States, in particular the declaration on the second front, which had "great importance for the people of the Soviet Union since the creation of a second front will constitute insuperable difficulties for the Hitlerite armies on our front. We hope that our common enemy will soon feel the full weight of the growing military cooperation of the three great powers"—a statement that, according to the official record, was met with prolonged, stormy applause.[28]

In the weeks that followed, Molotov's rhetoric sounded increasingly hollow. At the end of June Hitler launched Operation Blue—an invasion of southern Russia and the Caucasus. Hitler's armies advanced rapidly, just as they had done in the summer of 1941. By the end of July they had taken Rostov—the gateway to the Caucasus—and were approaching Stalingrad. Stalin's anxiety about this turn of events was expressed in a message to Churchill on July 23: "In view of the situation on the Soviet-German front, I state most emphatically that the Soviet government cannot tolerate the second front in Europe being postponed to 1943."[29] Churchill responded by suggesting a personal meeting in which he could talk to Stalin about Anglo-American plans for military action in 1942. Stalin agreed but asked the prime minister to come to Moscow. The prospects for the meeting were not good. In the weeks before Churchill's

Winston Churchill, Prime Minister of Great Britain, and Molotov review the guard of honor in Moscow in October 1944. Society for Cooperation in Russian and Soviet Studies

arrival, Soviet spies in Britain confirmed what Stalin and Molotov knew from their diplomatic sources: the British and Americans would not open a second front in Europe in 1942 and were instead planning a major military operation in North Africa.

Churchill arrived in Moscow on August 12 with, as expected, bad news: it would not be possible to invade France in 1942 because of a shortage of landing craft. Stalin pressed for some kind of second front, such as a small-scale landing on the Cherbourg Peninsula, but to no avail. Molotov had one meeting with Churchill in which he strongly backed up Stalin's arguments in favor of a second front in 1942, but he was careful to refer the prime minister to Stalin when it came to discussion of substantive issues.[30]

After Churchill left Moscow, Molotov wrote to Maisky, briefing him on the visit. "The negotiations with Churchill were not entirely smooth," Molotov told Maisky, but they were "followed by an extensive conversation in Comrade Stalin's private residence, making for close personal rapport with the guest. . . . Even though Churchill failed to come up with a satisfactory response on the main question [of the second front], the results can nevertheless be regarded as satisfactory."[31] Stalin's attitude soon soured, however. By the end of August the

Germans had reached the outskirts of Stalingrad. By the middle of September they were fighting in the city center. The growing danger that the Germans would capture Stalingrad magnified the consequences of no second front.

In early October Stalin caused a sensation when he issued a public statement that criticized the Allies' lack of support for the USSR, including their failure to open a second front. In private he was even more trenchant in his criticism. On October 19 he cabled Maisky in London:

> All of us in Moscow have formed the impression that Churchill is intent of the defeat of the USSR in order to come to terms with . . . Hitler . . . at our expense. Without such a supposition it is difficult to explain Churchill's conduct on the question of the second front in Europe, on the question of arms supplies to the USSR . . . on the question of Hess, whom Churchill seems to be holding in reserve, on the question of the systematic bombardment of Berlin . . . which Churchill proclaimed he would do in Moscow and which he did not fulfill one iota.[32]

Stalin's intemperate reference to Hess harked back to old Soviet fears that the British were plotting a separate peace with Germany and were proposing to use Hitler's former deputy as an intermediary. These fears were exacerbated by a British announcement in early October that Nazi war criminals would not be tried until after the war, thus saving Hess from any immediate punishment. Maisky tried to calm down his boss by suggesting that Churchill was seeking an "easy war" rather than the defeat of the USSR, but Stalin was adamant that "as a proponent of an easy war Churchill is easily influenced by those pursuing the defeat of the Soviet Union, since the defeat of our country and a compromise with Germany at the expense of the Soviet Union is the easiest form of war between England and Germany."[33]

Stalin was evidently feeling the strain of the battle for Stalingrad. In October 1942 the city was on the verge of falling to the Germans. However, in November 1943 the Red Army launched a massive counteroffensive that encircled German forces fighting in Stalingrad. By February 1943 the Germans had surrendered. The disaster at Stalingrad and the failure of Operation Blue ended any real hopes of a German victory on the Eastern Front. The Red Army seized the strategic initiative at Stalingrad and never lost it. That success was the beginning of the long march to Berlin that would culminate with the Red Army's capture of the German capital in April 1945.

The diplomatic consequences of the Soviet victory at Stalingrad were important, too. After that battle, Churchill and Roosevelt had to reckon with a Soviet ally that would emerge from the war as the greatest military power in Europe—and one whose political influence would be buoyed by popular admiration for the Red Army's heroic deeds and by growing support for the European communist parties, which had been in the vanguard of the resistance to the German occupation. In this new context the idea of an advance settlement of a number of postwar issues became increasingly attractive to Churchill and Roosevelt, who began pressing Stalin for a face-to-face meeting. Stalin was in no immediate hurry, as military affairs continued to consume his attentions. While an ultimate Soviet victory was inevitable, there were many more battles to fight before the war was won.

An early indicator of Stalin's political intentions was the decision in May 1943 to abolish the Comintern. By freeing the communist parties of direct control from Moscow, Stalin signaled that the political struggle for postwar Europe would be waged under the banner of a socially progressive patriotism. Another indication that Stalin was thinking again about postwar issues was the launch in June 1943 of a new, fortnightly journal devoted to foreign affairs—*Voina i Rabochii Klass* (War and the Working Class). Ostensibly published by the Soviet trade unions, it was, in effect, the house journal of the Foreign Commissariat. Indeed, much of the material published by the journal had started life as internal briefing documents, and its contents were tightly controlled by Molotov and Stalin.

After the Red Army's success in the great tank battle at Kursk in July 1943, Stalin began to focus more fully on the question of the postwar order. Within the Foreign Commissariat the new priorities were flagged by the creation that summer of three new policy commissions: the Commission on the Armistice Terms, headed by former defense commissar Marshal Voroshilov; the Commission on Peace Treaties and the Postwar Order, headed by Litvinov; and the Commission on Reparations headed by Maisky, who, like Litvinov, was recalled from his ambassadorial post in summer 1943.

Litvinov's recall from Washington took him out of the loop of Soviet-American relations and denied him access to secret diplomatic correspondence. This must have suited Molotov, who then made sure that Litvinov had access only to publicly available information. Indeed, most of the commission's reports, including those Litvinov wrote personally, were based on newspaper sources. On the other hand, Litvinov's commission did much valuable research, and its detailed findings and proposals shaped and influenced many aspects of Soviet foreign policy during and immediately after the war. Molotov's personal animosity toward Litvinov was one thing–his (and Stalin's) need to utilize the former foreign commissar's vast expertise was quite another.

THE MOSCOW CONFERENCE OF FOREIGN MINISTERS

The specific catalyst for establishing the planning commissions was Molotov's upcoming conference in Moscow with Eden and Hull. On August 9, 1943, Stalin agreed to meet Roosevelt and Churchill at a tripartite summit; two weeks later he consented to a preliminary meeting of the three foreign ministers. In agreeing to host the foreign ministers' conference, the Soviets' aim was to press again their case for the opening of a second front. Hence they submitted only one item for the agenda: "measures to shorten the war against Germany and its allies in Europe." It was clear, however, that the conference would occasion discussion of a wide range of political issues.

In preparations for the conference, Litvinov was particularly active. He drafted the main Soviet work plan for the conference, advised Molotov on conference tactics, and provided diverse memorandums and proposals on topics such as inter-Allied consultative machinery, international organization, Austrian independence, Polish-Soviet relations, and the geopolitical shape of postwar Eastern Europe. Litvinov was not the only contributor of the dozens of briefing papers and policy proposals that crossed Molotov's desk, but he was by far the most forthright in expressing his own opinion.[34]

On October 18 Molotov submitted to Stalin a summary document outlining the positions the Soviet delegation proposed to take at the conference.[35] Despite Litvinov's best efforts to foster a proactive approach, the positive policy content of the document was tentative, limited for the most part to reasserting preexisting Soviet positions (always the safest option when Stalin's precise wishes remained unknown). Molotov's advance view of the conference–as expressed in a strategy document prepared by another of his deputy commissars, Vladimir G. Dekanozov (the former ambassador to Berlin)–was that the British and Americans were trying to distract attention from the second front issue and were instead seeking information on Soviet policy, particularly toward the German question,[36] and Molotov was determined to find out what his allies were proposing before revealing his own hand.

Molotov's stance did not augur well for the Moscow conference, but it turned out to be one of the most important tripartite meetings of the war, on a par with the better-known summits of Tehran, Yalta, and Potsdam. This was largely due to the constructive approach taken by Molotov during the actual negotiations with Eden and Hull. Needless to say, everything Molotov said and did at the conference had Stalin's approval. Stalin did not personally take part in the conference, but Molotov and his delegation (including Litvinov) met him several times during its course. In addition, the Soviet dictator had his own meetings with Eden and Hull and hosted the closing conference dinner on October 30.

The conference opened on October 19 in the Spiridonovka Palace–the same venue at which the ill-fated military negotiations with the British and French had been held in August 1939. Molotov chaired the conference throughout.[37] The discussions and decisions shaped inter-Allied relations for the rest of the war. Among the more important resolutions were a declaration on the need to create a new international security organization after the war, a pledge to punish German war criminals, and a decision to establish a tripartite European Advisory Commission (EAC), based in London, to consider the armistice terms for Germany and other enemy states. On the second front issue, Eden and Hull gave reassurances there would be an Anglo-American invasion of France in spring 1944, and there was broad agreement on other military measures, such as trying to bring Turkey into the war on the Allied side. While there was no specific agreement on the postwar treatment of Germany, there was a broad meeting of minds on the need for the country to be disarmed, demilitarized, denazified, and dismembered–broken into a number of smaller states.

The Soviets were well satisfied with the results of the conference, which was hailed in the communist press as the harbinger of victory and of a long and stable peace guaranteed by the continuing cooperation of the Big Three. Internally Molotov instructed his diplomats that the conference was "a big event in the life of the People's Commissariat of Foreign Affairs," which "all PCFA workers must study in detail . . . and, if possible, make proposals on the realization of its decisions."[38]

Molotov's performance at the Moscow conference was a great hit with the British and Americans. According Archibald Clark Kerr, the British ambassador to Moscow,

Molotov conducted the proceedings with sustained tact and skill and growing good humour, deferring any matter that seemed to threaten prickliness
and only reverting to it when its thorns had been drawn by talks over food
and wine. The way he handled the debates compelled our respect and in
the end our affection also.[39]

The verdict of the American ambassador, Averell Harriman, was that the
conference "came pretty close to the type of intimacy that exists in the discussions between the British and ourselves," while his deputy, Charles Bohlen,
thought it "marked the return of the USSR as a fellow member of the society of
nations with the sense of responsibility that carried with it."[40] When Anthony
Eden, the British foreign secretary, reported to the House of Commons on the
conference, he was gushing in his praise of Molotov: "I have yet to sit under a
chairman who showed greater skill, patience and judgement than Mr Molotov,
and I must say that it was his handling of a long and complicated agenda that
[explains] a large measure of the success we achieved."[41]

Another of Molotov's fans was Harriman's daughter Kathleen, who accompanied her father on his mission to Moscow during the war. She thought
Molotov urbane, sophisticated, and the nicest of the Soviet leaders. "Moly,"
as she called him, had "a hellova sense of humor and nice twinkling eyes." It
was Molotov who usually presided over diplomatic dinners sponsored by the
Soviets. On one of these occasions, Stalin was present. "There were toasts to
everyone," related Kathleen in a letter to her friend Pamela Churchill (Winston's daughter-in-law), "and Stalin was very amusing when Moly got up and
raised his glass to Stalin with a short conventional phrase about 'our great
leader.' Stalin, after he'd drunk, came back with a 'I thought he was going to
say something new about me!' Moly answered with a rather glum, 'It's always
a good one,' which I thought very funny."[42]

The Czech historian Vojtech Mastny, not normally a fan of Molotov's, assessed the conference as follows:

The Moscow meeting stands out as the only one where the issues were
clearly defined, systematically discussed, and disposed through genuine
bargaining. . . . Molotov was at his very best at Moscow—a compliment
which can hardly be made to his British, much less to his American coun-
terparts. It was because of the superior Soviet diplomacy . . . that Stalin

could look forward with confidence to his impending talks with Roosevelt and Churchill at Tehran.[43]

FROM TEHRAN TO DUMBARTON OAKS

Iran had been occupied by Allied troops since 1941, and the Soviet embassy in Tehran was deemed a suitable venue for the coming summit because it allowed Stalin to maintain direct contact with his General Staff in Moscow. There was no fixed agenda and the conversations among Stalin, Roosevelt, and Churchill ranged far and wide. Early discussions were dominated by the second front issue as Stalin sought—and was given—a hard and fast commitment to an Allied invasion of France in spring 1944. In return Stalin promised to join the war against Japan as soon as he possibly could after the defeat of Germany.

For the future politics of the Grand Alliance, three particular discussions at Tehran were important. First, there was a further exchange between Roosevelt and Stalin about the president's idea for a great power directorate to police the postwar order—a proposal that was music to the Soviet dictator's ears. Second was Stalin's insistence during several conversations that a harsh, punitive peace be imposed on Germany. Stalin was convinced Germany would recover in fifteen to twenty years and start a third world war unless strong preventative measures were taken. Third was the reassertion of the Soviet claim to its June 1941 border with Poland. As compensation for the loss of Western Belorussia and Western Ukraine, Stalin was willing to cede German territory to the Poles, and, to sweeten the pill still further, he was also prepared to transfer back to Poland those Soviet-controlled areas along the border with a majority of ethnic Poles. But on the fundamental issue of retaining the territorial gains made during the Nazi-Soviet pact there would be no concessions.

While neither Churchill nor Roosevelt had any great objections to Stalin's plans for Poland, the question of Western recognition of the 1941 Soviet border with Poland remained unresolved. The same was true of all the other political issues raised at Tehran. Nonetheless, Tehran, together with the Moscow conference, marked the beginning of a new, tripartite phase in Soviet foreign policy—one dominated by the idea that the postwar world would be shaped by the wartime negotiations of the Big Three, who would then collectively police the international order they had created.

Driving Molotov and Stalin's pursuit of a peacetime Grand Alliance with Britain and the United States was their fear of renewed German aggression, which was hardly surprising given the devastation the USSR was suffering as a result of the war. This was the second time in a generation that Russia (now the Soviet Union) had been invaded by Germany. According to Stalin, after World War I the Allies had failed to impose upon Germany a sufficiently punitive peace. In his view the German danger would need to be contained on the long-term basis by permanently weakening the country. Central to that project was the policy of dismemberment, and the breakup of Germany was only conceivable—and sustainable—on the basis of long-term collaboration among the Big Three. Dismemberment also implied spheres of influence, since it was likely that the separate German states would come under the wing of one or another great power.

The question of how to ensure that spheres of influence did not lead to great-power conflicts was the central theme of Litvinov's musings on the postwar world. Litvinov's solution was to keep the interests of the great powers separate and to negotiate explicit agreements about spheres or influence, or "zones of security" as he called them. The cement binding these arrangements together would be the common interest of the great powers in maintaining peace and security.[44]

There is no reason to suppose that Stalin and Molotov disagreed with Litvinov's grand aspirations, but their outlook was more ideological than his and informed by expectations that in the postwar period the Western sphere would undergo an internal political transformation as communists and their left-wing allies increased their influence. In other words, Stalin and Molotov expected the character of the peacetime Grand Alliance to be shaped in a political context highly favorable to the Soviet Union.

The problem with Litvinov's approach was the absence of a practical diplomatic space in which to pursue a tripartite division of the postwar world. Neither the British nor more especially the Americans were prepared to engage in explicit bargaining about spheres of influence. A similar problem arose in relation to plans for dismembering Germany formulated by Litvinov's Commission on the Peace Treaties and the Postwar Order. There was general agreement among the Big Three that dismemberment was a good idea in principle, but how this would be achieved in practice did not figure in the active diplomacy of the Grand Alliance during the war. That diplomacy had a much narrower focus: preparations for the Allied occupation of the country. This was the job of the EAC, on which the Soviet representative was Fedor Gusev, Maisky's successor as ambassador to London. The governing assumption of the EAC's work was that Germany would be invaded and occupied by the Allies and subject to unilaterally imposed terms of unconditional surrender. By late 1944 those terms had been agreed upon, as had the division of Germany into American, British, and Soviet zones of military occupation (with a French zone to be partitioned off the American zone at a later date). Overseeing the occupation would be an Allied Control Council that would coordinate activities in the different zones, pending the determination of Germany's political future.[45]

More problematic were Soviet-Western discussions on the establishment of a new international security organization to succeed the discredited and all but defunct League of Nations. The prospect of the League's final demise pleased the Soviets. In December 1939, following its attack on Finland, the USSR had suffered the indignity of being the only state ever expelled from the League of Nations for aggression (Japan, Italy, and Germany had left of their own accord). The creation by the Grand Alliance of a new organization—destined to be called the United Nations—would not just be sweet revenge, but would also consolidate the status of the Soviet Union as a world power of the first rank.

Three-way discussions with the British and Americans began in early 1944 and culminated with the Allied conference at Dumbarton Oaks in Washington in August and September of that year.[46] Litvinov, a major contributor to Soviet preparations for the conference, identified three critical issues: First, the need to ensure that the decisions taken by the directing body of the new organization, the Security Council, were based on unanimity among the great powers. Second was the need to safeguard postwar security through a series of bilateral and multilateral agreements among the great powers separate from the constitutional structures of the UN. Litvinov's argument here was that the experience of the League showed the great powers were more likely to honor specific agreements among themselves than stick to general commitments on collective security. Third was the need to establish regional suborganizations with the UN framework as an infrastructure for the great power division of the world into spheres of influence.

Judging by Litvinov's complaints about his notes and memorandums being ignored, Molotov did not particularly welcome his contributions. An indicator of Molotov's thinking is contained in a contribution to the internal discussion by Yakov Malik, the Soviet ambassador to Japan, who was later to become one of his key lieutenants. Malik made two cautionary points. First, while the idea of the leading role of the great powers in the new organization was valid, the USSR should be wary of taking too much initiative on this issue, bearing in mind the likely objections from small states. Better to sound out the American and British position first, argued Malik. Second, the problem with a regional-based organization that divided the world into great power zones of responsibility was that the USSR could find itself excluded or marginalized in areas where it had vital interests, for example the Far East. Malik's analysis implied a looser set of great-power relationships than that advocated by Litvinov and a piecemeal approach to the construction of the new international organization.

Stalin had the last word, of course, and on July 20 Molotov submitted to him a draft of the directive for the Soviet delegation to the Dumbarton Oaks conference. It omitted mention of the separate great-power agreements that Litvinov was so keen on and dealt with the question of regional organization by saying that the great powers should have the right to participate in all the subsections of the new international security organization. In early August these instructions were amended in the light of further submissions from the British and Americans and resubmitted to Stalin on August 9 for final endorsement. Molotov drew Stalin's attention to two points. First, in accordance with American wishes, France was now included as a permanent member of the Security Council (along with Britain, China, the USA, and the USSR). Second, since Britain and the United States had reserved their position on the question of regional organizations, the Soviet Union should do so, too.[47]

Litvinov was not happy with this outcome, confiding to the Norwegian ambassador there were differences between his view and the official Soviet position, which "favored a looser international organization." In October 1944 he complained to Edgar Snow, a left-wing American journalist, that Litvinov's "original plan had been discarded; instead, at Dumbarton Oaks, the Soviet representative Andrei A. Gromyko had pulled out of his pocket an altogether different scheme."[48]

Gromyko was Litvinov's successor as ambassador to the United States and the leader of the Soviet delegation at Dumbarton Oaks. The scheme Gromyko pulled out of his pocket was based on the directives to the Soviet delegation. These mandated the delegation to seek the creation of an international organization to be dominated by an executive body of the great powers.[49]

There was no great gulf between the Soviet position and that of Britain and the United States, and a large measure of agreement was reached at Dumbarton Oaks. The main sticking point in the negotiations was the issue of the veto power wielded by the permanent members of the proposed Security Council. The Soviets stood by the principle of unanimity and rejected a British and American compromise proposal that the right of veto should not apply when a great power was directly involved in a security dispute. On September 9 Roosevelt appealed to Stalin to accept the Western position, but the Soviet dictator was unmoved, replying on the 14th that "the voting procedure in the Council will, I feel, be of appreciable importance to the success of the International Security Organization because it is essential that the Council should base its work on the principle of agreement and unanimity between the four leading Powers on all matters, including those that directly concern one of those powers."[50]

Although important, Dumbarton Oaks was not the only item on Molotov's diplomatic agenda that summer. As the conference approached, a crisis broke within the Grand Alliance about Soviet policy toward the Warsaw Uprising of August 1944. The uprising was an attempt by Polish nationalists to seize power in the capital before the arrival of the Red Army, rapidly approaching the city. Unfortunately, Soviet offensive operations petered out when confronted with a strong German defense of the city. The suspicion was that Stalin had deliberately paused the Soviet offensive to give the Germans time to crush the uprising and thereby dispose of the anticommunist Poles. This suspicion intensified when the Soviets refused to cooperate with British and American efforts to airdrop supplies to the insurgents. In fact, Stalin had expected to take Warsaw quickly and easily (the city did not fall until January 1945), and he was confident that the Red Army and his Polish communist allies would be able to deal with the nationalist challenge. In that context Stalin was even prepared to contemplate Soviet aid for the uprising. Only when the Red Army failed to take Warsaw and the Soviets were blamed by the Poles for the uprising's failure did Stalin's attitude harden. The British and American ambassadors in Moscow were horrified by Soviet obstruction of Western aid to the insurgents. After a meeting on August 17, Harriman reported that "my recent conversations with Vyshinsky and particularly with Molotov tonight lead me to the opinion that these men are bloated with power and expect they can force their will on us and all countries."[51] By September, however, relations had improved, and the Soviets were themselves air dropping supplies to the last remnants of the Polish resistance in Warsaw.

Poland was not the only country invaded by the Red Army in summer 1944. The August 20 invasion of Romania sparked an internal crisis there, and a coup overthrew the government and switched the country's allegiance to the Allies. On August 31 the Red Army captured Bucharest, and within days a Romanian delegation had arrived in Moscow to negotiate an armistice; a truce treaty was signed on September 12. Meanwhile, on September 5 the Soviet Union declared war on Bulgaria, the one member of the Axis that had not joined in the attack on the USSR but which collaborated with Germany in other ways, including by declaring war on Britain and the United States, the latter a purely symbolic gesture that had few practical consequences. Again there was an internal coup, and by the end of September Bulgaria had surrendered, signing an armistice a month later. As the Red Army invaded Slovakia and Yugoslavia and headed for their borders, the Hungarians sued for peace, too, but a German takeover prevented armistice negotiations, and it was not until February 1945 that Budapest fell to the Soviets.

THE CHURCHILL-STALIN PERCENTAGES DEAL

It was against this background that one of the most famous diplomatic meetings of World War II took place. On October 9 Churchill arrived in Moscow on his second visit to the Soviet capital. He went straight to the Kremlin for dinner, followed by a meeting with Stalin at which Churchill passed to him a piece of paper with a suggested division of the Balkans into British and Soviet spheres of influence, a division expressed in percentages: 90/10 for Russia in Romania; 90/10 for the British in Greece; Yugoslavia and Hungary 50/50; Bulgaria 75/25 in favor of Russia. Stalin ticked the list and passed the paper back to Churchill. Later in the meeting Stalin said the figures for Bulgaria should be amended 90/10 so that they harmonized with those for Romania. Stalin, or perhaps Molotov, had some further thoughts on the matter after the meeting. When Molotov met Eden the next day, he angled for 75/25 Soviet influence in Hungary. In return he was prepared to drop Stalin's demand for 90/10 in Bulgaria and reduce that to 75/25. Molotov also demanded a 60/40 share of Yugoslavia. The matter was finally settled at a further meeting on October 11, where it was agreed that Yugoslavia should remain 50/50, while Bulgaria and Hungary would be 80/20 in the Soviets' favor.[52]

But what did these percentages mean? The closest that Molotov and Eden came to a practical definition was in relation to the Allied Control Commission

(ACC) established to run the occupation of Bulgaria. The Soviets intended to apply to Bulgaria the model used in relation to Romania–an occupation controlled by an ACC but which excluded the British and American representatives from any real say in decision making. The rationale for this model was that whichever Allied country or countries militarily occupied an enemy state should be in control, the principle established by the Anglo-American occupation of Italy in 1943. Thus, the Eden-Molotov haggling about the Bulgarian percentages was a forlorn effort by the British to secure more say in the occupation regime (on the grounds that Bulgaria and Britain had been at war for three years). Molotov was prepared to make some symbolic concessions but none that would undermine Soviet control of the occupation regime. Hungary was another country the Soviets anticipated occupying militarily, and Stalin and Molotov were keen to assert in advance their occupation rights, hence the amendment to Churchill's proposal for a 50/50 split of that country. Yugoslavia was an allied rather than an enemy state, which meant it would not be subject to an occupation regime, so what the 50/50 British/Soviet split implied in its case was anyone's guess.

In truth, the only clear thing to emerge from the percentages discussions was that Stalin agreed to stay out of Greece. Churchill was afraid that Greece would be overrun by the National Liberation Front (EAM), the military wing of the Greek People's Liberation Army (ELAS), the communist-led partisan movement that already controlled large tracts of the country. The main issue from Churchill's point of view was Stalin's forbearance in relation to Greek affairs. He need not have worried. The Soviets had long ago decided Greece should be conceded to the British. Indeed, even before Churchill presented his "naughty document" about percentages at the meeting on October 9, Stalin had agreed with him "that England must have the right of decisive voice in Greece."[53]

Notwithstanding the retrospective hype generated by speculation about the meaning and consequences of the percentages discussion, Poland was actually the main topic of Stalin and Churchill's discussions in October 1944. Churchill was in Moscow to broker a deal to restore Polish-Soviet diplomatic relations. These relations had broken down in April 1943 following a German announcement about the discovery of the mass graves of Polish prisoners of war in the Katyn Forest. The POWs had been shot by the NKVD (Russian acronym of the People's Commissariat of Internal Affairs) in March and April

1940 on the instructions of the Politburo, and among the signatories of the Politburo resolution was Molotov. Moscow responded to the announcement by blaming the Germans for the killings, while the Polish government in exile in London called for an independent inquiry into the massacre. The Soviets were publicly outraged by the Polish position and severed diplomatic relations with the London Poles. Relations continued to deteriorate in 1944 when the Red Army entered Western Belorussia and Western Ukraine–territories the exile government claimed were still part of Poland. But Stalin and Molotov kept the door open to a deal with elements of exile government. Indeed, when the Warsaw Uprising erupted, the exile Poles' prime minister, Stanislaw Mikolajczyk, was in Moscow talking to Stalin. The Soviets offered a coalition government, including their communist allies, that would rule in liberated Poland pending the peace conference and postwar elections. In return Mikolajczyk would have to recognize the Curzon Line as the Polish-Soviet border.

The Stalin-Mikolajczyk talks went quite well, but any chance of a deal was dashed by the controversy surrounding the Warsaw Uprising. Stalin was willing to try again, and he agreed to Churchill's proposal that Mikolajczyk be invited to Moscow for further talks. In Moscow Mikolajczyk talked with Churchill, Stalin, and Molotov and with the leaders of the Polish Committee of National Liberation–the front organization for the communists and their allies that had established a provisional government based in Lublin to administer territories liberated by the Red Army (hence the appellation "Lublin Poles"). Mikolajczyk was inclined to do a deal but was constrained by the exile government in London. The talks in Moscow ended in failure, and a few weeks later Mikolajczyk resigned from his post.

A distant but very interested bystander during the Stalin-Churchill talks was President Roosevelt. He was represented in Moscow by Ambassador Harriman, who attended a number of the meetings on his behalf but not the one at which the percentages discussion took place. On the eve of Churchill's arrival in Moscow, Roosevelt had written pointedly to Stalin: "In this global war there is literally no question, military or political, in which the United States is not interested. I am firmly convinced that the three of us, and only the three of us, can find the solution to the questions unresolved. . . . I prefer to regard your forthcoming talks with the Prime Minister as preliminary to a meeting of the three of us."[54]

Roosevelt had been pressing Stalin for another summit since July. Originally Roosevelt hoped to hold the meeting in September, but Stalin demurred because of pressing military matters. Further delays occurred because of the American presidential elections in November 1944 (won handsomely by Roosevelt, who was inaugurated for a fourth term in January 1945). Eventually, it was agreed to convene a tripartite summit in February 1945 at the Black Sea port of Yalta.

PERSPECTIVES ON THE POSTWAR WORLD

Soviet policy preparations for Yalta were not nearly as extensive and systematic as they had been for the Moscow Conference of Foreign Ministers. The planning commissions were working well and churning out the necessary briefing documents, so there was less need for special preparations. Also, Soviet policy on most issues was settled and a matter of implementation rather than further elaboration.

Like Tehran there was no preset agenda for the Yalta summit, and on the eve of the conference Gromyko in Washington and Gusev in London submitted reports to Molotov on what issues were likely to arise. Both ambassadors identified the obvious points of contention: Poland, the German question, the United Nations, the Far Eastern war, etc. Their comments and advice were entirely predictable and stuck closely to existing Soviet policy.[55] More interesting were the broader speculations of Soviet officials on the likely shape of the postwar world and the light these shed on Stalin and Molotov's thinking of the eve of the Yalta Conference.

As early as January 1944, Maisky had sent Molotov a long memorandum setting out his views on the coming peace and the possible character of the postwar order. Maisky's starting point was that Moscow's postwar goal was a prolonged period of peace and security. To achieve that goal, the Soviet Union had to pursue a number of policies. The USSR's borders should be those extant in June 1941, and Finland and Romania should conclude mutual assistance pacts with the Soviet Union and permit Soviet military bases on their territory. French and Polish independence would be restored, but neither country would be allowed to become strong enough to pose a threat to the Soviet Union in Europe. Czechoslovakia would be strengthened as a key Soviet ally, and the mutual assistance treaty its exile government had signed with Moscow in December 1943 would be replicated with Yugoslavia and Bulgaria. Germany needed to be ideologically and economically disarmed as well as militarily weakened, with the aim of rendering it harmless for thirty to fifty years. The Soviet Union wanted Japan defeated, but it had no interest in becoming directly involved in the Far Eastern war and could achieve its territorial goals (the acquisition of South Sakhalin and the Kuril Islands) at the peace conference.

As long as there was no proletarian revolution in Europe, Maisky did not foresee big problems with Britain and the United States after the war, although there could be some tensions arising out of Soviet support for broad-based, progressive democratic regimes. Maisky thought the United States would be a dynamic and expansionist imperial power after the war, whereas Britain would be a conservative imperialist state interested in preserving the status quo. This meant there would be a good basis for close postwar cooperation between Britain and the USSR. Both countries would be keen on postwar stability, and the Soviets needed to keep Britain strong as a counterbalance to American power. The prospects were equally rosy for Soviet-American relations. There need be no direct conflicts between American and Soviet interests, and, in the context of its imperial rivalry with Britain, Washington would be concerned to keep Moscow neutral. Overall, the Soviet Union should be able to maintain good relations with both Britain and the United States.[56]

Gromyko, too, was thinking in broad terms. On July 14, 1944, he submitted a long document to Molotov entitled "On the Question of Soviet-American Relations," one of a number of such communications to Molotov on the theme of the wartime Soviet-American détente and its durability in the long run. Gromyko's outlook on Soviet-American relations was generally positive. He argued that Roosevelt's policy of cooperation with the Soviet Union had majority support in Congress, in the Democratic and Republican parties, and among the general public. Opposition to Roosevelt's policy came from the reactionary, anticommunist elements of the press and from the Roman Catholic Church. There were 23 million Catholics in the United States, Gromyko pointed out, including 5 million Poles who were especially exercised by issues in Polish-Soviet relations. Gromyko also highlighted American fears of communist revolution and sovietization, particularly in Eastern Europe. Gromyko thought that Soviet-American cooperation would continue after the war. Isolationist foreign policies had been abandoned in favor of involvement in European and international affairs. The United States, therefore, had a common interest with the Soviets in dealing with the German threat and in securing conditions for a prolonged peace. Gromyko also identified significant economic and trade reasons for postwar Soviet-American cooperation and concluded that "notwithstanding the difficulties which will probably arise from time to time . . . without doubt the conditions exist for the continuation of collaboration between the two countries. . . . To a large degree relations between the two countries in the postwar period will be determined by the relations shaped and continuing to be shaped in wartime."[57]

In a letter to Molotov ten days later, Gromyko analyzed the reasons why Henry Wallace had been replaced by Harry Truman as Roosevelt's vice-presidential running mate in the 1944 elections. Gromyko's view was that Wallace was too radical and had offended business interests and right-wing elements in the Democratic Party such as the "Southern bloc" of Democratic senators and congressmen. Truman, on the other hand, was supported by the Southern bloc and had some influential individual backers in the Democratic Party. He had also played an impressive role as chairman of the Senate committee charged with overseeing war production and mobilization. That work had established him as a serious political figure. Gromyko concluded that as far as foreign policy was concerned, Truman "always supported Roosevelt. He is a supporter of cooperation between the United States and its allies. He stands for cooperation with the Soviet Union. He speaks positively of the Tehran and Moscow conferences."[58]

As ever, Litvinov, too, was thinking in grandiose terms. In November 1944 he wrote a paper for Molotov entitled "On the Prospects and Possible Basis of Soviet-British Cooperation."[59] According to Litvinov the fundamental basis for postwar Anglo-Soviet cooperation would be the containment of Germany and the maintenance of peace in Europe. However, the war would bequeath a dangerous power imbalance in Europe arising from the Soviet defeat of Germany and from French and Italian decline. That problem could be resolved by the demarcation of British and Soviet security spheres in Europe. Litvinov suggested a maximum Soviet security zone of Finland, Sweden, Poland, Hungary, Czechoslovakia, Romania, the Balkans (but not Greece), and Turkey. The British security zone would consist of Western Europe, but with Norway, Denmark, Germany, Austria, and Italy constituting a neutral zone. According to Litvinov,

> This delimitation will mean that Britain must undertake not to enter into specifically close relations with, or make any agreements against, our will with the countries in our sphere, and also not to have military, naval, or air-force bases there. We can give the corresponding undertaking with regard

to the British sphere, except for France which must have the right to join an Anglo-Russian treaty directed against Germany.

Litvinov returned to the question of postwar Anglo-Soviet cooperation in a note to Molotov regarding "On the Question of Blocs and Spheres of Influence," dated January 11, 1945.[60] In this document Litvinov restated his proposal to divide Europe into British and Soviet spheres of interest, pointing out that tripartite discussions involving the Americans did not preclude bilateral arrangements and agreements between the great powers. Litvinov saw no reason for the United States to be involved in Anglo-Soviet discussions about zones of security given the antipathy of the American press and public opinion to blocs and spheres of influence. Litvinov pointed out, too, that when objecting to spheres of influence in Europe, the Americans chose to forget their Monroe Doctrine and the American position in Latin America. In conclusion Litvinov returned to his old theme that agreements on British and Soviet security zones in Europe should come from bilateral deals and not be dependent on the regional structures of an international security organization.

What Gromyko, Litvinov, and Maisky were saying and proposing were not necessarily what Stalin and Molotov were thinking. But in Stalin's USSR the terms of such internal discussions were highly restrictive. Even as independent a figure as Litvinov had to be careful not to overstep the mark of what it was permissible to say. Like future historians, these three mid-level policymakers tried to glean what was on Stalin's mind by reading the runes of his public statements, interpreting what was being said in the Soviet press, and making use of any confidential information at their disposal. One advantage they had over future historians was that they all had personal dealings with Stalin and with Molotov, who could always be relied upon to reflect the boss's views. It is reasonable to assume, therefore, that their speculations about the postwar world were not merely idiosyncratic but reflected the language and terms of the prevailing discourse within Molotov's Foreign Commissariat. True, their documents did not represent that discourse in its entirety; there also existed another, overlapping discourse of those officials whose language and thinking were infused with a more traditional, ideological perspective that anticipated a renewal of the antagonisms between the socialist and the capitalist world. But the reflections of Maisky, Gromyko, and Litvinov are strongly indicative of Stalin and Molotov's preference for continued tripartite collaboration after the war.

More direct evidence of Stalin's thinking on the eve of Yalta is contained in some conversations he had in January 1945 with a group of Bulgarian and Yugoslavian communists. The conversations dealt mainly with Balkan matters, but Stalin also expostulated on some broader themes. On January 28 he stated:

> The capitalist world is divided into two hostile blocs–democratic and fascist. The Soviet Union takes advantage of this in order to fight against the most dangerous [country] for the Slavs–Germany. But even after the defeat of Germany the danger of war/invasion will continue to exist. Germany is a great state with large industry, strong organisation, employees, and traditions; it shall never accept its defeat and will continue to be dangerous for the Slavonic world, because it sees it as an enemy. The imperialist danger could come from another side.
>
> The crisis of capitalism today is caused mainly by the decay and mutual ruin of the two enemy camps. This is favourable for the victory of socialism in Europe. But we have to forget the idea that the victory of socialism could be realised only through Soviet rule. It could be presented by some other political systems–for example by a democracy, a parliamentary republic and even by constitutional monarchy.[61]

Another version of Stalin's remarks was recorded in the diary of Georgi Dimitrov, the Bulgarian former leader of the Communist International:

> Germany will be routed, but the Germans are a sturdy people with great numbers of cadres; they will rise again. The Slavic peoples should not be caught unawares the next time they attempt an attack against them, and in the future this will probably, even certainly, occur. The old Slavophilism expressed the aim of tsarist Russia to subjugate the other Slavic peoples. Our Slavophilism is something completely different–the unification of the Slavic peoples as equals for the common defense of their existence and future. . . . The crisis of capitalism has manifested itself in the division of the capitalists into two factions–one fascist, the other democratic. The alliance between ourselves and the democratic faction came about because the latter had a stake in preventing Hitler's domination, for that brutal state would have driven the working class to extremes and to the overthrow of capitalism itself. We are currently allied with one faction against the other,

but in the future we will be allied against the first faction of capitalists, too.

Perhaps we are mistaken when we suppose that the Soviet form is the only one that leads to socialism. In practice, it turns out that the Soviet form is the best, but by no means the only, form. There may be other forms—the democratic republic and even under certain conditions the constitutional monarchy.[62]

Stalin's remarks about the two wings of capitalism have sometimes been interpreted to mean that he believed conflict with the democratic faction of capitalism was inevitable. But, as both quotations show, on Stalin's mind was the long-term German threat and the need for Slavic unity to confront it. Stalin's message to the Slavs was that they could only rely on themselves to deal with the Germans, not an enduring alliance with democratic capitalism. Equally, it is clear that in terms of communist political strategy, Stalin was advocating a moderate political course, one that focused on reform rather than revolution. This remained Stalin's policy for the communist movement for another two or three years; only when the strategy of gradual communist political advance was deemed a failure did he embrace a more militant and leftist approach to political action.

The auguries for tripartite cooperation at Yalta were good. Neither Stalin's diplomatic nor his political strategy presaged any major conflicts with Britain and the United States, at least not in the immediate future. The scene was set for serious negotiations with Churchill and Roosevelt to resolve a number of current controversies and create the basis for a durable, peacetime Grand Alliance.

THE YALTA CONFERENCE

At the Yalta summit (February 4–11, 1945) the plenary sessions of the Big Three were supplemented by meetings of the three foreign ministers—Eden, Molotov, and Edward Stettinius, Hull's successor as secretary of state—who teased out the details of decisions and agreements.

The first substantive discussion concerned the future of Germany. Stalin pushed hard for dismemberment and reparations but received only partial satisfaction. Both were agreed to in principle but referred to postconference committees for further discussion. The next discussion concerned the United Nations, and Stalin prevailed on the retention of the veto for permanent members of the Security Council. More difficult was the Polish question, specifically whether the West would recognize the Lublin Poles as the provisional government of Poland. Eventually it was agreed the Lublin government would be "reorganized on a broader democratic basis with the inclusion of democratic leaders from Poland itself and from Poles abroad."[63] In addition, the Curzon Line was accepted as the Polish-Soviet border, and the principle of transferring German territory to Poland accepted. But the details were left open for further discussion at the peace conference.

Most congenial were the discussions between Stalin and Roosevelt about the USSR's entry into the war in the Far East. Stalin agreed to attack Japan two or three months after the defeat of Germany. In return he would gain South Sakhalin, the Kurils, transit rights through Manchuria, and control of the Chinese ports of Dairen and Port Arthur. The only proviso was that the concessions affecting China would be subject to a separate Sino-Soviet agreement, a stipulation that neither Stalin nor Roosevelt expected to cause any difficulty.

Last but not least, there was the Declaration on Liberated Europe. This American-proposed document spoke of "the restoration of sovereign rights and self-government" to European peoples, to be achieved through "free elections of governments responsible to the will of the people."[64] It was the only major concession made by Stalin to soothe the democratic sensibilities of his Western allies. Even so, the Soviet interpretation of the document stressed its references to destroying the last vestiges of Fascism and Nazism rather than its commitment to Western-style democracy. In any case, the Soviets were convinced their communist allies would do well in the forthcoming elections and would emerge as important players in broad-based coalition governments.

The immediate postconference assessment of the results by the Soviets was very positive. Maisky, who had presented Soviet policy on reparations, drafted a circular to Soviet embassies for Molotov that concluded: "In general the atmosphere of the conference had a friendly character and the feeling was one of striving for agreement on disputed questions. We assess the conference as highly positive."[65] In the Soviet press the conference was lauded as yet another great historical turning point in the construction of a projected peacetime Grand Alliance.[66]

This post-Yalta euphoria did not last long. For one thing, Stalin was disappointed by his failure to gain a firm commitment from Churchill and Roosevelt to dismember Germany. If dismemberment was not going to happen, the Soviet Union should strive to avoid being blamed by the German people for pushing such a policy and seek instead to gain some political benefit from supporting Germany's reunification. On March 24 Molotov cabled Gusev, the Soviet representative on the Commission on Dismemberment, with instructions to drop the policy.[67] Henceforth Molotov and Stalin spoke publicly and privately only of a united Germany, albeit disarmed, demilitarized, denazified, and democratized.

A second disappointment was a prolonged wrangle about the composition of the new Polish provisional government. The Soviet interpretation of the Yalta agreement was that the Lublin government would be broadened by the inclusion of Polish politicians who were prepared to accept the Curzon Line and were willing to work constructively with the Soviets and their communist allies. Britain and the United States, on the other hand, wanted the creation of a completely new Polish government, to include a significant group of pro-Western political leaders. It was Molotov's job to resolve this dispute in negotiations with the British and American ambassadors. By April the negotiations had reached an impasse as both sides maneuvered for political advantage.

At the height of the dispute over Poland, the death of President Roosevelt cast further doubt about the future of the Grand Alliance. Stalin and Molotov seem to have been genuinely touched by Roosevelt's sudden demise. According to Harriman, when Molotov came to see him to give his condolences, he "seemed deeply moved and disturbed. He stayed for some time talking about the part President Roosevelt had played in the war and in plans for the peace. . . . I have never heard Molotov talk so earnestly."[68] On April 15 a memorial service was held for Roosevelt in Moscow, attended by Molotov and all his deputies except for Litvinov, who was ill. At Harriman's suggestion Stalin sent Molotov to the United States to meet the new president, Harry Truman, and to attend the founding conference of the United Nations in San Francisco.

MOLOTOV AND TRUMAN

Molotov's second visit to the United States turned out to be one of the most famous trips of his career, not because of what happened at the time but because of what was written about it later. In his memoirs, published in 1955, Truman described a very dramatic meeting that ended with Molotov complaining that he had "never been talked to like that in my life." "Carry out your agreements and you won't get talked to like that," Truman allegedly snapped back. As is often the case with good stories, this incident became the pivotal point for many historical narratives of the origins of the Cold War. The problem is that the story is not true.[69]

On the eve of his trip to Washington, Molotov received a telegram from Gromyko assessing the new president. While generally positive, Gromyko concluded on a note of caution: "How far he will continue the policy of co-operation with the Soviet Union and to what extent he will come under the influence of isolationist anti-Soviet groups is difficult to say at the moment."[70]

Molotov's first meeting with Truman on April 22 was very amicable. Truman began by saying that he wanted friendly relations between the Soviet Union and the United States to continue and the San Francisco conference to be crowned with success. Truman added, however, that American public opinion considered the resolution of the Polish question to be especially important. Molotov agreed, but pointed out to Truman that Poland was a neighbor of the USSR that had been used as corridor for German aggression and the resolution of the Polish question was of especially great importance for the Soviet Union. Molotov wanted to know if Truman stood by the decisions taken at Yalta and Dumbarton Oaks, and was very pleased to receive an affirmative reply. The meeting ended with a toast by Truman to Stalin and a proposal for a meeting with the Soviet leader. Molotov replied "that the Soviet government would be glad to see Truman in Moscow and the sooner the better. A meeting between Marshal Stalin and the President would have very great significance. Meetings between Roosevelt and Stalin always had very great positive significance. The establishment of personal relations between government leaders was always highly important."[71]

Immediately after seeing Truman, Molotov met Eden and Stettinius to discuss the Polish question. No headway was made as Molotov continued to insist the new Polish government be formed on the basis of the existing government and "must be friendly to the USSR." "Poland is situated in our zone of military action and our Red Army has spilt much blood liberating Poland from the Germans," Molotov told Eden and Stettinius. "France, Belgium and Holland are situated in the zone of action of [Allied military] forces and the Soviet government does not interfere in the business of forming governments in those countries."[72]

When Molotov met Truman again the next day, the talk was much tougher. Truman made a strong statement in support of the Western position on the Polish question, pointing out that failure to resolve it satisfactorily would "provoke doubts about our unity and our determination to collaborate in the post-war period." Molotov responded by saying that in the past there had been difficult questions in Soviet-American relations, but these had been resolved when the two sides had found a common language and did not attempt to impose their will upon one another.[73] It is at the end of this meeting that Molotov supposedly complained about his treatment by Truman. However, neither the Soviet report of the meeting nor the American record mentions the famous parting exchange recorded by Truman in his memoirs. The only real difference between the two official accounts is that while the Soviet document emphasizes Molotov's firmness in standing by the Soviet position on Poland, the American report stresses Truman's assertion of the Western viewpoint.

It would seem that Truman's memoir spin on the meeting–composed at the height of the Cold War–was purely a dramatic device to emphasize the toughness he displayed in his dealings with the Soviets. Equally certain is that Molotov–the man who had kept his composure in the face of Hitler's histrionics–would not have been fazed by a few sharp words with Truman.

At Truman's request, Molotov met Eden and Stettinius again, but there was no progress, and the talks had to continue in San Francisco.[74] In San Francisco Molotov gave a notable speech to the UN conference on April 26 in which he justified great-power domination of the nascent organization by reference to the Anglo-Soviet-American role in winning World War II and to the potential of the Grand Alliance to preserve the peace if it remained united and was supported by other states: "If the leading democratic countries demonstrate their ability to act in harmony in the postwar period as well, this will mean that the peace and security of nations have at last found their most effective bulwark and defense. But this is not enough. Are other peace-loving nations ready to rally around these leading powers and create an effective international security organization?–that is the question that must be settled at this conference." Molotov also reminded his audience that it was the Soviet Union "in bloody battles with German fascism" that had "saved European civilization."[75]

Meanwhile, the wrangling about Poland continued. Molotov's irritation at the continuation of fruitless discussions bubbled to the surface when he refused to allow his interpreter, Vladimir Pavlov, to compare translation notes with his British counterpart, A. H. Birse.[76] However, at a meeting on May 2 there was a small breakthrough in negotiations when Molotov announced that Mikolaj-czyk was an acceptable member of a reconstructed Polish government now that he had agreed to the Curzon Line.[77] The next concession came from Truman, who decided to send Harry Hopkins to Moscow to broker a deal. Hopkins arrived in the Soviet capital on May 25 and had several meetings with Stalin. Their discussions paved the way for an agreement that saw the reorganization of the communist-dominated Polish provisional government by the addition of four pro-Western cabinet ministers, including Mikolajczyk, who was named a deputy premier. The government was recognized by the British and Americans on July 5.

The dispute over Poland had soured Soviet-Western relations for several months, but in the end Stalin and Molotov extracted from Britain and the United States the concessions they considered vital to Soviet interests. This success suggested that the implicit spheres-of-influence agreement negotiated at Yalta remained valid and that the forthcoming Potsdam summit with Truman would continue tripartite cooperation.

THE POTSDAM CONFERENCE

The format of the Potsdam Conference (July 17 to August 2) was the same as at Yalta. The Big Three (Truman, Stalin, Churchill—replaced halfway through by Clement Attlee after the British general election)—met in plenary sessions for general discussions, while the foreign ministers (Molotov, new secretary of state James F. Byrnes, and Eden—replaced by Ernest Bevin) met separately to deal with the policy details.

The main discussion at Potsdam was about the future of Germany, and a detailed agreement was reached on the country's "complete disarmament and demilitarization" as well as the decentralization of its economic and political structures. On reparations—an issue very important to the Soviets—it was agreed that part of the $10 billion due to the USSR would be paid by industrial goods from the Western zones of military occupation.

More contentious was the treatment of Germany's allies during the war—Italy, Bulgaria, Finland, Hungary, and Romania. While the British and Americans sought special treatment for Italy, Stalin strove to protect the interests of states in his sphere of interest by gaining Western recognition for the friendly governments that had been established in Bulgaria, Finland, Hungary, and Romania. In the end, the issue was referred to the Council of Foreign Ministers (CFM)—a body established by the conference to negotiate the details of peace treaties for the Axis states.

The Soviets were disappointed by their exclusion from the so-called Potsdam Declaration, which demanded the Japanese surrender or face "prompt and utter destruction." That aside, there was very little discussion of the Far East except Soviet confirmation they would declare war on Japan by the middle of August.

In personal terms, relations among the Big Three did not achieve the level of intimacy of Churchill, Roosevelt, and Stalin, but they were generally friendly and good-humored. Although the British and Americans tended to line up against the Soviets in negotiations, there were Anglo-American differences as well. As Byrnes quipped, "One gets the impression that when we agree with our Soviet friends, the British delegation withholds its agreement, and when we agree with our British friends, we do not obtain the agreement of the Soviet delegation. (*Laughter*)"[78]

At the conclusion of the Potsdam Conference on August 2, 1945, the participants solemnly declared that it had "strengthened the ties . . . and extended the scope of their collaboration and understanding" and had renewed their confidence in their ability to deliver "a just and enduring peace." In the Soviet press Potsdam received the same adulatory treatment as Tehran and Yalta.[79] In private the Soviets were a little more restrained but still highly positive in their assessment of the conference. In a report circulated to Soviet ambassadors, Molotov wrote that "the conference ended with quite satisfactory results for the Soviet Union."[80] More revealing are the confidential statements recorded by the Yugoslavian ambassador to Moscow:

> According to Molotov and Vyshinsky at the conference it was possible to see, and to see in its results, that the English and Americans accept that they have lost Eastern Europe and the Balkans. . . . Molotov said that throughout the conference there was a good atmosphere, albeit not without harsh polemics and sharp words. Everyone tried to ensure that all questions were resolved by compromise decisions. . . . About Truman they said he was quite cultured and shows much understanding of European problems.[81]

Dimitrov recorded similar comments in his diary: "Spoke with Molotov about the Berlin conference, and in particular about decisions affecting Bulgaria and the Balkans. Basically, these decisions are to our advantage. In effect, this sphere of influence has been recognised as ours."[82]

As World War II drew to a close, Stalin and Molotov foresaw a great future for the Grand Alliance. The success of Potsdam seemed to bode well for the first meeting of the CFM that would be held in London in September. Tripartite cooperation had survived Roosevelt's death, and a number of difficult issues in inter-Allied relations had been resolved. The Soviet perspective was that great-power collaboration would continue in the long term to contain Germany and to maintain a stable setting for postwar reconstruction.

Stalin and Molotov were still Bolsheviks and far from abandoning their socialist goals, but these would be pursued on a gradual basis through the spreading influence of the communists and their allies. No doubt there would be tensions between Soviet diplomatic and ideological goals—there always had been—but peace and an equitable division of the spoils of war was the overriding interest of all the participants in the Grand Alliance, or so Molotov and Stalin believed. They were in for a rude awakening. The Grand Alliance began to disintegrate almost as soon as the war ended. The transition from a peacemaking scenario to a Cold War took just two years. While Stalin took this turn of events in stride, Molotov turned out to be a surprisingly reluctant cold warrior.

4

FIGHTING THE COLD WAR
(1946–1952)

Sometimes it is difficult to draw a line between the desire for security and the desire for expansion.

—V. M. Molotov (May 1946)[1]

At the end of World War II, Stalin took a long vacation, and it fell to Molotov to give the annual speech on the anniversary of the Bolshevik Revolution in November 1945. He began by making a point that was to feature strongly in Soviet public discourse after the war: the Anglo-Soviet-American coalition had won the war together, but the greatest contribution had come from the Red Army, which had turned the tide of the war in the Allies' favor a full year before the D-Day landings in France. It was the Soviet Union that had largely liberated Europe from German occupation and thereby saved European civilization.

The cost of that "liberation mission" had been extremely high, and Molotov recounted some stunning statistics of the damage inflicted on the USSR during the war: 1,710 towns and cities laid waste; 70,000 villages and 98,000 collective farms devastated; 6 million buildings and 31,850 factories destroyed; and 25 million people made homeless. Molotov did not mention the human casualties, which were too high to be officially admitted in the immediate aftermath of the war. Only after Stalin's death did the truth begin to come out: 8 million military dead and 16 million civilian fatalities—10 percent of the Soviet population. There were, in addition, the tens of millions of other Soviet citizens who had been wounded, widowed, orphaned, imprisoned, or enslaved by the

Germans. No wonder the Soviets thought they were the ones who deserved the greatest share of the credit for victory and a commensurate share of the spoils of war.

Molotov's other theme was that the test of war had shown the vitality of the Soviet system, increased popular support for the government, and deepened the unity of Soviet society. The task ahead, said Molotov, was the reconstruction of the Soviet economy, in particular economic recovery in those territories occupied and devastated by the enemy. Molotov was confident of success: "The enemy disrupted our peaceful, creative work. But we will, of course, make up for it and our country will prosper. We will have atomic energy and much else besides. (*Prolonged, stormy applause. All rise.*)" When it came to the future of the Grand Alliance, Molotov's assessment was more cautious: "The Anglo-Soviet-American anti-Hitler coalition . . . is now undergoing a test of its strength. Will this coalition prove as strong and capable of joint decisions under new conditions, when more and more new problems of the postwar period are arising?" But Molotov was confident problems would be overcome, as they had been during the war, and he defined the main task of Soviet foreign policy as strengthening cooperation with other peace-loving countries while remembering that "while we live in a 'system of states' and until the sources of fascist and imperialist aggression have been finally rooted out, we must remain vigilant in the face of the possibility of new infringements of the peace."[2]

POSTWAR PEACE NEGOTIATIONS

The first test for the Grand Alliance came at the London meeting of the Council of Foreign Ministers in September 1945. Consisting of the American secretary of state and the British, Chinese, French, and Soviet foreign ministers, the CFM had been established by the Potsdam Conference to negotiate the peace treaties for defeated enemy states.

The main task at the CFM's first meeting was to negotiate the terms of the peace treaties for Bulgaria, Finland, Hungary, Italy, and Romania–the five European states that had fought on Germany's side during the war. The Soviet delegation was instructed to make sure the five treaties were negotiated as a package. Since peace treaties could only be signed with recognized governments, that would require Western recognition of the pro-Soviet governments of Bulgaria and Romania. If the Western states objected that the Bulgarian

and Romania regimes were unrepresentative and should be replaced by newly elected governments, the Soviet delegation was instructed to counterraise
the situation in Greece where the progressive–that is, communist-led–forces
that had liberated most of the country from German occupation were being
repressed by a reactionary, pro-Western government. In relation to the Italian peace treaty, the Soviet delegation was mandated to support Yugoslavia's
claim to the Adriatic port city of Trieste and to seek a share in the trusteeships
that were to be established by the UN to run the former Italian colonies, in
particular Tripolitania (Western Libya). Another important issue for the Soviets
was the establishment of an Allied Control Council for Japan, where Stalin was
anxious to secure a role in the occupation.[3]

The CFM opened on September 11, 1945, and began in a friendly enough
spirit. In a gesture of conciliation, Molotov agreed that the French and Chinese
foreign ministers could take part in all the council's discussions. This procedure
was different from that agreed at Potsdam, which specified that China and
France would take part only in CFM discussions of peace treaties for countries
they had been at war with (which would have excluded the Chinese from all
discussion of the treaties for the minor Axis states and the French from all except that for Italy).

This was an auspicious opening for the conference, but the arguments
began soon enough. For a start the British and Americans were adamant in
their refusal to recognize the Bulgarian and Romanian governments and, as
expected, wanted to keep negotiations about an Italian peace treaty separate.
This raised the possibility that the Western states might decide to sign a peace
treaty with Italy rather than be forced to negotiate a package deal that would
entail recognition of the Bulgarian and Romanian governments. Such a prospect did not disturb Stalin. "What might happen under such conditions?" he
cabled Molotov on September 13. "Then we have a precedent. We would get
a possibility in our turn to reach a peace treaty with our satellites without the
Allies. If such a development would mean that current session of the [CFM]
winds up without taking decisions on major issues, we should not be afraid of
such an outcome either."[4]

Molotov continued to press for a quid pro quo–Western recognition of
Bulgaria and Romania in return for progress on the Italian negotiations–but
to no avail. "Why does the American government," Molotov asked James F.
Byrnes, the U.S. secretary of state, on September 19, "only want to reform the

government in Romania before elections and not in Greece? It seems that the United States does not want to interfere with the English in Greece, but it does with the Russians in Romania."[5] Molotov had similar exchanges with Ernest Bevin, the British foreign secretary, but he, like Byrnes, refused to accept the Greek analogy and continued to withhold recognition of the Bulgarian and Romanian governments until free elections had been held in those countries.

Another point of contention at the CFM was the Soviet demand for the trusteeship of Tripolitania. According to the British record of the discussion, Molotov made an impassioned plea about Tripolitania at the plenary session on September 15:

> The Soviet government claimed the right to active participation in the disposal of the Italian colonies because Italy had attacked, and had inflicted enormous damage upon, the Soviet Union. . . . Russia was anxious to have bases in the Mediterranean for her merchant fleet. World trade would develop and the Soviet Union wished to share in it. . . . The Soviet Government possessed wide experience in establishing friendly relations between various nationalities and was anxious to use that experience in Tripolitania. They would not propose to introduce the Soviet system in Tripolitania. They would take steps to promote a system of democratic government.[6]

As far as the Soviets were concerned, they had been promised a share of Italy's colonies by the Americans at the founding conference of the UN in San Francisco; it remained only to negotiate the practicalities. But there was no sign at the CFM that the Americans, or the British, were prepared to concede Tripolitania to Soviet control. Molotov, under strict instructions from Stalin to gain some kind of concession, continued to argue the Soviet case in private meetings with Bevin and Byrnes. On September 23 he complained to Bevin: "During the war we had argued but we had managed to come to terms, while the Soviet Union was needed. But when the war was over His Majesty's Government had seemed to change their attitude. Was that because we no longer need the Soviet Union?"[7] At a meeting with Bevin on October 1, Molotov attempted to bargain the transfer of the Dodecanese Islands to Greece in exchange for Soviet control of Tripolitania. Rebuffed, Molotov complained that the British did not want to give the USSR "even a corner of the Mediterranean."[8] Molotov received a more sympathetic hearing from Byrnes, but the American's tactic was to fob him off with talk of a Soviet role in an international council overseeing the trusteeship system.[9]

One positive development was a proposal from Byrnes on September 20 for a twenty-five-year pact on the demilitarization and disarmament of Germany. Molotov responded that he would have to report the proposal to his government but that he personally thought it was an interesting idea.[10] To Stalin, Molotov wrote: "I believe that we should support Byrnes' proposal on the four powers treaty in order to prevent new aggression by Germany, while not revealing excessive zeal. To be sure, this would be acceptable only if the Americans more or less move in our direction on the Balkan countries."[11] Stalin had other ideas. On September 22 he cabled Molotov instructions to counterpropose to Byrnes the simultaneous conclusion of a disarmament and demilitarization treaty with Japan. Stalin's evaluation of the Byrnes proposal was as follows:

> First, to divert our attention from the Far East; . . . second to receive from the USSR a formal sanction for the US playing the same role in European affairs as the USSR, so that the US may hereafter, in league with England, take the future of Europe into their hands; third to devalue the treaties of alliance that the USSR has already reached with European states; fourth, to pull out the rug from under any future treaties of alliance between the USSR and Rumania, Finland, etc.[12]

Rejection of Molotov's suggestion to negotiate with Byrnes followed hot on the heels of another rebuff from Stalin. On September 21 Stalin, annoyed by French and Chinese support for British and American positions at the conference, instructed Molotov to adhere to the Potsdam decision on the functioning of the CFM—that China and France should be mostly excluded from the discussions about the peace treaties. "I admit that I committed a grave oversight," responded Molotov. "I will take immediate measures [and] insist on immediate cessation of common sessions of five ministers . . . although it would be a sharp turn in the proceedings of the Council of Ministers." Molotov carried out his instructions the next day and that meant an end to negotiations about the peace treaties since the other foreign ministers were unwilling to change the procedure originally agreed.[13]

Molotov, however, had not given up hope of making some progress at the conference. On September 26 Byrnes proposed a compromise wherein the Soviet position on the procedural issue of rights to participation in CFM discussions would be accepted in return for the convening of a wider peace conference to consider the peace treaties. Molotov reported this proposal to Stalin and also suggested a compromise of his own: there would be further discussions about the Italian peace treaty in return for concessions on the establishment of an Allied Control Council for Japan. But Stalin was not for turning and had evidently decided that it would be best if the conference ended in failure. "The Allies are pressing on you to break your will and force you into making concessions," he wrote to Molotov on September 27. "It is obvious that you should display complete adamancy. . . . It is possible that the session of the Council would come to naught, in short, would be a failure. But even in this case we should not grieve." But Molotov had still not given up hope of a compromise. "I agree that the decisive moment has come," he wrote to Stalin on September 28. "I agree it is better to let the first session of the Council of Ministers end in failure rather than to make substantial concessions to Byrnes. . . . But if the American (and the British) give in on at least one of these questions [Japan or the Balkans], we should make a deal with them. Then the success of the work of the Council would be to our benefit."[14]

It seems that at this point Stalin decided to leave Molotov to his own devices and to allow the procedural wrangles to grind the CFM to a halt. They did, and on October 3 the meeting ended without even agreeing on the text of a closing communiqué. At his press conference the next day, Molotov tried to put as positive a spin as possible on the CFM's failure, saying that while the procedural dispute had prevented the council from concluding its work, many useful agreements had been reached during its thirty-three sessions. If there was a return to the procedure agreed at Potsdam, the council could resume its work. In conclusion Molotov stated, "The Soviet Union has emerged a victor from the last World War and occupies a fitting place in international relations. This is the result of the enormous efforts which were exerted by the Red Army and the whole Soviet people. . . . It is also the result of the fact that in those years the Soviet Union and the Western Allies marched side by side and collaborated successfully. The Soviet delegation looks ahead confidently and hopes that all of us will strive to consolidate the collaboration of the Allies."[15]

In private the Soviets were less sanguine about the outcome of the conference. An internal briefing for ambassadors noted that from the beginning of the conference, the USSR had faced a united front of the other powers seeking to undermine the decisions of Yalta and Potsdam. Truman's Democratic administration was castigated for allowing reactionary Republican elements to influence its foreign policy in an anti-Soviet direction, while the English Labourites were accused of being more conservative than the Conservatives in their defense of British imperial interests. The document concluded that the CFM had witnessed the

> failure of the first postwar diplomatic attack by American and English circles on the foreign policy gains made by the Soviet Union during the war. Further pressure on the USSR by the English and Americans is not excluded but we have every possibility of defending and consolidating the Soviet Union's foreign policy positions. We must display skillfulness, resourcefulness, steadfastness, and persistence, as the interests of the USSR demand.[16]

It is evident that Molotov was more inclined than Stalin to strive for agreement at the CFM, persisting with this attitude even when the boss had signaled an uncompromising stance. He was soon to be punished for this small act of defiance.

Not long after Molotov's return to Moscow, Stalin went on his vacation. As was his custom in the 1920s and 1930s, Stalin continued to receive documentation on the most important government decisions and relayed his views and instructions by letter or telegram. In Stalin's absence, Molotov, still the deputy premier as well as foreign minister, was nominally in charge. This made him vulnerable to criticism in the event of missteps, and Stalin, annoyed by Molotov's display of independence at the CFM, was on the lookout for mistakes. An early sign of what was to come was Stalin's complaint that the Soviet delegation did not have a stenographic record of the CFM: "We discover that the people in the leadership of the USA and England are much more familiar with the course of the conference than we, the Soviet leaders, are. . . . All this testifies to our backwardness and lack of experience in this area."[17]

Stalin's next complaint concerned a conversation Molotov had with Ambassador Harriman in which he appeared to concede too much control to the

Americans in running the occupation of Japan. "Molotov's manner of separating himself from the government, to picture himself as more liberal than the government is good for nothing," Stalin cabled members of the Politburo.[18] Then on November 9 *Pravda*, on instructions from Molotov, published a speech by Churchill that lavished praise on Stalin, who was not impressed. "I consider the publication of Churchill's speech . . . a mistake," he wrote to the Politburo:

> Churchill needs these eulogies to soothe his guilty conscience and to camouflage his hostile attitude to the USSR. . . . We only help these gentlemen by publishing these kinds of speeches. We now have quite a lot of high-ranking functionaries who burst into foolish raptures when praised by Churchills, Trumans, Byrneses, and, vice versa, become depressed when these gentlmen speak unfavorably of them. I regard such a mood dangerous as it develops servility toward foreign figures in this country. Hard struggle should be waged against servility toward foreigners. But if we continue to publish speeches like this we will only cultivate servility and fawning. I do not mention the fact that Soviet leaders have no need to be praised by foreign leaders. As for myself, this kind of praise only jars upon me.[19]

An even more serious rebuke was provoked by reports that Molotov had agreed to liberalize the censorship regime for foreign correspondents in the USSR. Stalin demanded an explanation, and when he did not get a satisfactory reply wrote he was "convinced that Molotov does not really care much about the interests of our state and the prestige of our government. He cares more about winning popularity among certain foreign circles. I cannot consider such a comrade as my first deputy."[20]

With Molotov's forced resignation in the cards, leading Politburo members met him for a session of criticism and self-criticism. They then cabled Stalin a list of Molotov's mistakes, including his role at the CFM where his behavior suggested that he "was for a policy of concessions, whereas the Soviet Government and Stalin were uncompromising."[21] Molotov sent his own groveling mea culpa to Stalin, but he was careful not to admit to specific mistakes in the sphere of foreign policy. After a couple of days Stalin relented and signaled the issue of Molotov's resignation had lapsed by bringing his deputy back into the loop of communications with Politburo members.

One reason for Stalin's change of heart in relation to Molotov was that he was in a better mood following a proposal from Byrnes that the American, British, and Soviet foreign ministers meet in Moscow and find a way around the problems encountered at the CFM. Stalin interpreted this development as a vindication of his hardline policy. "It is obvious that in dealing with such partners as the United States and Britain we cannot achieve anything serious if we begin to give in to intimidation or betray hesitation," he cabled the Politburo on December 9. "To obtain anything from these partners, we must arm ourselves with the policy of tenacity and steadfastness. The same policy of steadfastness and tenacity should guide our work at the forthcoming conference of the three [foreign] ministers."[22]

Stalin's strong words notwithstanding, the Moscow Conference of Foreign Ministers of December 1945 turned out to be a rather conciliatory affair. As was usually the case when Stalin conducted direct negotiations with foreigners, he assumed the good cop role while Molotov played the bad cop, steadfastly defending the details of the Soviet policy position. In relation to putting limits on France and China's participation in the CFM, the Soviets got their way but agreed in turn to Byrnes's proposal for a broader peace conference to consider the draft peace treaties. The logjam on Bulgaria and Romania was broken by an agreement on a broadening of the two governments leading to Western diplomatic recognition. Soviet demands in relation to Japan were satisfied through the creation of a Far Eastern Commission and an Allied Control Council, although the country's occupation regime remained under American control.

Stalin contributed by hosting the conference dinner and by meeting with Bevin and Byrnes on two occasions each. Later Byrnes recalled, "My talks with the Generalissimo [at dinner] that night, like those during the two earlier interviews, were marked by their encouraging combination of frankness and cordiality."[23] At his meeting with Stalin on December 24, Byrnes took the opportunity to mention his proposal for a pact on the disarmament of Germany. Stalin replied that such a pact could be signed, but there would have to be a similar agreement in relation to Japan.[24] At his meeting with Bevin that same day, Stalin was keen to discuss a Soviet trusteeship for Tripolitania and complained that if the CFM had agreed to this demand, "Great Britain would have lost nothing because she already had plenty of bases all over the world, more even than the United States. Could not the interests of the Soviet Government also be taken into account?" Later in the conversation Stalin said that "as he saw the situation, the United Kingdom had India and her possessions in the Indian Ocean in her sphere of interest [and] the United States had China and Japan, but the Soviet [Union] had nothing."[25]

In a message to Truman on December 23, Stalin expressed satisfaction with the progress of the conference and optimism about future relations with the United States.[26] Molotov's assessment of the conference, in a circular to Soviet embassies, was that the "decisions on Bulgaria and Rumania strengthen the situation of their democratic governments friendly to the Soviet Union" and "we managed to reach decisions on a number of important European and Far Eastern issues and to sustain development of the cooperation among the three countries that emerged during the war."[27]

During the Moscow conference Stalin signaled his intention to revive the CFM and to continue to negotiate the terms of the postwar peace settlement within the framework of the Grand Alliance. For Molotov the main task in the months ahead would be the negotiation by the CFM of the peace treaties for Bulgaria, Finland, Hungary, Italy, and Romania. Throughout these negotiations Molotov worked under the firm hand of Stalin, responding immediately and unreservedly to his guidance and instructions. For example, at the end of May Stalin thought Molotov had been too soft in a conversation with Byrnes when the American queried whether the Soviet Union was engaged in the search for security or expansion. Prompted by Stalin, Molotov went on the offensive at a meeting with Byrnes the next day:

> There is no corner of the world in which the USA cannot be seen. The U.S. has air bases everywhere: in Iceland, Greece, Italy, Turkey, China, Indonesia, and other places, and an even greater number of air and naval bases in the Pacific Ocean. The U.S. maintains its troops in Iceland despite the protests of the Icelandic government, also in China, while the USSR's troops have been withdrawn from China and other foreign territories. This is evidence of a real expansionism and expresses the striving of certain American circles toward an imperialist policy.[28]

In general, Stalin's tactical advice to Molotov was to force concessions from the other side by refusing to compromise, but to step away from confrontation if an uncompromising stance threatened to derail the negotiations altogether. Stalin also tutored his foreign minister on the importance of symbolism.

In August 1946 at the Paris Peace Conference—convened to discuss drafts of peace treaties prepared by the CFM—there was a military parade that Molotov attended but then abruptly left when he found himself seated in the second row among the representatives of small states. "You behaved absolutely correctly," Stalin told Molotov. "The dignity of the Soviet Union must be defended not only in big matters, but also in minutiae."[29]

One of Molotov's more notable contributions at the Paris Peace Conference came in a debate on the Italian-Yugoslav territorial dispute about Trieste, which revealed that he shared the pan-Slavic sentiments often expressed by Stalin during and immediately after the war:

> The time is past when Slav lands were material for partition among the European powers, when Slav peoples groaned under the yoke of Western and Eastern invaders. It is well known that the Slav nations have now found their place in the ranks of the Allied States and that political life in all the Slav countries is being built up along progressive democratic lines. Among the Slav and non-Slav states, Yugoslavia occupies a glorious place as a heroic fighter in the ranks of the anti-Hitlerite coalition."[30]

Despite Byrnes's best efforts to broaden its remit, the Paris Peace Conference was a consultative rather than a decision-making assembly. All decisions about the content of the peace treaties were reserved for unanimous agreement by the CFM. Notwithstanding its great length (July 29 to October 15), few issues were resolved, and in November the CFM reconvened in New York. At this point Stalin decreed to Molotov an abrupt change of tactics: "I advise you to make all possible concessions to Byrnes so that we can finally get the peace treaties over with."[31] Agreement was soon reached, and the peace treaties with Bulgaria, Finland, Hungary, Italy, and Romania were formally signed on February 10, 1947. In a circular letter to Soviet ambassadors at the end of December 1946, Molotov assessed the CFM negotiations as follows: "The preparation of peace treaties with Italy, Rumania, Bulgaria, Hungary and Finland took more than a year and required serious fighting, but as a result we succeeded in our principled positions and defended our interests and the interests of friendly states."[32]

The peace treaty negotiations were a surprising success story in the context of the overall deterioration of Soviet-Western relations in 1946. One barometer of the progressive disintegration of the Grand Alliance was the changing nature of Soviet discourse on the postwar world. By the end of 1946 that discourse was dominated by perceptions of the growth of hostile, anti-Soviet forces in the Western world.

One example of this discourse was a document of September 1946 drawn up by Nikolai Novikov, Soviet ambassador to the United States (his predecessor, Gromyko, had been posted to the United Nations). Novikov was a member of the Soviet delegation to the Paris Peace Conference, and Molotov asked him to compile a broad survey of the main trends in American foreign policy. Novikov's main contention was that under the influence of reactionary forces, the United States was striving for world supremacy. Roosevelt's policy of Big Three cooperation had been abandoned, said Novikov, and the Americans were now seeking to undermine the position of the Soviet Union, which posed the main obstacle to their supremacist plans. Within the United States a vicious anti-Soviet campaign was being conducted with a view to a possible war against the USSR.[33]

These themes were articulated publicly by Molotov, albeit in a more circumspect way, in a speech titled "The Soviet Union and International Cooperation" to the UN General Assembly on October 29, 1946. Without naming names, Molotov spoke of a struggle between two trends of international policy. Within the UN the conflict between these two trends was expressed in the struggle to maintain Great Power unanimity as the basis of the organization. Those seeking to end the veto system in the Security Council were attempting to destroy the UN and open the way to a bid for world supremacy by one bloc of powers, said Molotov.[34] This theme featured also in the speech by Soviet ideology chief, Andrei Zhdanov, on the twenty-ninth anniversary of the Bolshevik Revolution in November 1946. According to Zhdanov, the Paris Peace Conference had demonstrated the existence of "two tendencies in postwar policy. . . . One policy conducted by the Soviet Union is . . . to consolidate peace and prevent aggression. . . . The other policy . . . opening the path for the forces of expansion and aggression." Zhdanov's speech was also notable for this striking complaint about changing Western attitudes toward the Soviet Union:

One reads and wonders how quickly the Russians have changed. When our blood streamed in the battlefields they admired our courage, bravery, high morale, and boundless patriotism. And now that we wish, in cooperation with other nations, to make use of our equal rights to participation in international affairs, they begin to shower us with abuse and slander, to vilify and abuse us, saying at the same time that we possess an unbearable and suspicious character.[35]

The concept of an ongoing struggle between reactionary and progressive trends in the postwar world dated back to the London CFM, and the idea had been given a further boost by Stalin's response to Churchill's Iron Curtain speech in Fulton, Missouri, in March 1946. Churchill was in Fulton to collect an honorary degree from Westminster College. Missouri was President Truman's home state, and he sat on the platform as the former British prime minister pronounced what became for many people the Western declaration of the Cold War:

> From Stettin in the Baltic to Trieste in the Adriatic an *iron curtain* has descended across the Continent. Behind that line lie all the capitals of the ancient states of Central and Eastern Europe. Warsaw, Berlin, Prague, Vienna, Budapest, Belgrade, Bucharest and Sofia, all these famous cities . . . lie in what I must call the Soviet sphere, and all are subject in one form or another, not only to Soviet influence, but to a very high and, in some cases, increasing measure of control from Moscow. . . . The Communist parties . . . have been raised to pre-eminence and power far beyond their numbers and are seeking everywhere to obtain totalitarian control.[36]

Stalin responded to Churchill in an "interview" with *Pravda* on March 14. According to Stalin, Churchill was trying to provoke a new war and was an advocate of English-speaking domination of the world. Stalin did not mention the "Iron Curtain," but he frankly asserted the USSR's right to friendly regimes in Eastern Europe, given that these states had provided a platform for German aggression against the Soviet Union. In conclusion Stalin alluded to Churchill's role in the anti-Bolshevik coalition that had intervened in the Russian Civil War and promised that if "Churchill and his friends" succeeded in organizing a "new march against 'Eastern Europe,'" they "will be beaten again as they were beaten in the past."[37]

GREECE, IRAN, TURKEY

Adding to the tension in Soviet-Western relations in 1946 was a series of policy conflicts in an arc of crisis that encompassed Greece, Iran, and Turkey.[38]

The source of tension in relation to Greece was Soviet support for a communist-led insurgency against its pro-Western government. During the war Soviet support for the Greek partisans was constrained by the Stalin-Churchill percentages agreement of October 1944. By the time of the Potsdam Conference, however, the Soviet position was beginning to change. The Soviet delegation submitted a memorandum on the implementation of the Declaration on Liberated Europe, which criticized the reign of terror in Greece against the "democratic elements" and called for the immediate formation of a democratic government in Greece.[39] This memorandum presaged the main thrust of Soviet diplomacy on the Greek question for the next few months: criticism of Western policy in Greece, balanced by efforts to trade Moscow's reticence on Greek issues for Western recognition of the pro-Soviet Bulgarian and Romanian governments.

At the Moscow Conference of Foreign Ministers in December 1945, Soviet policy took another sharp turn with the demand for the withdrawal of British forces from Greece. This demand became part of a substantial Soviet campaign in 1946 for a general withdrawal of Western armed forces from foreign countries. But Soviet support for the Greek insurgents remained more rhetorical than real. Initially, Stalin did not agree with the militant tactics of the Greek communists, and it was not until after the outbreak of the Cold War in 1947 that the Soviets begin to offer substantial material aid to the communist side of the civil war. Even then, Stalin had his doubts. In February 1948 he told a delegation of Bulgarian and Yugoslavian communists:

Recently I started to doubt that the partisans could win. If you are not sure the partisans would win, the partisan movement should be restricted. The Americans and the English have a very strong interest in the Mediterranean. They would like to have their bases in Greece. They would use all possible means to support a government that would be obedient. This is an international issue of great importance. If the partisan movement is halted, they will have no excuse to attack you. . . . If you are confident that the partisans have good chances of winning, it is a different matter. But I have some doubts about this.[40]

Stalin's doubts were vindicated in summer 1949 when ELAS suffered a major defeat in northern Greece and was forced to retreat into Albania. Shortly after, in September 1949, Stalin met with the Greek communist leader Niko Zachariadis, who agreed to call off the armed struggle.[41]

The origins of the dispute over Soviet troop withdrawals from Iran in 1946 lay in the Allied occupation of the country during war. In August 1941 British and Soviet forces entered Iran with the aim of overthrowing German influence in the country, protecting oil supplies, and securing Allied supply routes to the USSR. Soviet troops occupied northern Iran and the British the south, while the Iranians remained nominally in control of the central region. Under a January 1942 treaty of alliance with Iran, the British and the Soviets pledged to withdraw their forces six months after the end of the war with "Germany and its associates" (later interpreted to include Japan).

The Soviets had long coveted an Iranian oil concession and took advantage of the occupation to further their interests in this sphere. In August 1944 Lavrentii Beria, the Soviet security chief, proposed to Stalin and Molotov that Soviet oil concessions be sought in areas occupied by the Red Army. The negotiation of such concessions was the task of a Foreign Ministry delegation to Tehran in September and October 1944. But the negotiations failed when the Iranians decided not to grant any more oil concessions until all Allied troops were withdrawn after the war.[42]

In February 1945 the Iranians offered to open negotiations on creating a joint Soviet-Iran stock company, but this was rejected by Moscow as inferior to the significant concessions already enjoyed by the British in the south. When the war in Europe came to an end in May 1945, the Iranians issued a note asking for an early withdrawal of all occupation forces, but the Soviets did not even bother to reply. Indeed, on May 25 Deputy Foreign Commissar S. I. Kavtaradze, who had led the Soviet negotiating team to Tehran, proposed to Molotov that the Red Army not withdraw from Iran until an oil concession had been extracted from the Iranians or a joint stock company controlled by Moscow had been created.[43]

At this point Moscow's desire to pressure Tehran into granting an oil concession intersected with nationalist pressures for unifying Soviet Azerbaijan with southern Azerbaijan–the area of northern Iran occupied by the Red Army. In April 1945 Mir Bagirov, the communist leader of Soviet Azerbaijan, drafted a plan for joining "southern Azerbaijan with Soviet Azerbaijan, or the formation of an independent southern Azerbaijani People's Republic, or the establishment of an independent bourgeois-democratic system or, at least, cultural autonomy in the framework of the Iranian state."[44] In early June 1945 Bagirov, along with Molotov and Kavtaradze, was directed by the Politburo to evaluate the feasibility of organizing separatist movements in southern Azerbaijan and other provinces of northern Iran. On July 6 the Politburo passed a resolution authorizing the establishment of such separatist movements, including the organization of a Democratic Party of Azerbaijan that would agitate for autonomy, albeit within the framework of the existing Iranian state.[45]

The Democratic Party of Azerbaijan (DPA) was formed in September 1945 and, aided by the Soviets, took control of southern Azerbaijan. In response Tehran proposed to send troops, but this move was blocked by the Soviets, who told the Iranians the Red Army would be able to guarantee order in southern Azerbaijan—an implicit threat to condone or facilitate disorder in the event of such an intervention.

Tehran's other tactic was to internationalize the crisis by appealing to the British and Americans for support and by threatening to take the matter to the United Nations. The Soviets responded to this pressure by insisting the movement for Azerbaijani autonomy was an internal Iranian matter; further, that their troops would be withdrawn in accordance with the 1942 treaty six months after the end of World War II (and because Japan had formally surrendered on September 2, that meant March 2, 1946).

At the Moscow foreign ministers' meeting in December 1945, there were informal talks about Iran, and Byrnes and Bevin attempted to secure agreement on a trilateral American-British-Soviet commission to oversee an accelerated withdrawal of all Allied troops from the country, but Molotov vetoed the idea.[46] Bevin and Byrnes also had the opportunity of discussing the Iranian crisis with Stalin, who told them the Soviet Union had no territorial claims against Iran and had no intention of incorporating any part of it into the USSR or of undermining the country's sovereignty.[47]

The Soviets tried to block discussion of the Iranian crisis at the UN, but in January 1946 the London meeting of the Security Council heard statements from Soviet and Iranian representatives, and an SC resolution urged bilateral Soviet-Iranian negotiations. This suited the Soviets, since a new government headed by Qavam as-Saltanah had come to power in Iran. Qavam had been elected premier with the support of the Tudeh Party—the front for the Iranian communists—and he was seen by the Soviets as a man they could do business with. On February 19 Qavam arrived in Moscow for talks and indicated that he might be willing to compromise on the question of an oil concession. In response the Soviets proposed that southern Azerbaijan be granted autonomy, that a Soviet-Iranian oil company be established in northern Iran (with control split 51/49 in Moscow's favor), and that Soviet troops be gradually withdrawn when order had been restored in northern Iran. These terms were not acceptable to Qavam, but discussions continued in Tehran. By early April the two sides had agreed that the Red Army would withdraw by early May, that there would be a Soviet-Iranian oil company (subject to parliamentary approval), and that there would be concessions to Azerbaijani demands for autonomy.[48] This brought to an end the "crisis" over Soviet troop withdrawals from Iran.

The third Soviet-Western clash in the Near East in 1946 concerned Turkey. Stalin had made no secret of his antagonism to the Montreux Convention of 1936 under which Turkey controlled shipping through the Black Sea Straits. The USSR was a signatory to the agreement, but during the period of the Nazi-Soviet pact Stalin had sought to agree with Hitler on a radical change in the straits regime—basically a transition from Turkish control to joint control with the USSR, including provision for Soviet military bases at the Bosporus and the Dardanelles.

At the percentages meeting on October 9, 1944, Stalin told Churchill that

> it was quite impossible for Russia to remain subject to Turkey, who could close the Straits and hamper Russian imports and exports and even her defence. What would Britain do if Spain or Egypt were given this right to close the Suez Canal, or what would the United States Government say if some South American Republic had the right to close the Panama Canal?[49]

Such references to the Suez and Panama canals cropped up again and again in Soviet-Western discussions of the straits, including at the Yalta conference in February 1945 when Stalin formally raised the question of revising Montreux and suggested the matter be considered by the American, British, and Soviet foreign ministers.[50]

After the Yalta Conference Soviet policy on Turkey took a more threatening turn. On March 19 Molotov announced that the USSR would not renew the 1925 Soviet-Turkish Treaty of Friendship and Neutrality when it expired in November 1945. The treaty, said the Soviet statement, "no longer corresponded to the new situation and needed serious improvement."[51] The Turkish response to the Soviet declaration was to seek negotiations about a new treaty. On June 7 the Turkish ambassador to Moscow met Molotov. Salim Sarper told Molotov that while Turkey would like to sign a mutual assistance treaty with the Soviet Union, it would be difficult to change the straits regime because there were other parties to that agreement. But, Sarper pointed out, under the terms of a Soviet-Turkish mutual assistance treaty, Turkey would be bound to defend the straits and the Black Sea. In response Molotov asked who would object if the Soviet Union and Turkey came to an agreement on the straits. Molotov then said that before there could be a new Soviet-Turkish treaty, the territorial pretensions of Armenia and Georgia against Turkey would have to be satisfied. Molotov was referring to the provinces of Kars and Ardahan. These were areas of eastern Turkey with Armenian and Georgian populations, which had been part of the Tsarist Empire from 1878 until 1921, when a Soviet-Turkish treaty transferred the two districts to Turkey. If agreement could not be reached on the territorial issue, said Molotov, then negotiations between the USSR and Turkey would have to be restricted to the straits issue.

Molotov met Sarper again on June 18 and made the same point: if Turkey could not satisfy Soviet territorial aspirations, there could be no mutual assistance pact between the two states, but there could be negotiations about the straits. In both conversations Molotov pointed to the comparison with Soviet-Polish relations. In 1921 the Soviet Union had been weak and had been forced to concede territory to Poland. The same had happened in relation to Turkey. But whereas Soviet-Polish differences had been resolved by redrawing the border, Armenia and Georgia's territorial claims remained unsatisfied.[52] Molotov's heavy-handed comparison between the positions of Poland and Turkey could not have reassured the Turks.

At Potsdam Stalin and Molotov spoke of their territorial demands on Turkey, but the formal Soviet proposal to the conference was restricted to demanding joint control of the straits, including provision for military bases.[53] While Truman and Churchill were prepared to contemplate a change in the straits regime, the Soviet demands went too far, and the conference protocol was restricted to the statement that Montreux should be revised as "not meeting present-day conditions."[54]

Soviet-Western exchanges on the straits continued at the London CFM meeting. On September 23, 1945, Molotov pointed out to Bevin that during

World War I, Britain had been prepared to concede Constantinople to tsarist Russia and that he could not understand the resistance to the Soviet demand for bases.[55]

In December 1945 Stalin reiterated Soviet demands to Bevin at the foreign ministers' conference in Moscow but said that "all talk of war against Turkey was rubbish."[56] In April 1946 Stalin told U.S. ambassador W. Bedell Smith (Harriman's successor) that "I have assured President Truman and have stated publicly that the Soviet Union has no intention of attacking Turkey . . . but Turkey is weak, and the Soviet Union is very conscious of the danger of foreign control of the Straits, which Turkey is not strong enough to protect. The Turkish Government is unfriendly to us. That is why the Soviet Union has demanded a base in the Dardanelles. It is a matter of our own security."[57]

Despite such reassurances, there were growing worries in the West that the USSR was preparing for war with Turkey over the straits or at least was intent on using the threat of Soviet military power to back its diplomatic demands.[58] That Stalin contemplated war against Turkey in 1946 seems far-fetched, but that he used Red Army maneuvers to pressure Turkey is more than likely.

When the Soviet-Turkish crisis over the straits finally broke on August 7, it was somewhat of an anticlimax. That day the USSR sent Ankara a diplomatic note on the revision of the Montreux Convention. Following a critique of Turkey's operation of the straits regime during the war, the Soviet note proposed that the straits always be open to merchant shipping; always be open to the warships of Black Sea powers; be closed to the warships of non–Black Sea powers, except in special circumstances; be under the control of Turkey and other Black Sea powers; and be jointly defended by the Soviet Union and Turkey.[59] On August 19, 1946, the United States challenged Moscow's contention that the straits regime was an exclusive concern of Black Sea powers and called for a multilateral conference to revise Montreux. The British expressed similar views two days later. On August 22 Turkey replied, echoing the British and American responses and stating in addition that the Soviet demand for joint defense of the straits was incompatible with the maintenance of Turkish sovereignty and security.[60] On September 24 Moscow responded with a memorandum reiterating the special rights of Black Sea powers in relation to the straits and denying that the Soviet proposals threatened or undermined Turkish sovereignty or security.[61] On October 9 the British and Americans reiterated their position, and on October 18 the Turks restated theirs. The USSR never replied to the Turkish note of October 18, and the "crisis" over the straits quickly petered out, notwithstanding suggestions from Soviet diplomats in Ankara that Moscow ratchet up the "war of nerves" with Turkey.[62]

According to Western Cold War lore, Stalin backed away from confrontation with Turkey because of strong British and American support for the Turks' stance on the straits issue. It is true that in the absence of such support, Stalin might well have been inclined to press his demands further. But it was not so much Western power that deterred Stalin as the broader, negative consequences of the prolongation and intensification of the straits crisis. In summer 1946 the Soviets were still locked into negotiations with the Western powers about the peace treaties for Bulgaria, Finland, Hungary, Italy, and Romania–agreements Moscow viewed as crucial to consolidating the Soviet and communist position in Eastern Europe. And the next item on the CFM's agenda–to be discussed at its Moscow meeting in March and April 1947–was the terms of a German peace treaty. Stalin and Molotov were both obsessed with the danger of a German revival and remained committed to the joint implementation with the West of the terms of the Potsdam Agreement on the denazification, demilitarization, and democratization of Germany.

THE MOSCOW CFM

The Council of Foreign Ministers opened in Moscow on March 10. Two days later, however, a huge shadow was cast over the conference by Truman's speech to Congress calling for financial aid to Greece and Turkey and for a global policy of defending the "free world" from armed minorities or outside pressures (i.e., the Soviet Union and the communists). The Soviets responded to the Truman Doctrine speech with critical articles in the communist press, but their reaction was subdued compared to the uproar that had met Churchill's Iron Curtain speech. Crucially, Stalin made no public comment; indeed, during the Moscow CFM he had a very friendly meeting with the new secretary of state, George Marshall. Using an analogy that Marshall, formerly U.S. Army chief of staff, would surely appreciate, Stalin described the Moscow CFM session as like "the first battle, a reconnaissance battle. When the partners have exhausted themselves then will come the possibilities of compromise. It is possible that the present session will not achieve any significant results. But don't despair. The results can be achieved at the next session. On all the main questions–

democratization, political organization, economic unity, and reparations—it is possible to achieve compromise."⁶³

Stalin had a similarly upbeat meeting a few days later with the visiting Republican politician Harold Stassen. He pointed out to Stassen that despite the differences in their economic systems, the Soviet Union and the United States had cooperated during the war and there was no reason why they could not continue to do so in peacetime. Stalin invoked Lenin's teachings in support of his belief in the possibility of peaceful coexistence between the socialist and capitalist systems. When Stassen pointed out that before the war Stalin had talked about "capitalist encirclement," the Soviet leader replied that he had never denied the possibility of cooperation with other states but had only spoken about the existence of actual threats from countries such as Germany. Each side supported its own social system, Stalin told Stassen, and history would decide which was the better. In the meantime both sides should stop sloganizing and name-calling. He and Roosevelt had never called each other "totalitarian" or "monopoly capitalists." "I am not a propagandist," said Stalin. "I am a man of business."⁶⁴

An important prelude to the Moscow CFM was the discussion of Byrnes's proposal for a "Twenty-Five-Year Treaty for the Disarmament and Demilitarization of Germany." Byrnes formally presented his proposal at the Paris CFM in April 1946. On his return to Moscow Molotov conducted an extensive consultation about the response to Byrnes's draft treaty. The consensus that emerged from this consultation exercise was that the Byrnes proposal was dangerous because it could lead to a premature end of the Allied occupation of Germany—before the country had been thoroughly demilitarized, denazified, and democratized, and before the Soviets had extracted their reparations.⁶⁵ This was the substance of Molotov's public response to the Byrnes proposal when the CFM reconvened in July 1946, but he did not completely close the door on the draft treaty, saying only that it required radical revision.

At this CFM meeting Molotov also made his first statement on the question of a peace treaty with Germany. His main points were that a peace treaty should only be signed when a new German government had been formed and when the occupying powers were satisfied that this government could ensure that Germany would remain a peace-loving and democratic state. To help achieve these goals, Molotov proposed to establish a central German admin-

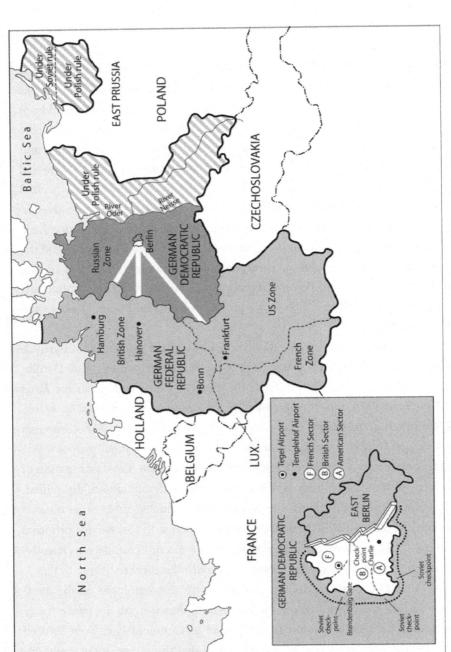

From Geoffrey Roberts, *Stalin's Wars: From World War to Cold War, 1939–1953* (London: Yale University Press, 2006).

istration to work toward the political and economic integration of the Allied zones of occupation.[66]

At the Moscow CFM the Soviets presented their own draft treaty, "On the Demilitarization of Germany and the Prevention to German Aggression," which formally stated their view that the country should remain occupied until it was safe for the Allied forces to leave. Molotov also elaborated on the Soviet proposal for a central German administration, saying the Allies should draft a constitutional document providing for the election of a provisional German government. This provisional government would be charged with drawing up a permanent constitution for the country and with the continuing implementation of the Potsdam agreement on the disarmament, denazification, and democratization of Germany. In due course the new German government would also negotiate the terms of a peace treaty.

The Western response to these Soviet proposals highlighted various economic issues—above all, the question of reparations deliveries to the USSR from western Germany—that had to be sorted out before there could be political unity. The Western powers also favored a German central government with weak powers relative to those of the German regions—a policy that suited their aim of excluding Soviet and communist influence from as much of Germany as they could.[67]

After six weeks of discussions the Moscow CFM closed without agreement. This did not unduly concern Molotov, who in closing the conference on April 24 spoke of the great preparatory work that had been done and said that he looked forward to the next round of negotiations. The *Pravda* editorial on the results of the conference echoed this line and emphasized that the basic issue remained the implementation of the Yalta and Potsdam agreements on Germany.[68] Unfortunately, by the time the CFM resumed in London six months later, the international political situation had changed dramatically. The Cold War had begun, the Grand Alliance had disintegrated, open ideological warfare had broken out between the Soviet Union and its erstwhile allies, and there were widespread fears that East-West tensions had significantly increased the danger of a new world war.

THE MARSHALL PLAN

The final catalytic event that led the Soviets to adopt a Cold War position was the "Marshall Plan," launched by the American secretary of state in a speech at

Harvard University on June 5, 1947. Marshall proposed a large-scale American aid program for war-torn Europe, with the funds being distributed on a coordinated basis by the Europeans themselves. Marshall's proposal was taken up by Britain and France. Bevin and Georges Bidault, the French foreign minister, met in Paris and on June 19 issued an invitation to the USSR to attend a tripartite conference to discuss a coordinated European recovery program backed by U.S. aid.

The Soviet response to these developments was mixed. The initial press response was negative, with the Marshall Plan being linked to the Truman Doctrine as yet another instrument for American interference in European affairs.[69] On June 21, however, the Politburo endorsed a positive reply to the Anglo-French proposal for a meeting to discuss the plan. Meanwhile, behind closed doors the Soviet leadership was considering the advice it was getting on the meaning of the Marshall Plan. An early contribution came from Ambassador Novikov in Washington on June 9, who cabled, "In this American proposal are the clear contours of a West European bloc directed against us." In a further dispatch on June 24, Novikov affirmed that "a careful analysis of the Marshall Plan shows that in the end it amounts to the creation of a West European bloc as an instrument of US policy. . . . Instead of the previous uncoordinated actions directed towards the economic and political subjection of European countries to American capital and the formation of an anti-Soviet grouping, the Marshall Plan envisages more extensive action aimed at resolving the problem in a more effective way."[70]

Different policy advice came from Eugene Varga, a prominent Soviet economist. Varga's view was that the Marshall Plan was primarily a response to America's postwar economic problems, particularly a lack of demand for its exports in Europe. The plan's purpose was to provide dollars to Europeans so they could buy American goods and services. Varga also pointed out the drawbacks of the Soviet Union not participating in the plan: it would facilitate American domination of Europe, strengthen the U.S. hand in relation to the economic future of Germany, and allow reactionaries to blame the USSR if the plan failed.[71] Varga's analysis implied that it could suit the Americans to provide loans and grants to Soviet bloc countries as well as to Western Europe. If so, the Soviets would have no objections, as long as there were no political strings attached. Was the Marshall Plan a political threat or an economic opportunity? Stalin's response to this conundrum was to keep an open mind and to see what happened. The Soviet delegation to the talks with the British and French was instructed to find out what American aid was on offer, to block any move that threatened interference in the internal affairs of aid recipients, and to make sure that discussion of the German question remained the prerogative of the CFM.[72]

Molotov arrived in the French capital at the end of June, bringing with him a large group of expert advisers–a sign that he intended to engage in serious negotiations rather than public propaganda polemics. But he quickly came to the conclusion that the Marshall Plan was intended to leverage Western influence on Eastern Europe and to undermine Soviet and communist control. The Soviets rapidly withdrew from the negotiations, with Molotov telling the conference on July 2: "The question of American economic aid . . . has . . . served as a pretext for the British and French governments to insist on the creation of a new organization standing above the European countries and intervening in the domestic affairs of the countries of Europe."[73]

Following the collapse of the Paris talks, the British and French invited other European states to a conference to establish an organization to supervise Marshall aid. After some hesitation the Soviets advised their communist allies in Eastern Europe to boycott the Marshall Plan negotiations. The Soviets then launched the so-called Molotov Plan–a series of bilateral trade treaties between the USSR and Eastern Europe–as a counter to the attractions of the Marshall Plan.

In September 1947 the Soviets launched the Communist Information Buro (Cominform)–a successor to the Comintern (abolished in 1943) aimed at co-ordinating the policies and actions of the major European communist parties. At the founding conference in Poland, Zhdanov used the Marshall Plan to illustrate his argument that the split in the postwar world between two trends or policies had solidified into the formation of two blocs, or camps:

> The further we are removed from the end of the war, the more clearly do the two basic orientations in postwar international politics stand out, corresponding to the division . . . into two basic camps: the imperialist and anti-democratic camp . . . and the anti-imperialist and democratic camp. . . . The principal leading force in the imperialist camp is the USA. . . . The fundamental aim of the imperialist camp is to strengthen imperialism, prepare a new imperialist war, fight against socialism and democracy,

and give all-around support to reactionary and anti-democratic, pro-fascist regimes and movements. For the performance of these tasks the imperialist camp is ready to rely on reactionary and anti-democratic elements in all countries and to back former war-enemies against its own wartime allies. The anti-imperialist and anti-fascist forces constitute the other camp, with, as their mainstay, the USSR and the countries of new democracy. . . . The aim of this camp is to fight against the threat of new wars and imperialist expansion, to consolidate democracy, and to uproot what remains of fascism.[74]

Zhdanov's two-camps speech, as it came to be known, was the Soviet riposte to the Truman Doctrine and the Marshall Plan, in effect a counterdeclaration of the Cold War.

This Cold War turn in Soviet foreign policy was reflected also in Molotov's speech on the thirtieth anniversary of the Bolshevik Revolution in November 1947, which bristled with hostility toward the Western powers. Britain and the United States were accused of surrounding the Soviet Union with a global chain of air and naval bases. "It is obvious," said Molotov, "that the creation of military bases in various parts of the world is not designed for the purposes of defense, but as preparation for aggression." He added, "Today, the ruling circles of the United States as well as of Great Britain head an international group which has made it its purpose to strengthen capitalism and to establish the domination of these countries over other nations."[75]

Against this background there was little hope of negotiating a breakthrough at the London meeting of the CFM in November and December 1947. At the conference Molotov pushed hard for an agreement on procedures for negotiating a German peace treaty. The Soviets envisaged forming a central German government that would be consulted on peace treaty terms to be negotiated at a multilateral peace conference along the lines of the Paris Peace Conference. The Western states responded, as they had done at the Moscow conference, that the economic principles of a united Germany had to be agreed upon before there could be any steps toward political unity. Since there was no meeting of minds on economic issues, not least on the question of reparations, the conference closed in failure on December 15.[76]

The Molotov Plan, the campaign against the Marshall Plan, and the establishment of Cominform were part and parcel of the process of consolidating

the communist bloc in Eastern Europe. Zhdanov's two-camps speech had signaled an acceleration of the process of imposing the Soviet model of socialism
on Eastern Europe: state-owned and controlled economies, centralized state
planning, collectivized agriculture, and tight, vigilant communist control of
civil society as well as political life. Already, however, strains were evident in
the unity of the bloc. In 1948 communist Yugoslavia, under the leadership of
the former partisan leader Josip Broz Tito, was expelled from the bloc. Marshal
Tito had been Stalin's favorite communist son, and his party seen as a model
of ideological purity and militancy. The headquarters of the Cominform was
located in Belgrade, and the Yugoslavian delegate had played a starring role in
the proceedings of its founding conference, attacking with relish the "reformist"
political strategy of the French and Italian communist parties.

It was Tito's desire to follow an independent policy in relation to neigh-
boring Balkan states that precipitated the split. He was a strong supporter
of the communist partisans in the Greek Civil War, while Stalin preferred a
more restrained policy that did not overly antagonize the West. Tito wanted
to dominate Albania, to which the Soviets did not object, as long as they were
consulted first. Tito also tried to form a federation with communist Bulgaria
without first obtaining Stalin's consent. In February 1948 Stalin and Molotov
met a Bulgarian-Yugoslavian delegation (Tito did not attend the meeting) and
instructed them to fall into line and accept Soviet leadership on the big questions of foreign policy. The Bulgarians obliged, but the Yugoslavians rebelled.
There followed an acrimonious correspondence between Belgrade and Moscow, culminating in Yugoslavia's expulsion from the Cominform in June 1948
on grounds that it had embarked on a nationalistic, anti-Soviet, and proimpe-
rialist policy.[77]

THE COLD WAR

By 1948 the Cold War was well and truly under way, but Stalin and Molotov
hesitated to break off all negotiations with the West. When Stalin received an
open letter from Progressive Party presidential candidate Henry Wallace in
May 1948, he responded positively. Wallace proposed a series of specific steps
to bring the Cold War to an end, including a peace treaty leading to the reunification of Germany. Wallace had been Roosevelt's vice president during
most of the war and had broken with Truman over policy toward the Soviet
Union. Stalin replied that Wallace's proposals represented a good basis for an

agreement between the Soviet Union and the United States and that "despite the differences in economic systems and ideologies the coexistence of these systems and the peaceful settlement of differences between the USSR and the USA are not only possible but absolutely necessary in the interests of universal peace." Wallace's open letter and Stalin's response were, in fact, concocted and coordinated by the two men via backchannel communications.[78]

The Wallace-Stalin exchange coincided with another development the Soviets seized on to keep open the possibility of negotiations with the West. On May 4 Molotov was approached by Ambassador Smith with a statement that the United States had no hostile or aggressive aims in relation to the Soviet Union. Molotov was so taken aback that he asked Smith to repeat what he had said. The ambassador did so and stated that the American aim in making this statement was to reduce tensions and stabilize the international situation. Molotov replied formally to the Smith statement at a further meeting on May 9. While the Soviet reply rejected American criticisms of Soviet foreign policy and complained about the growth of a Western military bloc directed against the USSR, it welcomed the U.S. statement as basis for further discussion and emphasized the possibilities of peace and cooperation between the two countries.[79] The next day TASS issued a statement on Soviet-American relations that revealed the contents of the Smith-Molotov exchange and suggested that it presaged bilateral negotiations between the two countries. This statement generated some dramatic newspaper headlines around the world—"No more cold war" declared one French paper—but it backfired when the Americans rapidly backed away from any suggestion they had called for talks with the Soviets.[80]

The Soviet peace offensive of May 1948 was soon overshadowed by the outbreak of the first Berlin crisis. On June 7 Britain, France, the United States, and the Benelux countries (Belgium, Netherlands, and Luxembourg) issued a communiqué from London announcing their intention to establish a federal German state in the Western zones of occupation. A few days later a new currency was issued in the Western zones, an act that threatened to undermine the much weaker Soviet-backed currency in East Germany. These events precipitated the Soviet blockade of West Berlin at the end of June. Although termed a "blockade" by the West, the Soviet action consisted of a limited set of restrictions on land access to the Western sectors of Berlin from West Germany. It did not preclude supplies to West Berlin from the Soviet zone of occupation, which continued to trickle into the city, nor was air access prohibited—hence the famous airlift.[81]

The goal of Stalin's pressure tactics was to force the Western states to rescind their London communiqué and return to the CFM negotiating forum. Stalin was quite frank about his aim in two conversations he held with the British, French, and American ambassadors in August 1948.[82] In January 1949 Stalin made this position public when he agreed with a Western interviewer that the blockade would be lifted if the West agreed to convene another CFM session devoted to the German question. In May 1949 the blockade was lifted when the Western powers agreed to reconvene the CFM in Paris.

By the time the blockade ended, Molotov was no longer foreign minister, having been removed from the post on March 4, 1949, following his dispute with Stalin about the expulsion of his wife from the Communist Party. His place was taken by his deputy, Andrei Vyshinsky. Molotov was given a new job: head of the Politburo's commission on foreign affairs. That meant he remained in overall charge of foreign policy. As ever, the last word on foreign policy was Stalin's, but the penultimate voice remained Molotov's, with whom Vyshinsky invariably consulted before submitting documents to the Soviet dictator.

THE STRUGGLE FOR A GERMAN PEACE TREATY

At the Paris CFM in June 1949, Vyshinsky's brief was to resist the further economic and political integration of the Western zones of Germany by seeking to restore four-power control of the whole country. A second goal was an agreement that the Soviet Union and the Western powers would, within three months, negotiate the draft of a German peace treaty.

There were two new wrinkles in Soviet policy on Germany: first, negotiation of a draft peace treaty was no longer tied to the prior formation of a united German government and, second, Allied occupation forces were to be withdrawn a year after the conclusion of such a treaty.[83] These changes represented a substantial policy shift. The Soviets had previously favored prolonged Allied occupation and a piecemeal process of negotiation leading to an all-German government and the signature of a peace treaty. Now they sought a rapid Allied withdrawal as a means of averting the further integration of western Germany into the Western bloc. That bloc had taken on a very definite military aspect with the establishment of the North Atlantic Treaty Organization (NATO) in April 1949. The Soviets saw NATO as an aggressive alliance directed against

*Molotov shakes hands with British Foreign Secretary Ernest Bevin on arrival at Lancaster
House in London for a meeting of the Council of Foreign Ministers (November 25, 1947).*
Society for Cooperation in Russian and Soviet Studies

the USSR and its East European allies. It posed no immediate military threat,
but the potential for a West Germany–NATO linkup was self-evident. Such an
alliance the Soviets did fear.

Like its immediate predecessors in Moscow and London, the Paris CFM
closed without any agreement. From the Soviet point of view the situation went
from bad to worse during the months that followed. In September 1949 the
process of forming an independent West German state was completed when
parliamentary elections were held in the new Federal Republic of Germany
(FRG). In October 1949 Stalin retaliated by founding the German Democratic
Republic (GDR). The division of Germany the Soviets had sought to resist was
now a reality. In May 1950 the American, British, and French foreign ministers
issued a statement urging the speedy integration of the FRG into the West European community. In August Churchill called for the creation of a European
army, and in September the Western powers paved the way for German participation in such an army when they terminated the state of war with Germany
and declared that an attack on the FRG would be an attack on them. In Oc-

tober the French government proposed the Pleven Plan for a European army with German contingents. Meeting in Brussels in December, the three Western foreign ministers agreed in principle to a West German military contribution to the defense of Western Europe.

The Soviets responded to these developments by convening a conference of East European foreign ministers that issued a declaration opposing the re-militarization of West Germany. The meeting, held in Prague in October 1950, called also for the negotiation of a peace treaty for Germany and the establish-ment of an all-German council of representatives of the FRG and the GDR that would be consulted about the treaty's terms and prepare the way for the formation of an all-German government.[84] The Soviets were represented at the Prague gathering not by Vyshinsky, but by Molotov, who took a very active part in the proceedings and displayed impressive skill in handling the discus-sion. He was clear the Soviet aim was a united, democratic, and peace-loving Germany and insisted the proposed all-German council had to involve demo-cratic forces in West Germany as well as the representatives of the GDR and FRG governments and parliaments.[85]

Needless to say, the Western powers ignored the Prague declaration and proceeded with their plans for the formation of a European army. The spec-ter of a remilitarized West Germany integrated into a Western military bloc loomed larger and larger. It was a nightmare scenario for the Soviets, who feared that a German military revival would lead to a third world war.

CHINA AND KOREA

On the other side of the world—in Asia—the outlook for the Soviets was some-what brighter. In 1949 Mao Zedong's Chinese communists finally triumphed in the long-running civil war with Chiang Kai-shek's nationalists. In Beijing in October 1949 Mao proclaimed the establishment of the People's Republic of China. Stalin had been skeptical of Mao's prospects for success, but he quickly grasped the significance of an alliance with the communist leadership of the most populous country in the world. At the end of 1949 Mao traveled to Mos-cow for talks with Stalin, and the result was the signature in February 1950 of the Sino-Soviet Treaty of Friendship, Alliance, and Mutual Assistance. Molotov played only a secondary role in the treaty negotiations, but there is no doubt he valued the Sino-Soviet alliance very highly and saw it as a mainstay of the Cold War struggle with the United States for global power and influence. As we shall see, when that alliance fell apart in the late 1950s and early 1960s, Molotov's sympathies were with the Chinese side of the Sino-Soviet split.

The communist triumph in China was the most important backdrop to a critical decision taken by Stalin in summer 1950: the initiation of the Korean War.

Until 1945 Korea was a Japanese colony. When Japan surrendered, the country was divided along the thirty-eighth parallel into Soviet and American zones of occupation. The intention was to reunite the country following national elections, but, as happened in Germany, the two occupation regimes hardened into competing states: an authoritarian communist regime in the North headed by Kim Il-sung and an authoritarian capitalist regime in the South headed by Syngman Rhee. In 1949 Soviet and American troops withdrew, and the scene was set for a clash between Kim and Rhee, each of whom aspired to reunite Korea under his leadership.

The main architect of the Korean War was Kim Il-sung, who persuaded Stalin that an attack on the South would result in an easy victory and would be greeted by a popular revolutionary uprising by the country's downtrodden masses. Flush with the communist success in China, Stalin was inclined to share these illusions.

Initially the North Korean invasion of June 1950 was quite successful, and much of South Korea fell to Kim's armies. Stalin and Kim expected the Americans to acquiesce to this outcome and were surprised when, with UN backing, the United States intervened to save South Korea. American-led forces soon launched a series of successful counteroffensives and forced the North Koreans to retreat back across the thirty-eighth parallel. It seemed that Kim's regime was about to collapse. Luckily for Stalin, help was on hand from the Chinese communists. With the help of Chinese "volunteers," the North Koreans were able to stabilize their position, and the war turned into a battle of attrition along the border with South Korea. The Soviets did not intervene directly in the war, but they continued to be the major military supplier of the Chinese and North Koreans. Stalin favored a continuation of the war as long as there was a chance of gaining a decisive military advantage, but by mid-1951 he had come to accept the necessity of armistice negotiations.[86]

The North Korean attack was seen in the West as an expansionary Soviet move, and it precipitated a significant acceleration of Western rearmament programs. There was a commensurate development on the Soviet side. In January 1951 Stalin convened a meeting of the communist leaders of Bulgaria, Czecho-

slovakia, Hungary, Poland, and Romania accompanied by the defense ministers of those countries. The meeting was chaired by Molotov, and its purpose
was to agree to plans for a rapid and substantial rearmament of the communist
bloc. The rationale for this policy was that the United States was bogged down
in Korea, and this provided a breathing space of two to three years to prepare
for war. Stalin did not consider war with the United States inevitable, but he
did believe the best way to deter an "imperialist attack" on the communist bloc
was to be well armed.[87] By 1953 the armies of the USSR's East European allies
numbered over a million, while the Soviet armed forces increased from under
3 million in 1948 to over 5 million.

The other prong of the USSR's defensive military buildup was the continuation of the Soviet A-bomb program. The Soviets had first tested an atomic
bomb in August 1949, and there were two more such tests in 1951. By the time
of Stalin's death in 1953, the Soviets possessed fifty to a hundred atomic weapons–
a significant arsenal but minuscule compared to the thousands of bombs of the
Americans. Stalin's general attitude to the Bomb–which seems to have been
shared by Molotov–was that while it was important to possess atomic weapons,
their importance in modern warfare was exaggerated. Conventional armies
and navies were still needed to win wars, and countries as big and powerful as
the Soviet Union could survive a nuclear attack. Stalin had a point. The real
revolution in military technology lay ahead–in the mid-1950s with the development of the hydrogen bomb–a weapon thousands of times more powerful
than the A-bombs dropped on Hiroshima and Nagasaki in 1945–and long-
range missiles capable of delivering nuclear weapons to targets thousands of
miles away.[88]

THE PEACE MOVEMENT

His evident bellicosity in Korea notwithstanding, Stalin's main international
interest in the late 1940s and early 1950s was the communist peace movement,
which grew into a mass political movement in a number of European countries.

The movement was launched in August 1948 at a World Congress of Intellectuals for Peace in Wroclaw, Poland, which attracted the participation of a
number of famous Western intellectuals, artists, and scientists including Pablo
Picasso, Bertolt Brecht, Aldous Huxley, and Frédéric and Irène Joliot-Curie.
From this gathering was elected an International Liaison Committee of Intellectuals for Peace, with headquarters in Paris and national committees in

forty-six countries. This was followed by the First World Congress of Partisans of Peace, which opened in Paris on April 20, 1949. Attended by nearly two thousand delegates, the congress claimed to speak for 600 million people in seventy-two countries and passed resolutions condemning NATO, opposing the rearmament of Germany and Japan, and calling for the prohibition of nuclear weapons. The meeting elected a Permanent Committee of the Partisans of Peace (PCPP), which eventually evolved into the World Peace Council (WPC).[89]

The two main Soviet figures involved in the peace movement were Alexander Fadeyev, the head of the Soviet Writers' Union, and the writer and journalist Ilya Ehrenburg. From Molotov's archives we know the two men submitted detailed reports to the Soviet leadership on the activities of the peace movement and were given specific instructions on policies to be pursued by the PCPP and its successor, the WPC.[90]

In ideological terms the place of the peace movement in communist political strategy was expounded by Mikhail Suslov, Zhdanov's successor as Soviet ideology chief at the third and final conference of the Cominform in November 1949 (Zhdanov had died in 1948). Suslov spoke on "The Defense of Peace and Struggle Against the Warmongers," and his message was that "the entire policy of the Anglo-American imperialist bloc is now devoted to preparing another world war." That meant the struggle for peace was now the primary task of the communist movement. Suslov highlighted, in particular, the need for a peace campaign on the broadest possible political basis: "The power of the movement of the partisans of peace consists in the fact that it embraces hundreds of millions of people from the working class, the peasantry, the intelligentsia, and the urban middle strata, regardless of race and nationality and religious or political beliefs."[91]

In March 1950 the WPC met in the Swedish capital and issued the Stockholm Appeal—a petition demanding the prohibition of nuclear weapons. According to Soviet records, by the end of the year the petition had nearly 500 million signatures. In November 1950 the Second World Peace Congress was convened in the Polish capital and the Warsaw Appeal was launched—a petition centered on demands for an end to the war in Korea, which secured more than 560 million signatures. At its Berlin meeting in February 1951, the WPC launched the third of the peace movement's great international petition campaigns–the demand for a five-power peace pact between Britain, China, France, the Soviet Union, and the United States. By December nearly 600 million people had signed this appeal.[92] The proposal for a five-power peace pact had first been presented by Vyshinsky in a speech at the UN in September 1949 but did not feature centrally in peace movement campaigning until after an interview by Stalin in February 1951 in which the Soviet leader highlighted the demand for a great power peace pact. This had been the cue for a sustained mass campaign for the five-power peace pact, and the Politburo's instructions to Fadeyev and Ehrenburg in 1951–1952 reflected the high priority attached to this policy demand.[93]

The peace campaign featured prominently at the nineteenth congress of the Soviet Communist Party in October 1952–the first such gathering since 1939. Just before the congress Stalin published a series of articles in *Pravda* under the heading "Economic Problems of Socialism in the USSR," which were then collected together in a booklet of the same name. In a section entitled "Inevitability of War between the Capitalist Countries" Stalin reaffirmed traditional Soviet doctrine that while intra-capitalist wars were inevitable, war between the USSR and the capitalist states was not. The latter assertion rested on the belief that a capitalist attack on the USSR could be averted by a combination of Soviet power, political struggle, and capitalist fear of revolutions in their own countries. As far as intra-capitalist wars were concerned, while these were generally inevitable in theory, Stalin said that in practice the peace movement could prevent each particular capitalist war. The point of this convoluted reasoning was to emphasize that the struggle for peace could be won within the framework of capitalism: "The object of the present-day peace movement," wrote Stalin, "is to rouse the masses of people to fight for the preservation of peace and for the prevention of another world war. Consequently, the aim of this movement is not to overthrow capitalism and establish socialism–it confines itself to the democratic aim of preserving peace. In this respect, the present-day peace movement differs from the movement of the time of the First World War for the conversion of the imperialist war into civil war, since the latter movement went further and pursued socialist ends."[94] It should be noted that Stalin's implicit revision of the traditional Marxist doctrine of the inevitability of capitalist war reflected the shift in Soviet discourse that had already taken place in the context of the peace movement–which explicitly argued that political struggle could prevent wars.

Georgii Malenkov, the deputy premier and Stalin's number two in the party apparatus, presented the Central Committee report at the congress. The struggle for peace was one of the main themes of the foreign policy section of the report, and Malenkov summarized Soviet peace policy as follows:

> There exists another perspective, the perspective of preserving peace, the perspective of peace between people. This perspective demands the prohibition of war propaganda . . . the prohibition of atomic and bacteriological weapons, progressive reductions in the armed forces of the great powers, the conclusion of a peace pact between those powers, the growth of trade between countries, the restoration of a single international market, and other such measures in the spirit of strengthening peace.[95]

Stalin's only direct contribution to the congress were some brief concluding remarks urging the foreign fraternal delegates to raise the banner of national independence and make the Communist Party the leading patriotic force of their nation—invocations that were an established feature of Soviet discourse on the struggle for peace.

Molotov's role at the congress was minor. He chaired the opening session and gave a short speech but contributed little else. He was out of favor with Stalin following the failure of a major initiative to resolve the German question.

THE "MOLOTOV NOTE" OF 1952

When the Western powers ignored the Prague Declaration of October 1950, the Soviets proposed a CFM meeting to discuss the question of German rearmament. The Western powers agreed, as long as the CFM could also discuss the basic causes of tension with the Soviet Union (in their view, communist aggression). This diplomatic exchange led in March 1951 to a deputy foreign ministers' meeting in Paris charged with preparing the agenda for a future CFM meeting. The Soviet representative at the conference was Andrei Gromyko, whose brief was to secure an agenda that dealt with the following: (1) the implementation of the Potsdam Agreement on the demilitarization of Germany; (2) the rapid conclusion of a peace treaty with Germany and the withdrawal of occupation forces; and (3) the improvement of the atmosphere in Europe and steps toward the reduction of armaments.[96]

Judging by Gromyko's directives, the Soviet intention was to have a serious, constructive negotiation, if the Western powers were prepared to step away from their plans for German remilitarization. It was to no avail; the Paris discussions dragged on until June, with no agreement reached on convening the CFM, let alone an agenda for such a meeting.

In September 1951 Molotov, Vyshinsky, and their Foreign Ministry officials decided on a new strategy: they would put pressure on the Western powers by persuading the German people of the virtues of peace treaty negotiations. The plan was that the GDR government and the German communists would campaign for a peace treaty and call for the formation of an all-German council to discuss the issue. If the Bonn government refused to play ball, the GDR would then call on the four occupying powers to negotiate a peace treaty. The USSR would respond positively to this proposal and would issue its own draft of a peace treaty, with the aim of strengthening the political campaign within Germany for reunification and adding to the pressure on the Western powers to return to the negotiating table.

Broadly speaking, this was the sequence of events that actually unfolded in late 1951 and early 1952. On March 10 the Soviets issued a note on the German question.[97] Often called the Stalin Note, it should, as the Russian scholar Alexei Filitov has suggested, really be called the Molotov Note, since all the archive documentation on its conception and execution bears Molotov's imprimatur.[98]

The main innovation of the Molotov Note was that it contained a Soviet draft of the principles of a German peace treaty. According to the Soviet proposal, there would be a united Germany, Allied occupation forces would be withdrawn within a year of the signing of a peace treaty, Germany's armed forces would be limited to levels necessary for national defense, and, crucially, Germany would pledge not to enter into any coalition or military alliance directed against states it had fought during the last war—that is, the country would not be allowed to participate either in NATO or in the European Defence Community (EDC) that the Western powers were planning to form. This Soviet offer to the West—a united Germany in exchange for its disarmament and neutralization—was to remain on the table for the next three years.

The Western powers' response on March 25 was to propose free all-German elections to elect a government that would then negotiate a peace treaty—a government that would be free to enter any defensive associations it liked. This was unacceptable to the Soviets, but on April 9 they did agree to discussions on free all-German elections. This was not much of a concession, since the Soviets had long been on record as supporting democratic elections as part of the process leading to German reunification. Indeed, at the Moscow CFM in 1947 Molotov had argued publicly that such elections should be based on the model of the Weimar Constitution. The Soviets had since shifted to the position that the elections should be based on the electoral laws of the FRG and the GDR as well as those of the Weimar Republic, but the stumbling block in the negotiations with the Western powers was not the principle of free all-German elections—it was the Soviet demand for advance guarantees that a united Germany would not join the Western bloc. While the West wanted a united Germany that would be free to decide its own (pro-Western) foreign policy, the Soviets wanted an agreement that would preclude a revival of German aggression.

Casting a pall over these diplomatic exchanges was the Western decision in May 1952 to sign the Paris-Bonn Agreements on the establishment of the EDC. The exchange of diplomatic notes continued for another few months, but the gulf between the two sides could not be bridged. By the end of the year the Soviets had lost interest and did not even bother to reply to the final Western note of September 1952.[99] The last Soviet note in the sequence was issued on August 23. That same day Vyshinsky met with Walter Ulbricht, the East German communist leader. Ulbricht welcomed the note, saying that it would strengthen the GDR's struggle for a united Germany. Some people, said Ulbricht, thought that since the GDR had embarked on the course of building socialism, there would be no more talk of German unity, but the Soviet note had made it clear the aim remained a united, democratic Germany.[100] If, as some historians say, the March note was purely a propaganda exercise designed to disrupt or delay West German rearmament and the formation of the EDC, Ulbricht was not privy to this information. Of course, the Soviets intended to do all they could to buttress the position of their supporters in a united Germany, but that did not preclude a serious political compromise with the West. That might mean loss of communist political control in East Germany, but the prize of the long-term containment of German aggression made even that price seem worth paying, at least to Molotov.

Stalin supported the campaign for a German peace treaty, but he was skeptical about the prospects for success. In his last known comments on the German question in April 1952, Stalin told a delegation of GDR leaders:

Whatever proposals we make on the German question the Western powers won't agree with them and they won't withdraw from West Germany. To think that the Americans will compromise or accept the draft peace treaty would be a mistake. The Americans need an army in West Germany in order to keep control of Western Europe. . . . The Americans are drawing West Germany into the [NATO] pact. They will form West German forces. . . . In West Germany an independent state is being formed. And you must organize your own state. The demarcation line between West Germany and East Germany should be considered a frontier, and not just any frontier but a dangerous frontier.[101]

Stalin allowed the Molotov Note initiative to run its course, but the stark reality was that by the end of 1952, the Soviet Union faced the prospect of a rearmed West Germany fully integrated into the Western bloc.

Stalin's displeasure at the failure of the Molotov Note was signaled by Molotov's minor role at the nineteenth party congress and by the way he was treated after the congress. Although Molotov was reelected to the Central Committee and to the Presidium of the Central Committee (the new name for the Politburo), he was excluded by Stalin from the Presidium Buro—a smaller body that would be in charge of day-to-day affairs. Molotov also lost his responsibilities in the area of foreign policy,[102] and at the Central Committee's first meeting after the congress Stalin openly attacked him for past mistakes, including his support for a Jewish autonomous region in the Crimea. Stalin also criticized him as being a capitulationist in the Cold War struggle with the West—a veiled reference, perhaps, to Molotov's longstanding support for a German peace treaty.[103] Thereafter, relations between the two men worsened. As Molotov told Chuev years later, "In 1953 Stalin no longer invited me to attend official or informal comradely gatherings, to spend an evening together or to see a film. I was cut off."[104]

By the end of 1952 both Soviet diplomacy and the peace movement were at an impasse. The war in Korea continued, albeit at a lower level of intensity. There was little prospect of a negotiated settlement of the German question. The peace movement had scored some propaganda points and mobilized support for Soviet foreign policy, but it had failed to deflect the West from its Cold War course. Within the Soviet leadership Molotov—the leading advocate of diplomatic negotiations with the West—had been isolated and marginalized by Stalin. Then, somewhat unexpectedly, Stalin died of a stroke in March 1953. The way was open for a revival under Molotov's leadership of the Soviet campaign for a German peace treaty and, even more radically, an end to the Cold War itself.

5

PARTISAN OF PEACE
(1953–1955)

The Soviet Union stands for the reunification of Germany—reunification on a peace-loving and democratic basis. In a united Germany the regime that exists in Eastern Germany should not prevail, and neither should the regime that exists in West Germany. Which regime should and will prevail in a united Germany is a matter that must be decided by the German people themselves in free all-German elections.

— V. M. Molotov (June 1955)[1]

When Stalin died the new Soviet leaders took the opportunity to relaunch their international peace campaign. At the dictator's funeral on March 9, 1953, the three main speakers were Georgii Malenkov, the new prime minister; the security chief, Lavrentii Beria; and Molotov, who had just been reappointed foreign minister. Each emphasized the Soviet Union's commitment to peaceful coexistence with the capitalist world. Molotov said, "Our foreign policy, known throughout the world as a Stalinist peace-loving foreign policy, is a policy in defense of peace between peoples, an unshakable policy of preserving and strengthening peace, a policy of struggle against the preparation and unleashing of a new war, a policy of international cooperation and the development of businesslike relations with all countries."[2]

The Soviet peace offensive was a continuation of Moscow's peace campaigns of the late 1940s and early 1950s. More innovative were the accompanying changes in Soviet foreign policies: a virulent anti-Zionist campaign that had led to a break in diplomatic relations with Israel was discontinued; demands for

Turkish territorial concessions were dropped, as was the claim to a share in the control of the Black Sea Straits; the conflict with Tito's Yugoslavia was ended and ambassadors exchanged with Belgrade, thus paving the way for a full-scale reconstruction of Soviet-Yugoslavian relations; and, most importantly, the Korean War was terminated when a truce was agreed in July 1953.

Stalin's death, the Soviet peace offensive, and the changes in Moscow's foreign policy raised expectations of a fundamental reconstruction of East-West relations, including, possibly, an end to the Cold War. This respite in the Cold War lasted for two years, culminating in the July 1955 Geneva Summit between the leaders of Britain, France, the Soviet Union, and the United States. The Geneva meeting was the first great power summit since the end of World War II. It had few practical results, but there was much talk of the "spirit of Geneva"–the hope that there could be a prolonged détente in the Cold War.

Historical narratives of the post-Stalin détente usually cast Malenkov in the heroic role of progenitor of the spirit of Geneva. Another favored figure is Nikita Khrushchev, Stalin's successor as leader of the Communist Party, credited with being a strong proponent of détente, architect of the normalization of Soviet relations with Yugoslavia, and responsible for the breakthrough in diplomatic negotiations that led to the Austrian State Treaty of May 1955. The villain of the piece is invariably Molotov who, it is said, continued to follow the inflexible and intransigent policies of the Stalin era.

In truth, the architect of détente on the Soviet side was Molotov. For Molotov there was no more important goal than the achievement of a peace treaty that would contain the German danger and attenuate the threat of new world war. To achieve that goal he was prepared to explore and to sanction innovative and radical policy approaches, including a deal with the West on the German question that might have led to a loss of communist control in East Germany. In exchange for this sacrifice Molotov sought a comprehensive system of European collective security that would neutralize the Western bloc's threat to the Soviet Union. The achievement of European collective security would end the Cold War and create a prolonged East-West détente. That new context would provide a favorable environment for the Soviets and their communist allies to continue the pursuit of their socialist goals.

While Molotov believed the advent of socialism on a global scale was inevitable in the long run, in the short term he was prepared to accept peaceful coexistence with capitalism and peaceful competition for global power and influence. Such a perspective had informed Soviet views of world affairs since the 1920s. In the 1950s the urgency of Molotov's pursuit of détente was motivated both by fear of a German revival and his belief that the Soviet Union had the diplomatic and political capacity to force the Western powers to do a deal.

Molotov's attempts to settle the German question and end the Cold War were supported by Malenkov but opposed by Khrushchev, who was not prepared to pay the price of giving up the GDR, a move he foresaw would threaten the stability of the whole Soviet bloc. Khrushchev was more sanguine than Molotov about the German threat and confident the Soviet Union's growing nuclear arsenal would nullify German militarism and deter a new world war. Khrushchev also sensed that the critical issue for the USSR was not the resolution of the German question and a European settlement—Molotov's priority—but the management of Soviet relations with the new power in world politics, the United States. Khrushchev's perspectives were more global and future-oriented than Molotov's, whose horizons tended to be Eurocentric and bounded by the unfinished business of the war. This difference in perspective was hardly surprising given the years Molotov had devoted to the postwar peace negotiations. His dogged pursuit of a German peace treaty after Stalin's death had a strong personal element: the search for a successful end to his long quest for an enduring peace settlement.

THE GERMAN QUESTION REVISITED

Molotov and his Foreign Ministry officials began to contemplate a new initiative on the German question as early as April 1953. On April 18, 1953, Ivan Tugarinov, head of the Soviet foreign ministry's intelligence-gathering committee, issued an information note on Western policy and the German question. Tugarinov pointed out that while the Western powers were trying to push through the ratification of the Paris-Bonn Agreements on the establishment of the EDC, they were facing growing political opposition in France and West Germany.[3] That same day Georgii Pushkin, former head of the Soviet diplomatic mission to Berlin, and Mikhail Gribanov, head of the Third European Department of the Foreign Ministry (responsible for Germany), sent Molotov a memorandum proposing a new initiative on the German question. Their most important proposal was the formation of a provisional all-German government composed of representatives of the two existing German governments, who would be charged principally with drafting an election law for the conduct of all-German elections.[4]

This new proposal for a provisional all-German government was the centerpiece of a further series of internal memorandums,[5] culminating in a note to Molotov on April 28 signed by Yakov Malik, former Soviet representative at the UN (and soon to be the new ambassador to the United Kingdom), and Vladimir Semyonov, former political head of the Soviet control commission in Germany, as well as by Pushkin and Gribanov. The four officials argued that to regain the initiative on the German question, the USSR should not only propose a provisional all-German government, but also the immediate withdrawal of all occupation forces after the formation of such a government. This dual proposal would, the memorandum argued, undercut Western demands for all-German elections prior to the negotiation of a peace treaty.[6]

In a further memorandum to Molotov on May 2, Semyonov stressed the political advantages of proposing a withdrawal of occupation forces upon the formation of an all-German provisional government, as opposed to the existing Soviet policy of withdrawal a year after the signature of a peace treaty. His point was that the negotiation of a peace treaty could delay the withdrawal of occupation forces for years, whereas the formation of a provisional all-German government offered more immediate prospects for withdrawal, an option that would appeal to German public opinion and help the Soviets regain the initiative in the struggle for Germany's reunification on a democratic and peaceful basis. Semyonov, like the other Foreign Ministry officials, advanced tactical reasons for a new policy initiative, but he was also clear about its strategic purpose:

> The crux of the German question during the postwar period has been the matter of the national reunification of Germany. A struggle between the Soviet Union and the GDR on the one side, and the United States, England, France, and the Bonn government on the other has occurred. . . . Since 1945, the entire postwar policy regarding the German question has been built on defending demands for German reunification on a peaceful and democratic basis, and later also on demands for a swift conclusion of a peace treaty, to be followed by the withdrawal of all occupation forces from Germany.[7]

On the basis of these internal ruminations, Molotov and the Foreign Ministry drafted proposals for the Presidium in early May outlining the need for a new initiative on the German question, the core of which was the call for a provisional all-German government.[8] However, by this time the leadership's attentions were elsewhere. There was a growing refugee crisis in the GDR, caused by the massive migration of East Germans to West Germany: more than 120,000 in the first four months of 1953 alone. Migration on such a scale was politically debilitating, economically threatening, and a major contributor to growing social discontent in the GDR. The contingent cause of the migration crisis was the accelerated construction of socialism in the GDR and the associated higher work requirements imposed upon the population. Faced with mounting evidence of popular dissatisfaction with the East German government, Moscow moved to stabilize the situation. On June 2 the Soviet government adopted a resolution, drafted by Molotov, Malenkov, and Beria, "On Measures to Improve the Health of the Political Situation in the GDR." The East German communists were ordered to abandon the forced construction of socialism and to implement a series of economic and political reforms designed to recover their popularity and authority. Among the measures proposed were "to put the tasks of the political struggle to reestablish the national unity of Germany and to conclude a peace treaty at the center of the attention of the broad mass of people both in the GDR and in West Germany."[9] That same day a delegation of East German communist leaders arrived in Moscow for three days of talks with the Soviet leadership. Among the participants was Malenkov, who had prepared a statement to read to the East German delegation:

> The question of perspectives on the development of the German Democratic Republic cannot be seen in isolation from the task of uniting East and West Germany into a single German state. It should be emphasized that the most important problem of the present international system is the restoration of German unity, of Germany's transformation into a peaceful democratic state. Some people, it seems, are inclined to think that we put forward the question of the restoration of Germany's unity in pursuance of propaganda ends only, that we are not really striving to end the division of Germany, that we are not interested in the restoration of a united Germany. This is a profound error. . . . We consider the unity of Germany and its transformation into a democratic and peace-loving state as the most

important condition, as one of the essential guarantees, for the maintenance of European and, consequently, of world security. . . . Profoundly mistaken are those who think that Germany can exist for a long time under conditions of dismemberment in the form of two independent states. To stick to the position of the existence of a dismembered Germany means to keep to the course for a new war. . . . To struggle for the unification of Germany under certain conditions, for its transformation into a peaceful and democratic state means to keep to the course for the prevention of a new world war. . . . On what basis can the unification of Germany be achieved in the current international situation? In our opinion, only on the basis that Germany will be a bourgeois-democratic state. Under present conditions the national unification of Germany on the basis of Germany's transformation into a land of the dictatorship of the proletariat in the form of people's democracy is not feasible. . . . Consequently, it is necessary to choose: either the course for the accelerated building of socialism in the GDR, for the independent existence of two Germanies, and that means the course for a third World War; or the abandonment of the accelerated building of socialism in the GDR and the course of the unification of Germany in the form of a bourgeois-democratic state on condition of its transformation into a peaceful and democratic country. This is why, in our opinion, the most pressing task for our German friends is to implement swiftly and decisively the measures which we are recommending for the normalization of the political and economic situation in the GDR and for safeguarding the future successful solution of the task of unifying Germany and transforming it into a peaceful and democratic state.[10]

This remarkable statement by Malenkov was the most frank exposition ever of the political logic of the Soviet position on the German question. In public pronouncements and in the internal Foreign Ministry documentation, the likely political consequences of German reunification for the GDR were consistently elided. The implicit assumption was that a successful struggle for a peaceful and democratic Germany would strengthen the position of the GDR and the West German communists, and impact positively on the social and political character of the new German state, which would then emerge as a left-wing regime sympathetic to the Soviet Union. No one asked what would happen if this rosy scenario did not materialize and the Soviets had to choose between the strategic advantages of a neutral, united Germany and the political imperative of holding on to the communist position in the GDR.

While the degree of clarity in Malenkov's statement was—and remained—unique, his comments were in accordance with long-established Soviet policy and with the outcome of the revisiting of the German question by Molotov and his foreign ministry in April and May 1953. However, events during the next few weeks had the effect of further narrowing the terms in which the German question could be discussed within Soviet policymaking circles.

The first such event was the June uprising in East Germany. The GDR government's announcement of a "New Course"—moderation of the pace of socialist construction—was interpreted by some sections of the population as a sign of weakness. When the government refused to scale back the higher work requirements, there was a popular revolt, which blossomed into a full-scale, nationwide political rebellion on June 16–17, 1953. According to one Soviet internal report on the revolt, 450,000 people went on strike and 330,000 participated in anti-regime demonstrations.[11] The strikes and demonstrations were relatively easily quelled by Soviet armed forces stationed in Germany and at a relatively low cost in human terms. According to the aforementioned report, there were 29 fatalities (including 11 party/police/government officials) and 350 wounded. But the revolt had exposed the political vulnerability of the East German communist regime and led to a redoubling of Soviet efforts to prop up the GDR economically and politically.

The second event was Beria's fall from grace and his denunciation at a special plenum of the Central Committee on July 2–7, 1953. The main charges against Beria related to his role in domestic politics and his supposed strivings, in conjunction with foreign imperialists, to seize power. The accusation that he wanted to give up the GDR to the capitalists also played a role in the proceedings, although not as prominently as other charges. Malenkov gave the opening report at the plenum on the "Criminal Anti-party and Anti-state Activities of Beria." In a section on the German question, Malenkov said that Beria "did not propose the course for the accelerated building of socialism be corrected; he proposed that any course for the building of socialism in the GDR be abandoned. Given what now is known about Beria, we must reevaluate this point of view. It is clear that this fact characterizes him as a bourgeois renegade."[12]

The next speaker in the discussion was Nikita Khrushchev, the new head of the Soviet Communist Party. He ratcheted up the condemnatory rhetoric on Beria and the German question:

> The clearest display that he was a provocateur, not a communist, was in relation to the German question when he raised the question of giving up the construction of socialism in order to make concessions to the West. He was asked: what does this mean? It means that 18 million Germans are given up to the Americans? Yes, he replied, it is necessary to form a neutral, democratic Germany. How could there be a neutral, bourgeois Germany between us and America? Is this possible? . . . Beria said that we will conclude an agreement. But what would this agreement be worth? We know the value of agreements. An agreement remains in force if it is reinforced by cannons. If an agreement is not reinforced it never stands. If we were to talk about such an agreement they would laugh at us, would think us naïve. But Beria is not stupid or a fool. He is clever and cunning and treacherous. So he was doing something, perhaps a task given to him, perhaps, the devil only knows, he was given other tasks by his residents. I can't guarantee not. Therefore, I repeat again that he is not a communist, he is a provocateur and he conducted himself like one.[13]

Molotov spoke next, attacking Beria on grounds that he had said there could be a peace-loving, bourgeois Germany. Molotov accused Beria of attempting to distort the position of the Presidium on the construction of socialism in Germany, pointing out that in the discussion he (Molotov) had insisted that the accelerated construction of socialism had been mistaken, but *not* the construction of socialism per se. Beria's statements on the German question showed, said Molotov, that he had "nothing in common with our party, that he was a person from the bourgeois camp, an anti-Soviet person."[14]

Molotov was followed by Nikolai Bulganin, the defense minister, who said that Beria favored the liquidation of the GDR and the restoration of a bourgeois Germany.

In his concluding remarks Malenkov did not return to the German question but the Plenum's formal resolution condemning Beria noted that he had "rejected the course of building socialism in the German Democratic Republic" and wanted to turn the GDR into a bourgeois republic.[15]

The denunciation of Beria's supposed views on the German question was linked to the June events in the GDR. Those disturbances had been characterized by the Soviet authorities, publicly and privately, as the work of foreign provocateurs.[16] By linking Beria with the idea of surrendering the GDR, his former comrades added to the case that he was not only a political renegade and would-be dictator, but an imperialist agent.

The immediate impact of the Beria affair on the direction of Soviet foreign policy was contradictory. While there was no more talk of a united but bourgeois-democratic Germany, the aim of reunifying the country as a peaceful and democratic state remained official policy. Soviet support for the GDR as a socialist state strengthened, but, equally, there was no hard and fast commitment by Moscow to its long-term existence as a separate state under communist control.

There was a pause in Foreign Ministry deliberations on the German question during the Beria affair, but when policymaking resumed at the end of July, there was a return to the positions hammered out in April and May. The spur was the receipt on July 15 of a Western diplomatic note proposing a foreign ministers' conference on the German question. On July 30, Andrei Gromyko, Molotov's deputy, presented him with a draft note on the German question. Gromyko's note proposed measures to strengthen the Soviet position in Germany, enhance the authority of the GDR "as the basis for the restoration of a united Germany as a peace-loving and democratic state," and create difficulties for Western plans to divide the country and use it as an agency of the West's aggressive plans in Europe. Among the measures proposed were (a) to agree to a foreign ministers' conference, (b) to issue a note on the German question proposing the formation of a provisional all-German government, (c) to implement previously proposed economic and political measures to bolster the GDR, (d) to convene a conference of people's democracies to issue a statement on the German question and conclude a collective pact of friendship, and (e) to invite a GDR delegation to Moscow for talks. On August 2 Molotov forwarded the Gromyko draft to the Presidium. All of the Foreign Ministry's proposals were ratified, except that for a conference of the people's democracies.[17]

The Soviet reply to the Western note of July 15 was issued on August 4. It agreed to a foreign ministers' conference to discuss the German question but insisted that discussions would also deal with measures to ease international tensions.[18] On August 15 the Soviet government issued a further note, this time specifically on the German question. It said "the restoration of the national unity of a democratic Germany remains a fundamental problem for the German people, the solution of which all the peace-loving peoples of Europe are interested in. . . . There must be no delay in adopting measures which might assist at least the gradual solution of the problem of uniting Germany, of forming an all-German democratic government." To this end the Soviets proposed that a conference be held within six months to discuss a peace treaty with Germany and the creation of a provisional all-German government:

> Such a government might, by direct agreement between East and West Germany, be set up to replace the existing governments of the German Democratic Republic and the German Federal Republic. If this should prove difficult at the present time, the Provisional All-German Government might be set up even though the governments of the GDR and the FRG remained in existence for the time being, in which case the Provisional All-German Government would evidently possess only restricted functions. Even so, the formation of a Provisional All-German Government would represent a real step forward towards the union of Germany, which would be consummated by the formation of an All-German Government on the basis of really free all-German elections.[19]

On August 20 a delegation from the GDR arrived in Moscow for discussions with the Soviet leadership. When it left three days later, a communiqué was issued outlining a series of Soviet concessions that strengthened the East German regime's economic position: reparation payments were to cease from January 1954, Soviet enterprises in Germany would be transferred to the GDR government, Soviet occupation charges would be reduced, all GDR debt to the USSR would be expunged, and trade would be increased between the two countries, including through the provision of Soviet loans to the GDR. The Soviet diplomatic mission to the GDR was raised to ambassadorial status, and Moscow also agreed to expedite the release of German POWs still held in the USSR. In his toast to the GDR delegation at a dinner in the Kremlin on August 22, Malenkov emphasized the need to resist Western plans to divide Germany and the importance of the struggle for German unity on a peace-loving and democratic basis.[20]

TOWARD COLLECTIVE SECURITY

The publication of the Soviet notes of August 4 and 15 was followed by a round of rancorous public diplomatic exchanges with the West, but by the end of 1953 there was agreement on convening a foreign ministers' conference.

Throughout these exchanges the Soviets insisted the German question had to be discussed alongside measures to reduce international tensions. As Molotov said at a press conference on November 13, "The settlement of the German problem is intimately bound up with European security and, consequently, with a relaxation of international tensions." Three days later, the Western powers issued a note accusing the Soviet Union of making proposals that "would entail the abandonment by France, Great Britain, and the United States of all their plans to safeguard their own security. A defenseless Western Europe appears to be the price demanded by the Soviet government for participation in a conference." Evidently stung by this Western counterattack, the Soviet reply on November 26 stated:

> The security of the West European countries will be firmly safeguarded if it is based not on the setting up of the West European countries in opposition to the East European countries, but on concerted efforts to safeguard European security. . . . The Soviet Union is prepared, together with other European countries, to make every effort to safeguard European security through the instrumentality of an appropriate agreement embracing all the countries of Europe, irrespective of their social system.[21]

Here was the germ of Soviet proposals for pan-European collective security. Adding urgency to this new policy direction was Soviet perception of the tactical need to preempt Western proposals on European collective security. Throughout the autumn of 1953, Soviet analysts reported on discussions taking place in the Western press about the creation of a system of nonaggression pacts in Europe—a proposal aimed at meeting Moscow's concerns about West German rearmament and the EDC. Soviet observers traced these discussions back to Churchill's May 1953 proposal for a "new Locarno," a reference to the Locarno Pact of 1925 that had assuaged French fears of a German revival by providing a security guarantee for France's eastern borders. The idea was to offer the Soviet Union a similar guarantee in the form of the Western powers' acceptance of the frontiers established in 1945 (i.e., taking into account German territorial losses to Poland and to the USSR), together with various East-West nonaggression agreements. There was also talk of withdrawing all foreign forces from a united Germany, of establishing demilitarized and neutral zones in Central Europe, and Western guarantees of Soviet security.[22] Similar commentaries and analyses figured in Foreign Ministry briefing documents on the likely positions the Western powers would adopt at the foreign ministers' conference. The conclusion was that the Western powers would propose guarantees of Soviet security in exchange for progress on the German question and the EDC.[23] These Soviet analyses and reports, brought together in a composite note from Semyonov and Pushkin to Molotov on January 5, concluded by drawing attention to Western speculation that the USSR would put forward its own plan for European collective security.[24]

The first draft of a treaty on European collective security drawn up by the Foreign Ministry was dated December 22, 1953. The basic proposition was for all European states to sign a collective security treaty pledging to support each other in the event of aggression.[25] At this stage, however, the Soviets remained locked into the idea that European security revolved around the resolution of the German question. Only incrementally did pan-European collective security become the major Soviet policy plank at the foreign ministers' conference. Indeed, Molotov's first draft of the directive for the Soviet delegation, sent to Malenkov and Khrushchev on January 3, omitted any mention of European collective security. This draft directive defined Soviet aims at the conference as (1) to exploit the contradictions between the imperialist powers to disrupt West German rearmament and the formation of the EDC, (2) to strengthen the international position of the Soviet Union, (3) to reduce international tensions, including by convening a five-power conference that the People's Republic of China would attend, and (4) to discuss the question of a peace treaty with Germany and the establishment of a democratic and peace-loving German state. The next day, however, Molotov sent Malenkov and Khrushchev a supplement to this draft, which specified that if no agreement were possible on the German question, the Soviet delegation would introduce a new proposal on "Safeguarding Security in Europe"–a proposal specifically designed to combat Western propaganda in favor of a "new Locarno." The addendum stated that, pending the signature of a peace treaty with Germany, (1) occupation forces should be withdrawn (but the Allies would retain the right to intervene in the event of the threat of German aggression), (2) German armaments should be limited, and (3) there should be an agreement on European collective security.

Molotov's amended draft was considered by the Presidium on January 7. It is not known what transpired at the meeting, but on January 12 Gromyko and Pushkin produced a new draft of the directive, which Molotov submitted to Malenkov and Khrushchev the next day. The new draft contained a paragraph on European collective security but only in the context of a very detailed set of instructions. On January 15 the Presidium passed a resolution on the draft directive. Again, the contents of this resolution are unknown, but two days later Gromyko submitted to Molotov the draft of a detailed proposal for a European collective security treaty. On January 20 this draft was in turn submitted to Malenkov and Khrushchev for their approval.[26] Hitherto, tactical preparations for the foreign ministers' conference had concentrated on the German question, with the Foreign Ministry producing extensive documentation analyzing Western policy on Germany and defending the Soviet policy position.[27] Now attention switched to possible Western objections to a pan-European collective security treaty.[28]

THE BERLIN CONFERENCE OF FOREIGN MINISTERS

The foreign ministers' conference (January 25 to February 18, 1954) was held in Berlin on Soviet suggestion. Molotov went with a large delegation of deputies and expert advisers, including Gromyko, Malik (now ambassador to the UK), Pushkin, and Semyonov (back in Germany as high commissioner). The United States was represented by Secretary of State John Foster Dulles, Britain by Foreign Secretary Anthony Eden, and France by Foreign Minister Georges Bidault.

Discussions at the twenty-seven public sessions of the conference ranged far and wide but centered on the German question and turned out to be mostly a reprise of the Soviet-Western public polemics of the preceding months, with the Western powers demanding free, all-German elections as a precondition for the negotiation of a peace treaty, while the Soviets insisted on the establishment of a provisional German government that would organize those elections.[29]

Publicly, the Western powers characterized Molotov's performance at the conference as typically dogmatic, uncompromising, and negative, and many historians have been content to accept this judgment. A more dispassionate reading of the proceedings suggests that Molotov displayed considerable flexibility and made strenuous efforts to reach agreement.

In his very first contribution to the discussion, Molotov said, "We have gathered here to arrive at some compromises. We have not assembled to make categorical statements but to listen to one another with a view to reaching agreement on some questions." In this spirit Molotov refuted Western claims that the Soviet proposal for a provisional government was aimed at delaying all-German elections and said that a short timetable leading to elections could be agreed upon. Molotov also denied the Soviet aim was to stage East German–style elections in which the results would be manipulated. Molotov even proposed a referendum in Germany on the choice between joining the EDC and concluding a peace treaty leading to reunification. There was also a new Soviet proposal on the table: occupation forces, apart from a token presence, would be withdrawn prior to elections (i.e., the process could begin before the signature of a peace treaty). On innumerable occasions Molotov said that all the Soviet proposals were up for detailed discussion and amendment.

In private, Molotov was even more friendly and accommodating. At dinner with Dulles on February 6, Molotov said that "he thought there was a possibility of some success on Germany . . . along the lines of a small German army, with a German government which would be directed neither against the United States, France, Great Britain nor the Soviet Union. He wondered if that possibility was totally excluded." Later in the conversation Molotov "repeated his view that a limited German army, with a government which was directed against none of the four powers, was a possible line of development." Toward the end of the conversation, Molotov made the same point again "but he left the impression that if this was excluded, other courses might be considered."[30]

Molotov displayed similar flexibility on the question of a peace treaty with Austria. Here the Soviet proposal was that a peace treaty ending the Allied occupation and restoring Austrian independence could be signed on two conditions: (1) that Austria would not join any military coalition or allow the establishment of foreign military bases on its territory and (2) that the final withdrawal of occupation forces was delayed until the signature of a peace treaty with Germany–a proposal directed at precluding an *Anschluss* uniting the two countries, as had happened in 1938.

Another set of discussions at the conference centered on the Soviet proposal for a pan-European system of collective security, introduced by Molotov on February 10.[31] The Soviets had evidently been expecting the Western states to put forward their own proposals for a system of nonaggression treaties and held back on presenting their own position until quite late in the day. The Western response was predictably hostile, particularly when Molotov made clear the proposed collective security system was an explicit alternative to the EDC. A particular bone of contention was that under the terms of the Soviet draft treaty, the United States would not be a member of the new collective security organization but merely, together with Communist China, an observer.

According to C. D. Jackson, a member of the U.S. delegation and Eisenhower's adviser on psychological-political warfare, this was a gross tactical error by Molotov: "Then came the block buster. The US was specifically excluded from the collective security pact. . . . At that point we all laughed out loud and the Russians were taken completely by surprise at our reaction. Molotov did a double take and finally managed a smile, but the Russian momentum was gone."[32] The laughter is often cited in Cold War historiography but not Molotov's subsequent statements that this clause in the Soviet draft treaty could be looked at, changed, and the United States accorded a different status in the collective security treaty.

At the session on February 10 Molotov said, "If the idea [of collective security] is unacceptable then our proposal will fail. If the idea is not rejected but requires another draft or corrections to our draft–that is another matter." At the session on February 15 Molotov said specifically in relation to U.S. membership of a European collective security organization: "One can have a different formulation of this point or its exclusion altogether. In any case we are prepared to examine another proposition on this question." At the same session Molotov was conciliatory in relation to NATO, saying that it was disinformation to suggest the European collective security treaty was directed against NATO when the proposed treaty was actually directed against the EDC and German rearmament. Goaded by critical remarks by Bidault and Eden, Molotov returned to the NATO question at the session on February 17:

> The Soviet delegation can only repeat that the draft general agreement [on European collective security] is an alternative to the EDC. Regarding the question of its compatibility with [NATO] the Soviet delegation has

already replied that we are prepared to study this question. Don't forget that in relation to [NATO] there are different views. Eden has more than once emphasized that in his view [NATO] has a defensive character. Bidault also spoke about this. The Soviet government has a different estimation of [NATO]. That is why it is necessary to study this question. Moreover, it is not to be excluded that [NATO] could be amended and the differences about the character of the agreement eliminated. A reply to Bidault's question about the compatibility or incompatibility of [NATO] and the general European question will only be possible after we have jointly studied this question.[33]

Integral to the Soviet proposal on collective security was that discussions on a pan-European agreement would be part of the process leading to the conclusion of a peace treaty for Germany. Indeed, pan-European collective security arrangements were the essential context for the signature of the peace treaty and the formation of a united Germany. In other words, there would be no EDC, no German rearmament, and the peace would be secured by a collective guarantee against aggression. As Molotov said in his speech introducing the collective security proposal:

> The creation of a system of collective security in Europe cannot and should not detract from the importance and necessity of settling the German question as speedily as possible in accordance with the requirements of maintaining peace in Europe. Moreover, the establishment of a system of collective security would help to create more favorable conditions for the settlement of the German question, inasmuch as it would rule out the involvement of either part of Germany in military alignments, and would thus remove one of the chief impediments to the creation of a united, peaceable, and democratic German state.[34]

The Western powers saw things very differently. For them the EDC was a defensive organization and a method to contain Germany while at the same time strengthening Western defenses against the Soviet threat. Western representatives at the conference gave no credence to Soviet proposals on either the German question or on European collective security, viewing them as a cover for more sinister designs. In his radio and television broadcast on the conference to the American public on February 24, Dulles described Soviet aims as the achievement of a communist-controlled Germany and a Soviet-controlled Europe from which the United States would be excluded. He ridiculed Molotov's collective security proposal as "so preposterous that when he read it laughter rippled around the Western sides of the table to the dismay of the Communist delegation."[35] In his private report to the National Security Council (NSC) two days later, Dulles was no less scathing, arguing that the conference showed that the neutralization of Germany and Austria was not possible because the Soviets would accept nothing less than full control of those countries. What the Soviets wanted, said Dulles, was a division of the world with the United States, under which the United States would be restricted to the Western Hemisphere while the USSR dominated Eurasia. Dulles informed the NSC that "Molotov had spoken with an evident show of personal authority. The Soviet Foreign Minister no longer appeared a mere subordinate, as he had when Stalin was alive. He appeared, comparatively at least, free to make his own decisions with a minimum of reporting back to Moscow for instructions." Dulles also warned the NSC that in Berlin Molotov had been "very clever and artful throughout the meeting. He is one of the shrewdest and wiliest diplomats of this century or, indeed, of any century."[36]

The Berlin Conference had its lighter sides, as shown by this ditty dedicated to "Auntie Mollie," composed by an unknown member of the British delegation (to be sung to the tune of "Lili Marlene"):

> Please Mr Dulles, this is now the Spring,
> We have talked of Germany, and almost everything.
> We have exhausted item one,
> And Auntie, he's just begun,
> Oh please, can't we go home,
> Oh please, can't we go home.
>
> Please Mr Bidault, can't we leave the rest,
> We've polished off Albania and now we're on Trieste.
> We have discussed the Mau Mau race,
> And next on Auntie's list is space.
> Oh please, can't we go home,
> Oh please, can't we go home.

Please Mr Eden, Parliament's on hol,

If we cannot break it off,

Suggest a hol to Mol.

We have discussed each continent,

Our energies are all spent,

Oh please, can't we go home,

Oh please, can't we go home.

Please dear Auntie Mollie,

Won't you be a friend,

We'd do almost anything to see this Conference end,

If going home is what you fear,

Let's agree to call it a year,

Then you come home with us,

Then you come home with us.[37]

After his return from Berlin, Molotov presented a report on the conference to a plenum of the Party's Central Committee. The report was highly critical of Western policy, but Molotov saw hope in growing popular opposition to the EDC, especially in France and West Germany.[38] Far from abandoning the collective security proposal in the face of Western rebuff, the Soviets saw the Berlin Conference as a launching pad for a campaign in favor of European collective security.

The Soviet delegation had monitored Western press reports and commentary on its proposals throughout the conference. They took particular note of the great and favorable interest shown in the proposal for European collective security.[39] Foreign Ministry officials assessed how to further the collective security proposal,[40] and Molotov moved to deal with the question of U.S. participation in a European collective security system and the issue of Soviet relations with NATO. Gromyko was tasked with formulating a new policy. After a number of drafts, corrected in detail by Molotov, the end result was a dual proposal: the United States could join the European collective security organization, and the USSR could join NATO.

On March 26 Molotov sent a long note to Khrushchev and Malenkov explaining the rationale for the proposal. This document is worth discussing at length since it is a rare example of a detailed discursive document prepared by Molotov for the Presidium. Usually he forwarded the documents drawn up by his officials to the Presidium without comment, except for a request they be approved. In this case he evidently felt the need to present in writing the arguments in favor of a daring policy initiative.

Molotov began by emphasizing the positive response provoked by the Soviet proposal for European collective security, especially in France. However, opponents of the Soviet proposal were saying that it was aimed at dislodging the United States from Europe. Molotov then recounted a conversation between the Soviet ambassador to Paris, Sergei Vinogradov, and A. Palevsky, one of the leaders of the Gaullist movement:

> According to Palevsky attitudes to the Soviet proposal would change if the Soviet government declared the United States could take part in the system of collective security in Europe as an occupying power in Germany, bearing in mind that the occupation of Germany would not continue indefinitely. On the basis of Palevsky's statement the United States' participation in the General European Agreement on a system of collective security would be temporary and limited to the period until the conclusion of a peace treaty with Germany.

But, wrote Molotov, it would not be expedient to specify the temporary character of the United States' participation because it would harm the struggle against the EDC. A related argument against the Soviet proposal, continued Molotov, was that it was directed at undermining NATO. The USSR should, therefore, propose simultaneously the United States' participation in a system of European collective security and the possibility of Soviet membership of NATO. Molotov assessed the probable outcome of this dual proposal:

> Most likely the organizers of the North Atlantic bloc will react negatively to this step of the Soviet government and will advance many different objections. In that event the governments of the three powers will have exposed themselves once again as the organizers of a military bloc against other states and it would strengthen the position of social forces conducting a struggle against the formation of the European Defence Community. Such an attitude toward the initiative of the Soviet government could, of course, have its negative side for us insofar as it affected the prestige of the

Soviet Union. Taking this into account, the Foreign Ministry proposes that the Soviet note should not state directly the readiness of the USSR to join the North Atlantic bloc but limit itself to a declaration of its readiness to examine jointly with other interested parties the question of the participation of the USSR in the North Atlantic bloc.

Of course, if the statement of the Soviet government meets with a positive attitude on the part of the three Western powers this would signify a great success for the Soviet Union since the USSR joining the North Atlantic Pact under certain conditions would radically change the character of the pact. The USSR joining the North Atlantic pact simultaneously with the conclusion of a General European Agreement on Collective Security in Europe would undermine plans for the creation of the European Defence Community and the remilitarization of West Germany.

The Foreign Ministry considers that raising the question of the USSR joining NATO requires even now an examination of the consequences that might arise. Bearing in mind that the North Atlantic Pact is directed against the democratic movement in the capitalist countries, if the question of the USSR joining it became practical it would be necessary to raise the issue of all participants in the agreement undertaking a commitment (in the form of a joint declaration, for example) on the inadmissibility of interference in the internal affairs of states and respect for the principles of state independence and sovereignty.

In addition the Soviet Union would, in an appropriate form, have to raise the question of American military bases in Europe and the necessity for states to agree to the reduction of military forces, in accordance with the position that would be created after the USSR's entry into the North Atlantic Pact.[41]

It is evident from these remarks that while Molotov did not expect the Soviet initiative to succeed, he did not rule out the possibility that it might. In that event the USSR would be prepared to join NATO, if the terms were right.

These internal deliberations and the move toward a more flexible position in relation to the United States and NATO found public expression in the March 1954 election campaign for the Supreme Soviet. In their election speeches both Malenkov and Molotov highlighted the importance of the struggle for European collective security. Malenkov was particularly forthright:

The Soviet government stands for a further reduction of international tensions and a firm and lasting peace, and is resolutely opposed to the policy of Cold War, the policy of preparation for a new world war, which, with modern methods of warfare, means the ruin of world civilization. . . . The main obstacle on the path toward lessening international tensions is the Western powers' approach to important international questions as a closed military group, which places aggressive military and strategic considerations above all else. This is the only explanation of the Western powers' attitude to the proposed General European Treaty on Collective Security in Europe. . . . We may rest assured that, given a real desire to guarantee security in Europe, it would be possible to surmount the obstacles to concluding the General European Treaty on Collective Security in Europe.

In his speech Molotov took on the criticism that the Soviet treaty proposal excluded the United States from the proposed collective security organization, pointing out that "during the Berlin Conference nobody denied the possibility of considering appropriate amendments to the draft presented."

The tone of Khrushchev's election speech was a little different. He noted that at the Berlin Conference the "Soviet Union brought forward concrete proposals for easing tensions in international relations," but he did not specify what these were. His main foreign policy theme was the growing importance of the countries of the socialist camp, and he concluded with the peroration that "like a mighty giant, the Soviet state, in friendly cooperation with the countries of people's democracy, is confidently proceeding toward its great goal, winning victory after victory. There is no force in the world which could deter our victorious advance to communism."[42]

Moscow's willingness to engage in further negotiations with the West, as expressed in the Molotov and Malenkov speeches, was taken up in the Soviet press. An article in *Novoe Vremya (New Times)* said "the conclusion that an all-European system of collective security is 'incompatible' with the Atlantic alliance is purely a product of Western propaganda."[43]

At the end of March the Soviet government issued a new policy note on collective security in Europe, announcing two amendments to the draft treaty it had submitted to the Berlin Conference. First, the United States would not be excluded from formal participation in a system of European collective security. Second, if NATO relinquished its aggressive character, the USSR would itself consider participation in the organization. In those circumstances, concluded the note, NATO "would cease to be a closed military alignment of states and would be open to other European countries which, together with the creation of an effective system of European collective security, would be of cardinal importance for the promotion of universal peace." Not unexpectedly, on May 7 the Western states rejected the Soviet note on the grounds that the USSR's participation in NATO would be incompatible with the democratic aims of the organization.[44]

Alongside continuation of the collective security campaign, the Soviets considered what to do next on the German question. Since negotiations with the West were at an impasse, Moscow focused on measures to strengthen the position of the GDR. In a note to Molotov on February 27, Pushkin and Semyonov made various proposals to enhance the status and authority of the GDR government. Many of their suggestions found public expression in a Soviet statement on relations with the GDR issued on March 26. This announced that the Soviet Union's relations with the GDR would henceforth be on the same basis as those with other sovereign states and that the East German government would be free to determine its internal and external affairs. To this end, Soviet supervision of GDR government agencies was abolished, while the scope and role of the Soviet high commissioner in Germany—the occupying authority in East Germany—were significantly reduced.[45]

Another illustration of the Foreign Ministry's thinking was Gribanov's memo to Molotov on July 16, 1954. Gribanov argued that the Soviet Union should stick to the position on the German question set out at the Berlin Conference—a provisional all-German government, negotiation of a peace treaty, the withdrawal of occupation forces, etc.—but if there was no progress, the Soviets should try to reach agreement with the West on other issues, including the temporary withdrawal of occupation forces to the borders of Germany, the organization of an all-German conference on economic and cultural links between the two German states, and all-Berlin elections. That same day Gribanov had composed another document for Molotov: an analysis of the impact the Soviet proposals for European collective security had on Western public opinion. Gribanov's theme was that the Soviet proposals remained at the center of Western public attention, particularly after Moscow had issued its March note proposing the USSR join NATO. According to Gribanov, Soviet proposals were making a considerable impact on the growing popular movement against the ratification of the Paris-Bonn Agreements, especially in France.[46]

FROM COLLECTIVE SECURITY TO THE WARSAW PACT

In the spring and early summer of 1954, a lot of Molotov's time was taken up by a prolonged conference in Geneva on Korea and Indochina.[47] However, the conference's success in brokering an end to France's war in Vietnam provided a new opening for the Soviet collective security campaign. The conference ended on July 21, and the next day the Soviets issued a statement highlighting the conference's lessons for other international negotiations:

> The results of the Geneva Conference confirm the Soviet government's conviction that there are now no disputed issues in international affairs that cannot be settled by negotiation and by agreements intended to promote international security, relaxation of international tensions, and peaceful co-existence of states irrespective of their social systems.[48]

On July 24 the Soviets published their belated reply to the Western note of May 7. The Soviet note contained two new proposals. First, that the draft treaty on European collective security be expanded to include an agreement on economic as well as political cooperation and, second, that a conference be convened to discuss establishing a system of collective security in Europe. The United States, as well as all European states, would be invited to participate and Communist China would be asked to send observers.[49]

On August 30 the French National Assembly rejected the plan for the EDC by a large majority. In a statement published on September 10, the Soviet Union warmly welcomed "the collapse of this projected military bloc" and reiterated proposals for a European collective security system to facilitate the reunification of Germany as a peaceful and democratic state.[50] On the same day, however, the Western states issued their reply to the July 24 Soviet note. The response restated Western demands for all-German elections and for the immediate conclusion of a peace treaty with Austria, and it held out the possibility of convening a foreign ministers' conference on European security if these matters could be resolved. By the time the Soviets issued their reply on October 23, the London-Paris Agreements on the direct admission of West Germany into NATO–the alternative to the collapsed EDC project–were in the process of being concluded. Moscow responded by warning that "if these decisions are carried out, it will no longer be possible to regard West Germany as a peaceable state, and this will make the reunification of Germany impossible for a long time." The Soviet note agreed to a foreign ministers' conference as long as it examined (1) all-German elections leading to Germany's reunification as a peaceful and democratic state, (2) withdrawal of occupation forces from Germany, and (3) the convening of a pan-European conference on collective security.[51]

Faced with no progress on their proposal for a conference on European collective security, the Soviets decided to press on alone. On November 13 they issued a note stating that such a conference would be convened in Moscow on November 19 or in Paris if the Western powers agreed to participate.[52] Invitations to attend were issued to the United States and all European states, but the Western powers refused to participate on the grounds that the Soviet proposals contained nothing new on either the German question or European security. The Western note counterproposed the immediate signing of a peace treaty with Austria and clarification of the Soviet position on all-German elections prior to convening another foreign ministers' conference. If that conference were successful, said the Western note, there was the prospect of a wider gathering on European security. In other words, there could be no East-West deal on collective security before the resolution of the German question.

The "Conference of European Countries on Safeguarding European Peace and Security," attended only by the USSR and its Eastern bloc allies, took place in Moscow from November 29 to December 2, 1954. It featured all the familiar Soviet arguments against the EDC, NATO, and West German rearmament. But there was an important new theme, stated by Molotov in his speech to the conference: "The peaceable states cannot ignore the fact that the aggressive elements in some of the Western countries are seeking to prevent the establishment of a system of collective European security. They are now redoubling their efforts to create military alignments which constitute a danger to peace. . . . We cannot, therefore, ignore or underestimate the fact that ratification for the Paris agreements would necessitate further weighty measures with a view to providing proper defense for the peace-loving states." This point was reiterated in the communiqué issued at the end of the conference: "If these military alliances in Europe should enlarge their land, air, and other forces . . . the other

European states will inevitably be compelled to take effective measures for their self-defense, to guard themselves against attack."[53]

Immediately after the conference the Soviet foreign ministry began hammering out yet another new set of policies on the German question and European security. Indeed, on the day the conference ended Semyonov submitted to Molotov a series of proposals on "further measures of the USSR in connection with the ratification of the Paris agreements." Semyonov's main proposal was to convene a second conference of the people's democracies with a view toward concluding an agreement on collective defense, including the establishment of a joint military command. A related proposal was the signature of a mutual defense treaty between the GDR and the USSR, and between East Germany and the other people's democracies.[54]

The Foreign Ministry worked on these proposals throughout December and January. On February 25 Molotov sent a draft to the Presidium, together with a note suggesting a second Soviet–East European conference on European collective security. Among the draft proposals was a treaty clause on the establishment of a joint military command—a provision worked on further by Molotov and Defense Minister Marshal Georgii Zhukov. While East Germany was to be a treaty signatory, the question of its participation in the joint military command was put aside for the moment, and in a note to the Presidium on May 9 Molotov said that it would be expedient for the GDR government to state that a future united German state would not be bound by the multilateral mutual assistance pact.[55]

Moscow publicly signaled its intentions in a statement on January 15, 1955, on the German question that warned "if the Paris agreements are ratified a new situation will have arisen, in which the Soviet Union will take measures not only to strengthen its friendly relations with the German Democratic Republic, but also, by the joint efforts of the peaceable European states, to strengthen the peace and security of Europe."[56] In a speech to the Supreme Soviet on February 8, Molotov further spelled this out:

> The Soviet Union and other peaceable states against whom the Paris agreements are directed will not sit with folded arms. They will have to adopt appropriate measures for the more effective safeguarding of their security and protection of peace in Europe. . . . Primarily these measures include

. . . a treaty of friendship, cooperation, and mutual assistance . . . so as to
lose no time, consultations on this point are already in progress. To the new
military blocs and alliances being formed in conjunction with German
militarism, we shall retaliate by further cementing our ranks, strengthening our ties of friendship, improving our cooperation generally and, wherever necessary, by extending the scope of our mutual assistance.[57]

The second Conference of European Countries on Safeguarding European
Peace and Security was held in Warsaw from May 11 to 14, 1955. It concluded
with the signing of a multilateral Treaty of Friendship, Cooperation, and Mutual Assistance. The rationale for the treaty was the Bonn parliament's ratification
of the Paris-London Agreements on West Germany's admission to NATO. But
the door to a negotiated settlement of the German question remained open,
and the campaign for pan-European collective security continued.

Bulganin, who had replaced Malenkov as prime minister in February
1955, gave the main speech at the conference. Malenkov had been dismissed at
Khrushchev's behest because of differences over economic policy. Khrushchev
also used the dismissal as an opportunity to air his views on the German question. In an unpublished speech to Communist Party deputies to the Supreme
Soviet in February 1955, Khrushchev said:

> To abandon socialism in the GDR, this means to abandon East Germany,
> to unite [and] send it to the West. Some people have said that there will
> be a unified German state, a neutral country between the Soviet Union
> and the bourgeois capitalist world. . . . Will Germany be a neutral country
> in our current conditions? This is impossible. Either it ought to go with
> us or go against us. . . . It would have been naïve to think that we, for
> example, would give up East Germany and we would right away have
> friendly relations with the British and Americans. Is this possible? No,
> this is impossible. You just give the enemy a finger and he will grab your
> hand. You give him Eastern Germany and he will say: get out of Poland
> and Czechoslovakia.[58]

Khrushchev had yet to fully establish his dominance of foreign policy, and
when Bulganin spoke he echoed the existing policy of support for the reunification of Germany. The Soviet Union, he said, was "prepared to lend its utmost

assistance to the restoration of German unity and to the conclusion of a peace treaty with Germany on an acceptable basis."[59]

The Warsaw Treaty Organization (WTO) has often been characterized as a military counter to NATO—which is certainly what it became—but its inspiration was the campaign for European collective security, and its initial purpose was political: to act as an exemplar of a pan-European collective security system. Indeed, the final article of the Warsaw Pact spelled this out: "Should a system of collective security be established in Europe . . . the present treaty shall cease to be operative from the day the General European Treaty enters into force."[60]

Despite the setback of the FRG's admission into NATO, Molotov remained hopeful that the campaign for European collective security could succeed, not least because of some positive straws in the wind, notably the imminent signature of a Soviet-Western agreement on the reunification of Austria.

The logjam in Soviet-Western negotiations about a treaty to end Allied occupation of Austria was broken by Molotov in his February 1955 speech to the Supreme Soviet. At the Berlin Conference a year earlier, Molotov had specified two conditions for an Austrian treaty: a guarantee of the country's neutrality and the retention of a token Soviet occupation force until a peace treaty for Germany was signed. Molotov modified this position in his Supreme Soviet speech by saying that if there were guarantees against a new *Anschluss*, then all troops could be withdrawn prior to the signature of a peace treaty with Germany. Molotov also called for a Soviet-Western conference that would examine both the Austrian and German questions, thus maintaining a link between the two projected treaties.[61] A few days later, however, Norbert Bischoff, Austrian ambassador to Moscow, suggested to Semyonov that separate bilateral negotiations with the Soviets about a treaty were possible. Molotov was instructed by the Presidium to pursue this possibility, and on February 25 he called in Bischoff and pointed out to him that the statement to the Supreme Soviet was a new position that was open to further negotiation.[62] There were further diplomatic conversations, and in mid-April Austrian chancellor Julius Raab arrived in Moscow for negotiations. Raab's visit produced a joint Austrian-Soviet communiqué in which the Austrians promised permanent neutrality and the Soviets agreed to withdraw their forces by the end of 1955 if the text of a treaty could be agreed to by the four occupying powers.[63] There followed four-power negotiations in Vienna between Britain, France, the United States, and the USSR, and the signature on May 15 of the Austrian State Treaty. In his speech at the signing ceremony, Molotov said, "The conclusion of the Austrian Treaty will be conducive to relaxation of international tension, and therein lies its special significance."[64]

It is commonly asserted that Molotov was opposed to the Austrian State Treaty and that his hand was forced by others in the Soviet leadership who favored an initiative to improve the prospects for East-West détente. The origins of this story can be traced to the July 1955 Central Committee plenum.[65] This plenum featured an extensive discussion of Soviet-Yugoslavian relations that centered on Molotov's opposition to the reestablishment of party-to-party relations with the Yugoslavian communists. Molotov was not opposed to a political-diplomatic rapprochement with Yugoslavia, but he did not agree with a complete repudiation of the former Soviet critique of Tito as a renegade from Marxism-Leninism. Molotov was criticized at the plenum for his oppositional stance in Presidium discussions during the previous few months,[66] a critique that was incorporated into the formal resolution passed by the Central Committee.

Khrushchev concentrated on Yugoslavia in his opening speech at the plenum and did not mention the Austrian question, but the first speaker after Molotov's initial reply to Khrushchev was Bulganin, who extended the attack on Molotov to other foreign policy errors, such as that in relation to Austria. Bulganin's remarks were taken up by Anastas Mikoyan, the trade minister, who expounded a detailed account of Molotov's resistance to a change of policy on Austria. A number of other speakers also mentioned Molotov's mistaken position on the Austrian question. In his concluding speech Khrushchev devoted quite a long section to the Austrian question, the theme being that Molotov obstructed the conclusion of a treaty and was intent on keeping Soviet troops in Austria for no good reason.

Molotov's reaction to this attack was both contrite and defiant. He defended the former Soviet policy on Yugoslavia as a legitimate critique of Tito's nationalist deviations and pointed out that in the recent past Belgrade had adopted foreign policy positions quite different from those of the USSR. Molotov retreated somewhat in his concluding remarks at the end of the discussion, confessing to the sin of opposition in relation to the Yugoslavian question and pledging his eternal loyalty to the party and its leadership, but he made no protracted confession. On the Austrian question he had this to say:

I must say, comrades, that I never had any doubt that this question had to be resolved. It's possible that the Ministry of Foreign Affairs tarried for a few months and that in our haste to find fault we were slow to change our position on this question. We objected, demonstrating that we were working normally, etc. Of course, on our part there was tardiness and we didn't change enough. . . . If on my part there were objections to particular points, for example, in relation to timing, these were not substantial objections. . . . It was recalled here that in the original draft we proposed to retain the right of the Soviet Union to reintroduce troops in Austria in the event of complications in connection with the militarization of West Germany. Actually, we put forward this proposal but did not insist upon it and it would have been mistaken had we done so. The rest of the differences on this issue I have not retained in my memory since they did not have any fundamental importance. True, not all our proposals were correct and the Presidium of the Central Committee corrected us, on the Austrian question and on other questions, demanding of us clearer, corrected drafts, than those we brought forward. But this happens in practical work.[67]

The files in the Foreign Ministry archive support Molotov's version of events. The proposal to separate the issue of Soviet troop withdrawals from Austria from the question of a peace treaty for Germany was first formulated by Molotov's officials in January 1955. In subsequent drafts of the emerging new policy position, Gromyko and other officials softened the Soviet stance even further, including by reducing the time for troop withdrawal from two years to six months.[68] Presidium discussions no doubt played a part in this process of reformulation, and it seems likely that Molotov was keener than the rest of the leadership on retaining a link with the conclusion of a German peace treaty. But the changes in the Soviet position on the Austrian treaty should not be exaggerated. The issue was whether or not to keep a token occupation force in Austria until a German peace treaty was signed. The previous position had made sense as providing a bargaining chip in negotiations about a German peace treaty with the Western powers. But by early 1955 it seemed less and less likely there would be any such discussions. In that new context the tactical advantage shifted toward signing a treaty with Austria that would provide an exemplar for an eventual settlement on Germany.

Post hoc polemics apart, there is no evidence that Molotov had any difficulty in accepting the new policy on Austria. If there were doves and hawks
in the Soviet Presidium in 1955–and things were much more complex than
that–then Molotov was in the former camp and Khrushchev was the hardliner.
As Khrushchev made clear, particularly in his closing remarks at the July plenum, what drove his determination to mend bridges with Tito was not détente
with the West, but his concept of the importance of strengthening the fraternal
friendship of the socialist camp:

> After the Second World War states with a combined population of 900
> million split from the imperialist camp. Popular revolution triumphed in
> great countries such as China. These countries coordinate their actions.
> . . . The Soviet Union, the People's Republic of China, and the other coun-
> tries of people's democracy must proceed from the common interests of
> the working class and all toilers, from the interests of the struggle for the
> victory of communism. Therefore we must take care to take advantage of
> all material and spiritual possibilities for the strengthening of our socialist
> camp. . . . Understand that the socialist countries are obliged to help one
> another so as to strengthen the friendship between us. . . . The historical
> experience of the Soviet Union underlines the teaching of Lenin that dif-
> ferent countries, united in their safeguarding of the victory of socialism,
> can choose different forms and methods of resolving the concrete prob-
> lems of socialist construction, depending on their historical and national
> peculiarities.[69]

It was this sense of priorities that led Khrushchev to also prefer the certain-
ties of a socialist GDR and a divided Germany to the political risks of a negotiated settlement of the German question. Molotov and the Foreign Ministry,
however, continued to strive for constructive negotiations with the West that
would establish a pan-European collective security system and neutralize the
threat of a united Germany.

THE TWO GENEVAS
The final phase of Molotov's campaign for European collective security
spanned the Geneva Summit (July 18–23, 1955) and the Geneva Conference
of Foreign Ministers (October 26 to November 16, 1955). The policy on European

collective security put forward by the Soviet Union at these two meetings was similar to that presented at the Berlin Conference but with some important additions and amendments, policy inflections designed to constrain the polarizing impact of NATO expansion, on the one hand, and the WTO's creation, on the other.

The invitation to a summit to discuss world problems was issued by the Western states on May 10, and the Soviets accepted on May 24. Intersecting with this development was a reformulation of Moscow's German policy. On May 27 Pushkin sent Molotov a note entitled "On the Question of a New Soviet Proposal in Relation to the Unification of Germany." Pushkin's starting point was the new situation created by West Germany's accession to NATO. Since it was unlikely West Germany would or could be forced to leave NATO in the short term, a new approach to German unification was required. At the center of Pushkin's proposed policy perspective was the concept of a process of rapprochement between the GDR and the FRG, with Germany's unification being achieved gradually.[70] This concept of a lengthy transition to German unity had two implications. First, it underlined the importance of the need for a common collective security system to provide essential context for the constructive coexistence of the two German states. Second, if the GDR was to coexist and seek rapprochement with West Germany, then so too should the Soviet Union.

The Soviets had, in fact, stated their willingness to normalize relations with the FRG in a statement on the German question back in January 1955 and had issued a decree declaring the state of war with Germany formally terminated. This latter declaration aimed to facilitate the signature of a Soviet-GDR treaty of alliance, but it also opened the door to the normalization of diplomatic relations with the Bonn government. On June 8, 1955, the Soviets published a statement proposing to establish direct political, trade, and cultural relations with the FRG and inviting Konrad Adenauer, the West German chancellor, to Moscow for talks. The West Germans responded positively to this overture but suggested unofficial negotiations to clarify a number of issues before entering into formal discussions. Continuing contacts eventually led to Adenauer going to Moscow in September 1955 to establish diplomatic relations between the USSR and the FRG.[71] Balancing this development was the signature on September 20 of a treaty between the GDR and the USSR that pledged friendship, cooperation, and continuing efforts to achieve "the reunification of Germany on a peaceful and democratic basis." Simultaneously the Soviets announced the abolition of their high commission in Germany and the transfer of control of the GDR's borders to the East Germans.[72]

The concept of a staged approach to the achievement of Soviet goals also featured centrally in the reformulation of policy on European collective security. The directive for the Soviet delegation to the Geneva Summit defined the USSR's overriding aim as the reduction of international tensions and the development of trust between states.[73] On collective security, Western objections to previous Soviet proposals were to be dealt with by the introduction of new arrangements in two stages: during the first stage (two to three years), the agreements and structures underpinning NATO and the Warsaw Pact would remain in force, except that the two sides would pledge nonaggression and political cooperation; only in the second stage would existing institutions be replaced by a new system of pan-European collective security. On the German question, the Soviet delegation was instructed not to raise the matter on its own initiative and to resist any linking of the issue of Germany's reunification to discussions of collective security. This seems a curious position for the Soviets to adopt, given their past insistence on the indivisibility of European security and resolution of the German question. But the Soviets wanted to avoid yet another argument with the West about all-German elections, which would distract from their priority of discussing European security issues. All-German elections were off the Soviet agenda—at least for the immediate future. It was self-evident that such elections would produce an all-German government intent on keeping Germany in NATO, an outcome that was completely unacceptable to Moscow.

Arms control and nuclear disarmament were the other Soviet policy priorities at the Geneva Summit. On May 10, 1955, the Soviet Union had published proposals calling on the United Nations to establish an international control agency to supervise dramatic reductions in armaments and armed forces, and initiate a process leading to the prohibition of nuclear weapons.[74] The Soviet delegation was instructed to pursue these proposals and to press the Western states for an agreement.

The Soviet delegation to the Geneva Summit was led by Bulganin, who was accompanied by Khrushchev, Molotov, and Zhukov. In his opening speech Bulganin echoed Molotov's opening remarks at the Berlin Conference: the purpose of the conference was "not to level accusations against each other, but to explore ways and means of easing international tensions and creating an atmosphere of confidence in relations between states." Later in his presentation Bulganin outlined the new Soviet proposal for a staged approach to European security. Bulganin also argued that European collective security was the key to the resolution of the German question. It was a point he returned to in his closing speech at the summit. The emergence of two separate German states and their respective memberships in NATO and the Warsaw Pact meant there could be no "mechanical merging" of the two parts of Germany. What was required, said Bulganin, was the creation of internal and external conditions conducive to German unity. The external condition was European collective security, while internally what was needed was a rapprochement of the two German states.[75]

While Bulganin conversed with Eisenhower, Eden (now British prime minister), and Edgar Faure (the French prime minister), Molotov was involved in parallel foreign ministers' discussions with Dulles, Antoine Pinay, and Harold Macmillan. Their talks centered on what should be discussed, both at the summit itself and at a future foreign ministers' conference. Predictably, the Western representatives wanted to discuss Germany and the question of all-German elections. Molotov, sticking to his brief, insisted that European security be discussed first and kept separate from the German question. The ensuing prolonged wrangle was resolved by a decision to discuss European security *and* the German question as the first item on the agenda of a future foreign ministers' conference, leaving ambiguous whether the two issues would be considered together or separately.[76]

The atmosphere at the summit was good, especially in private sessions and meetings.[77] But in spite of all the talk about the cooperative "spirit of Geneva," the only concrete result of the summit was an agreement to hold a foreign ministers' conference at the same venue in October to discuss European security, the German question, disarmament, and the development of East-West contacts. There was some movement on the question of European security during the discussion. In his opening speech, Eden offered the Soviet Union a security pact, an agreement on the level of forces and armaments in and around Germany, and discussions about the creation of an East-West demilitarized zone in Central Europe. Faure talked about the establishment of a general security organization in Europe in return for Soviet acceptance of a unified Germany. Eisenhower was less forthcoming at the summit itself, but he had already raised the idea of a neutral belt in Central Europe in a speech in May.[78] At the summit Bulganin brushed aside these overtures, saying the USSR had no need for Western security guarantees. But these Western statements did provide important clues and openings for a further reformulation of Soviet policy on European collective security. Most importantly, the directive from the heads of government to the foreign ministers included instructions to consider a European security pact at their forthcoming conference.[79]

By the time of the Geneva Summit, Khrushchev had established his supremacy in the Soviet leadership, including in the field of foreign policy. The dispute over Yugoslavia had been a severe blow to Molotov's prestige and position in the leadership, and impacted negatively on his ability to retain initiative and control in foreign policy. A telling example of the new power relationship between Khrushchev and Molotov occurred a few days before the Geneva Summit, during a Presidium discussion of a draft Foreign Ministry statement on the German question. The statement had been drafted in response to Western claims that the Soviet Union had lost interest in a united Germany. It refuted this suggestion and reiterated Soviet support for German unity but argued this could only be achieved in the context of European collective security and gradual rapprochement of the GDR and the FRG. There was nothing exceptional about the statement; its language and tone were normal in Soviet terms and its policy content in line with the current evolution of Moscow's line on the German question and European security. But Khrushchev rejected the draft as being too "pugnacious" and "blunt," while according to Bulganin the statement was "dry," its tone "impatient," and its conclusions inconsistent. The draft was "returned" to the Foreign Ministry, never to see the light of day.[80]

Around the same time, Molotov received another rap on the knuckles. In his February speech to the Supreme Soviet, he had spoken of the "foundations" of a socialist society having been built in the USSR. This formulation was considered incorrect by the rest of the leadership, and Molotov had to write a letter to the party's theoretical journal *Kommunist* withdrawing this remark and stating that a socialist society—not just its foundations—had already been built in the Soviet Union and that the country was now in transition to communism (i.e., an advanced form of socialism in which there would be material abundance).[81]

On their way back from the Geneva Summit, Bulganin and Khrushchev stopped off in Berlin for talks with the GDR leadership. The conclusion of their visit on July 27 occasioned a joint communiqué in which the USSR and the GDR reaffirmed their commitment to the reunification of Germany in the context of rapprochement between the two German states and movement toward European collective security. This statement was consistent with Soviet policy at the Geneva Summit. However, Khrushchev also gave a speech in Berlin, reportedly to a mass meeting of 250,000 people, in which he signaled a significant hardening of the Soviet position on the German question:

> The German question cannot be resolved at the expense of the GDR (*prolonged applause*). We are confident that the working people of the GDR will not agree with a point of view that only takes into account the interests of the Western countries, to the detriment of the interests of the GDR. Could the GDR agree to its incorporation into the North Atlantic pact and the West European Union and its involvement in the burden of an arms race? Could the working people of the GDR accept the liquidation of all their social and political achievements, the liquidation of their democratic reforms? We are convinced that the working people of the GDR will not agree to go down such a path (*prolonged applause*).[82]

Khrushchev's statement may be compared to an answer Molotov gave to a question at a press conference in San Francisco in June 1955. There to celebrate the tenth anniversary of the founding of the UN, Molotov was asked whether the Soviet aim was a united Germany with the same social system as in the GDR. He replied: "In a united Germany the regime which exists in Eastern Germany should not prevail and neither should the regime that exists in West Germany. Which regime should and will prevail in a united Germany is a matter that must be decided by the German people themselves in free all-German elections."[83]

It was Khrushchev's view that prevailed in Moscow, however, and when Bulganin reported to the Supreme Soviet on August 4, he said, "Nor must it be forgotten that both these states have differing social and economic structures. In the German Democratic Republic, the workers and their allies . . . are in power, having adopted the path of socialist construction, fully convinced of the correctness of the path they have chosen. It is quite understandable that the people of the German Democratic Republic declare that they cannot endanger the achievements they have gained during this period."[84] Such sentiments were also evident in a Foreign Ministry draft of a message to the governments of the people's democracies on the results of Geneva, which stated that the resolution

of the German question would not be at the expense of the GDR's socialist achievements and that a rapprochement between the two German states
would take ten years. The message also made it clear there was no question of
accepting a united Germany integrated into NATO in exchange for Western
guarantees of Soviet security.[85]

Khrushchev's hardening of Soviet policy on the German question meant
there could be little hope of achieving any deal with the West on European
collective security. The dilemma for Molotov and the Foreign Ministry officials as they prepared for the Geneva foreign ministers' conference was how
to maintain negotiations with the West on collective security while at the same
time responding to pressures from the Khrushchev camp to support further
integration of the GDR into the socialist bloc.

The Foreign Ministry's response to this challenge was yet another policy
innovation: the proposal that East and West Germany form a German confederation aimed at facilitating a rapprochement between the two states and
preparing the ground for future reunification. Presenting this proposal to Molotov on behalf of the drafting group (which included Gromyko and Pushkin),
Semyonov said on October 8:

> In our view the question of forming a German confederation is the prin-
> cipal new issue and it would be advisable to have an exchange of views
> with the leading comrades before introducing a draft to the Presidium. For
> our part, we think that since the GDR and the FRG would retain their full
> sovereignty in a German confederation, such a proposal meets the task of
> strengthening the GDR as a sovereign state as well as the task of keeping
> the banner of a united Germany in our hands.[86]

In a separate document the Foreign Ministry officials elaborated the role
of the proposed German confederation: it would be formed on terms agreed
to between the GDR and the FRG, there would be an elected consultative assembly and all-German bodies to coordinate policy, and it would facilitate cooperation between the two German states and the negotiation of an agreement
leading to the reunification of Germany as a democratic and peace-loving state,
including the holding of all-German elections.[87] The Presidium did not accept
this proposal, however, and the final draft of the delegation's instructions incor-

porated a notable change: the paragraph proposing a German confederation was omitted, and in its place was substituted the following:

> In the examination of the German question at the conference the delegation must proceed from the fact that in present conditions the fundamental task in relation to the German question is the consolidation of the social system forming in the GDR, as well as strengthening the foreign policy position of the GDR as a sovereign state. In this connection it is necessary to rebuff all attempts by the three Western powers to resolve the German question at the expense of the GDR and its social achievements.[88]

As this directive shows, the tendency toward a two Germanies policy in which the priority was strengthening the GDR as a member of the socialist camp had solidified into a definite policy position. But Molotov had not given up the idea of a negotiated resolution of the German question linked to a deal on European collective security, and during the Geneva foreign ministers' conference he was to make one last effort to persuade the Soviet leadership to adopt a more conciliatory approach to negotiations with the Western powers.

Another element of the Foreign Ministry's preparations for the conference was more successful: a further refinement of the staged approach to the achievement of European collective security. While the original Soviet proposal on pan-European collective security was to be reintroduced at the conference, if the West rejected an all-embracing pact Molotov would then propose a security treaty for a smaller group of countries—perhaps only the four great powers and the two Germanies. Under this proposal there would be no time limit set for the liquidation of existing groupings such as NATO and the Warsaw Pact. If this proposal was rejected, too, the Soviets would next propose a four-power nonaggression treaty and, if that was unacceptable, there could be a simple nonaggression agreement between NATO and the Warsaw Pact. In addition, the Soviets were prepared to contemplate the establishment of controlled military zones in Central Europe, including in both parts of Germany. The Soviet delegation was also instructed to pursue previous proposals on arms control and nuclear disarmament.[89]

In arriving at this more flexible position on European security, the Soviets had, in fact, placed themselves on a path of convergence with the Western powers who were preparing proposals that went beyond their previous offer of a security guarantee. Soviet propaganda and campaigning had been successful, and the pressure of public opinion was bearing down on Western governments, particularly the growing popularity of the idea of pan-European collective security. An analysis of public opinion polling data prepared for the Eisenhower administration soon after the Geneva Summit concluded the results "raise disquieting doubts about the future of NATO." The most telling data concerned the question, "Suppose it were proposed that NATO be replaced by a security system including both the US and the USSR and other European nations. Would you favor this proposal, or do you prefer present arrangements for West European defense?" In response 38 percent of respondents in Britain, France, Italy, and West Germany said they would favor a new system, while only 19 percent favored retaining NATO and 43 percent had no opinion. Numbers favoring mutual troop withdrawals by the United States and the Soviet Union from Europe were even higher. Among "upper socio-economic groups" the percentages favoring pan-European security and troop withdrawals were higher still. "NATO, in fact, appears highly vulnerable from the opinion point of view," concluded the analysis. "At the least, it appears the people of Western Europe are now willing to consider security arrangements alternative to NATO."[90]

In response to these and other political pressures, the Western powers decided to propose a European security treaty under which the signatories would renounce the use of force, limit armaments and armed forces, and pledge to act collectively against aggression, irrespective of whether the attackers or the victims were NATO members.

The prime Presidium directive to the Soviet delegation was to build on the perceived success of the Geneva Summit and to seek a further reduction of international tension. The opening sessions of the foreign ministers' conference seemed to bear out hopes for further progress toward détente. The first item on the agenda was European security. Molotov presented the various Soviet proposals for a staged approach to the achievement of European collective security, while the Western representatives presented their "Outline Terms of Treaty of Assurance on the Reunification of Germany," which offered a security pact in exchange for all-German elections leading to the reunification of the country. During the course of discussion both sides welcomed each other's proposals, noting the convergence of positions since the Berlin Conference and the Geneva Summit. Molotov welcomed the West's acceptance of the need for European collective security and adopted a conciliatory tone, even while criticizing the linkage of the offer of a "Treaty of Assurance and German Reunification."[91] Dulles was almost gushing in his appraisal of progress toward an agreement, saying on November 2, "As I have examined in parallel columns the proposals put forward by the Western powers . . . and compared them with the proposals and positions advanced by Mr. Molotov . . . I found that there was a very considerable parallelism in our thinking. . . . We have, I think, achieved a quite remarkable degree of parallel thinking with respect to the concept of European security. . . . It seems to me that we have reached a point where as a result of constructive thinking on both sides we can see a realizable vision of security in Europe."[92] But, as Dulles went to say, there was a stumbling block, and that was the failure to agree on the German question.

From the beginning of the conference, Western representatives pressed Molotov on the question of all-German elections, pointing out that the directive agreed at the Geneva Summit stated that "the settlement of the German question and the re-unification of Germany by means of free elections shall be carried out in conformity with the national interests of the German people and the interests of European security." They also reminded Molotov that he had been in favor of all-German elections at the Berlin Conference. In response Molotov repeated the Soviet line that the issue had changed since Berlin and that progress toward elections had to be based on the recognition of the existence of two German states with different social systems. Molotov further argued that European security should come first and would provide the foundation for Germany's reunification as a democratic and peaceful state. The way forward, said Molotov, was the rapprochement of the two Germanies, and to this end he proposed the establishment of an all-German council of representatives of the GDR and the FRG. Molotov did not rule out all-German elections in the long run but made it clear that in no circumstances would a united Germany in NATO be an acceptable proposition. The continued participation of the FRG in NATO was another matter, and the implication of Soviet proposals for a NATO–Warsaw Pact nonaggression pact was that West Germany could remain a member of the Western alliance for the foreseeable future.

These exchanges between Molotov and the Western foreign ministers on the German question were cordial and well reasoned on both sides. But it became obvious that there could be no further progress on negotiations for a European security pact in the absence of a deal on all-German elections. At this point in the proceedings Molotov returned to Moscow for consultations with the Soviet leadership. At a meeting of the Presidium on November 6, he introduced a resolution on "European Security and Germany" that was designed to unblock the impasse on all-German elections. Molotov's resolution in effect proposed a return to the earlier Soviet position on the German question: there could be elections and a united Germany, provided it remained neutral. Crucially, the resolution specified that the GDR and the FRG would discuss and prepare for all-German elections in the shortest possible time. This commitment to elections was hedged with restrictions—for example in relation to the protection of the "democratic and social reforms and freedoms" of the German people—but the important point was that it opened the door to further discussions with the West. The document concluded that in order to facilitate the freest possible elections, all foreign troops (apart from some limited detachments) should be withdrawn from Germany within three months. This was all too much for the Soviet leadership, who rejected Molotov's proposal and instead resolved to reaffirm existing directives to the Soviet delegation in Geneva.[93] According to notes of the Presidium discussion on November 6, Khrushchev objected to Molotov's proposal in these terms:

> The course of the conference is normal. The delegation has done everything. What is proposed is not worth going for. Many hidden dangers. Dulles is maneuvering. They could go for a withdrawal of troops. The Germans will be disoriented if we leave with nothing. It doesn't matter, we can live with it another year.

Molotov replied that "this proposal arises from the fact that to the Germans it looks like [the West] is for elections and we are not. Tactically we should not place ourselves in a less favorable position. We demand from them the repudiation of the Paris agreements."

Khrushchev, however, was supported by the rest of the Soviet leadership, and he spoke again at the end of the discussion:

> The cry will go out that the position of power has prevailed. The Germans from the GDR will say "you have betrayed us." We can't take the risk. Twenty million Germans we have in our confidence. In the center of Eu-

rope. New tactics must be worked out. Patience and persistence must be displayed. No change in the position.

The discussion continued at the Presidium meeting the next day, with Khrushchev arguing:

A year ago we raised the question of elections. Then they did not accept. Now the position has changed. Now from a position of power they want to talk about elections. It is necessary to confront them with our arguments. You [Molotov] say "if the FRG leaves NATO"; don't get involved in this discussion. Better to pass this question to the Germans. The question of European security is a general question and it can be resolved with two Germanies. We want to preserve the system formed in the GDR–this should be said.[94]

Khrushchev was supported by the other Presidium members, and the door was firmly closed to further negotiations about all-German elections. Molotov returned to Berlin and, in line with his brief, gave a speech on November 8 that not only ruled out all-German elections for the foreseeable future, but gave East Germany a virtual veto on Germany's reunification:

A mechanical merging of the two parts of Germany through so-called free elections . . . might result in the violation of the vital interests of the working people of the German Democratic Republic. . . . Naturally one cannot agree to the factories and mills, the land and its mineral wealth being taken away from the working people of the German Democratic Republic.[95]

Harold Macmillan wrote in his memoirs that at the Geneva foreign ministers' conference, he "could not help feeling there was some conflict of view and purpose inside the Soviet Government. Molotov had seemed at first uncertain what line to follow. It was only after his return from his visit to Moscow that he launched into the most intransigent and violent of his diatribes."[96] Another witness is Oleg Troyanovskii, a junior member of Molotov's delegation in Geneva, who recalled: "Molotov and Gromyko went to Khrushchev, who was on holiday in the Crimea. I don't know why, but they took me with them. On the journey and from their conversations I found out that they had the text of an

important proposal which could lead to the success of the conference. However, after talking to Khrushchev they came back depressed and angry. The
[Foreign] Ministers' Conference turned out to be fruitless."[97] At the time, Dulles
correctly gauged the magnitude of the shift in the Soviet position:

> Yesterday Mr. Molotov, just returned from Moscow, made a statement
> on behalf of the Soviet Union. It had such grave implications that I asked
> that we should suspend our meeting until today so as to be able to give
> his statement deliberate thought. . . . The Soviet Union says in the most
> categorical manner that the security of Europe is best assured by a con-
> tinued division of Germany, at least until Germany can be united under
> conditions which would sovietize the whole of Germany. . . . I would
> be less than frank if I did not say that, as far as the United States is con-
> cerned, what has happened here has largely shattered such confidence as
> was born with the summit conference at Geneva.[98]

With no prospect of a deal on all-German elections, the Western offer of
a European security pact was off the table, and the conference closed without
agreement. The terse communiqué issued at the end of the conference noted
that there had been a "frank and comprehensive discussion" and that the four
foreign ministers had agreed to recommend to their governments that future
discussions be conducted through diplomatic channels. The Soviet foreign
ministry's assessment of the conference in a draft telegram to other socialist
countries was that it showed that the Western states were not interested in collective security—only "the liquidation of the GDR, the remilitarization of all
Germany, and the inclusion of a united Germany in a Western military bloc."[99]

The public Soviet verdict on the conference was delivered by Khrushchev
in a speech to the Supreme Soviet at the end of December:

> The most acute question today is the question of European security. The
> settlement of other international questions depends on the resolution of
> this question. You know, however, that our partners in negotiations—the
> USA, England, and France—counterposed the German question. Their
> position was that in order for West Germany to unite with the GDR the
> social gains of the GDR would have to be liquidated, the country armed
> to the teeth and Germany included in NATO. Under such conditions they

would have no objection to signing an agreement on European security, even though in that event not only would there be no safeguarding of European security, there would be an increase in the threat of the outbreak of a new war in Europe, with grave consequences for its peoples.[100]

According to Khrushchev the Western aim in the negotiations was not only to strengthen NATO, but to force the USSR and the socialist camp to capitulate and accept their conditions. "Some security!" was Khrushchev's sardonic comment. Khrushchev also repeated the argument he had made at the Presidium meeting in November: the fact that Germany's reunification was not possible in the present circumstances ought not impede an agreement on European collective security, as it was a separate issue. In this regard he made favorable mention of Eden and Faure's comments on European security at the Geneva Summit, saying that these statements constituted a basis for negotiations. However, it was precisely on the issue of linkage between the German question and European security that negotiations at the foreign ministers' conference had broken down. Khrushchev said nothing about how this difference between the Western and Soviet positions might be bridged.

The Soviet campaign for European collective security did not end in 1955. At the twentieth party congress in 1956, Khrushchev reiterated the Soviet program for collective security in Europe, including the gradual reunification of Germany on the basis of a rapprochement between the two German states. The Soviet campaign continued, indeed, for another twenty years and culminated with the Conference on Security and Cooperation in Europe in 1975. Under the terms of the 1975 Helsinki Final Act, Europe's borders were frozen, and there were pledges of peace, cooperation, and consultation across the Cold War divide.

When Chuev put it to Molotov that the pan-European conference was an old idea of his, he readily agreed.[101] But freezing Europe's Cold War divisions was a far cry from Molotov's ambition in the 1950s to dissolve the Cold War blocs and replace them with all-embracing pan-European collective security structures.

Did Molotov really believe that an all-European security agreement would lead to détente and an end to the Cold War? Certainly, that is what he said in public, and there is nothing in the archive record to suggest he was being disingenuous. Of course, as an orthodox Marxist Molotov believed, too, that the political struggle between capitalism and communism would continue. It is moot whether that struggle could have been contained within a stable framework of détente and European security. Historically Gorbachev ended the Cold War by giving up the struggle for communism and dissolving the Soviet bloc. That dazzling dénouement has blinded observers to the possibility of different historical outcomes, including Molotov's vision that the Grand Alliance could be re-created in the 1950s and Germany contained within a common security framework.

There has also been a tendency to see the Cold War as a zero-sum game that could only end with victory for one side. To a certain extent Molotov shared that mentality. According to his ideological worldview, communism would eventually triumph over capitalism. But he also feared a German revival and the dire threat that posed in the Cold War context. His fears proved unfounded, but he did not know that at the time. Molotov's ideological orthodoxies made him see threats that perhaps did not exist, but they also led him to embrace imaginative solutions to the very real dangers of the Cold War.

6

DEFIANT IN DEFEAT
(1956–1986)

In time Stalin will be rehabilitated in history. There will be a Stalin museum in Moscow. Without fail! By popular demand.

—V. M. Molotov (January 1985)[1]

Molotov had lost control of Soviet foreign policy to Khrushchev by the end of 1955, and his removal as foreign minister was inevitable. During preparations for the twentieth party congress in February 1956, he and Khrushchev clashed repeatedly over the latter's proposal to conduct a wide-ranging critique of Stalin at the congress. At the Presidium meeting on February 1, Molotov said that as well as criticizing Stalin, it was necessary to recognize he was a great leader who had continued the work of Lenin and that under Stalin's leadership socialism had been victorious. The Presidium discussion on Stalin continued on February 9, when Molotov argued that "for thirty years we lived under the leadership of Stalin—and industrialization was victorious. After Stalin there was a great party. There was a cult of personality but we should also speak about [that for] Lenin and Marx."[2]

Molotov received some support from Presidium members, but Khrushchev's special report to the congress on "the cult of the personality and its consequences" went ahead. Delivered at a closed session of the congress, Khrushchev's famous secret speech electrified delegates with its revelations of the mass repressions of the Stalin era. Most shocking to delegates was the number of loyal party and state officials killed by Stalin. At the seventeenth party congress in 1934, reported Khrushchev, 139 people were elected to the Central

Committee. Some 70 percent of these CC members were arrested and shot, mostly from 1937 to 1938.

As well as delivering the dramatic secret speech, Khrushchev also presented the public report of the Central Committee to the congress. The foreign policy section of this report contained a notable amendment to Soviet doctrine: the repudiation of the idea that war was inevitable as long as capitalism and imperialism existed. War was not inevitable, argued Khrushchev, because the Soviet Union and the forces of the peace movement were strong enough to prevent it. This argument was linked to the perspective that it was possible to achieve socialism in the advanced capitalist countries by peaceful means, by the utilization of parliaments and other democratic institutions.

Molotov mostly remained on the sidelines at the congress, but he did give one of the more interesting speeches of his political career. While Molotov echoed Khrushchev's argument that war was no longer inevitable under capitalism, he also stressed the continuing danger of war: "We must not minimise the danger of war or abandon ourselves to the illusion that peace and tranquility are guaranteed to us. . . . We must always be vigilant and closely follow the imperialists' aggressive plans. We must not fall into complacency and think that the imperialist can be persuaded by good words and peace-loving plans." Molotov also called for innovation in the methods used to conduct the struggle for peace:

> In order to expand the struggle for peace as much as possible our party and the Soviet government have waged this struggle under the banner of easing international tension. . . . The policy of easing international tension is the most effective and flexible method of struggling for peace, and under the present circumstances it opens up the widest possibilities for attracting various strata of society to this cause, regardless of differences in political views. This policy takes the struggle for peace beyond the usual limits; it embraces the field of economic and cultural interests and the relations of states and private bodies but also of private individuals. Not only diplomats and politicians can help ease international tension, but also economic and cultural leaders.[3]

Khrushchev's secret speech was not published in the press or made available for foreign consumption (although it soon leaked out), but it was circulated internally and read out at party meetings all over the Soviet Union. It provoked a variety of responses. Some party members were very supportive, others hostile to the critique of Stalin, while many were confused and uncertain. In Georgia the speech provoked pro-Stalin demonstrations with some protesters carrying placards demanding "Molotov for Prime Minister" and "Molotov to Head the CPSU."[4]

In response to these pressures the party leadership retreated somewhat from the radical critique of Stalin enunciated by Khrushchev at the congress. One sign of this retreat was the publication in June 1956 of a Central Committee resolution, "On Overcoming the Consequences of the Personality Cult," which emphasized Stalin's positive qualities as a leader as well as his faults.[5]

Another telling sign of the faltering of the anti-Stalin campaign was Molotov's appointment in April 1956 to chair a Presidium commission charged with investigating the political show trials of the 1930s–trials that had resulted in the execution of many high-ranking Old Bolsheviks opposed to Stalin. As Stalin's key lieutenant in the 1930s, Molotov had been intimately involved in the decisions to stage these rigged trials. Even more extraordinary, the commission's remit was broadened to include investigation of the assassination of Sergei Kirov in December 1934. Kirov was the head of the Leningrad communists, and his death had been the pretext for the wave of terror against the anti-Stalinist opposition that started the cycle of show trials. At the twentieth congress Khrushchev had hinted at a Stalin conspiracy to murder Kirov. If there was such a conspiracy, then Molotov must have been involved since he had accompanied Stalin to Leningrad immediately after Kirov's death to help the dictator conduct a personal investigation of the circumstances of the assassination.

Molotov's commission was supposed to report within a month, but its work dragged on until the end of the year. It is possible that Molotov deliberately delayed proceedings, but it is more likely that his tardiness was the result of the complexity of the multiple investigations and of his typically slow and painstaking working methods. When the commission did report in December 1956, its findings did not please Khrushchev. According to the commission, the victims of the show trials may have been innocent of the charges of murder, sabotage, and high treason that had resulted in their execution, but they were guilty of opposition to the party and the Soviet system. As to Kirov, a lone assassin–Leonid Nikolaev–rather than a conspiratorial group, had killed him, but the anti-Soviet atmosphere engendered by the anti-Stalin opposition had encouraged his action.[6]

Khrushchev's setback on the anti-Stalin front did not save Molotov from dismissal as foreign minister. Matters came to a head on the eve of a visit by Tito to Moscow in June 1956. At the Presidium meeting on May 25, Molotov indicated that he had not revised his negative view of the Yugoslavian communists. Khrushchev accused him of sticking to his old positions and of not having changed his view of Tito since he was censured at the July 1955 plenum. At the Presidium meeting on May 26, Khrushchev raised the question of Molotov continuing in post, accusing him of being a weak foreign minister—an "aristocrat" who liked being a patron but did no work. Apart from his "lordliness" Molotov had nothing to commend him, Khrushchev told the Presidium. Two days later the Presidium again discussed Molotov's removal as foreign minister. Everyone was in favor, but some members worried that such a sudden move would not be understood by the Soviet public and suggested instead the appointment of a deputy who would work with Molotov before taking over as foreign minister. It was decided to postpone the decision until a better-attended meeting of the Presidium.

However, on June 1 Molotov was replaced by Dmitrii Shepilov, a close associate of Khrushchev's and the editor-in-chief of *Pravda*.[7] Shepilov was primarily an ideologist, but he had begun to branch out into foreign policy. In May 1955 he had accompanied Khrushchev on his visit to Yugoslavia and was subsequently heavily involved in Soviet relations with Egypt, including the negotiation of a major arms deal with President Gamal Abdel Nasser.

Molotov was down but not out. He was given no replacement post but remained a member of the Presidium and active in its decisions and discussions. From that position he was able to make a partial political comeback during the Polish and Hungarian crises of October and November 1956.

THE POLISH AND HUNGARIAN CRISES

The Polish crisis originated in June 1956 with workers' riots in Poznan and the shooting of hundreds of demonstrators by the Polish security forces. The protests were economic in origin but with definite overtones of a challenge to communist power. The Polish communists responded to the crisis by bringing Wladyslaw Gomulka back into the leadership. Gomulka, the party's former leader, had been arrested in 1951 for the sin of "national communism." The

Poles also proposed to sack the minister of defense, the Polish-born but Soviet Marshal Konstantin Rokossovsky. These developments alarmed Moscow, particularly as they were accompanied by growing popular demonstrations in favor of political reform.

At the height of the crisis in October 1956, Khrushchev flew uninvited to Warsaw to demand talks with the Polish party leadership. In the delegation were Molotov and Lazar Kaganovich, another member of the Presidium who had expressed reservations about the critique of Stalin at the twentieth party congress. As Khrushchev biographer William Taubman noted, "the presence of Molotov and Kaganovich showed how profoundly the crisis had undermined Khrushchev's authority." According to Taubman the talks with the Poles went badly, and Khrushchev, strongly supported by Molotov, decided to send Soviet troops into the country to restore order and shore up communist power, but later changed his mind.[8] There is, however, no firsthand evidence to support this story and no reason to suppose that Molotov did not support the political solution outlined by Khrushchev at the Presidium meeting on October 24. Gomulka had promised to stabilize the situation, and Khrushchev proposed to trust him because while "it would be very easy to find a reason for conflict, the resolution of such a conflict would be very difficult."[9]

One reason the Soviet leadership was keen to avoid becoming embroiled in a military intervention in Poland was that a much more serious crisis was developing simultaneously in Hungary. On October 23 Hungarian security police opened fire on crowds attempting to storm Budapest's main radio station. In response an armed revolt broke out across the city, and the communist government asked for Soviet military assistance to suppress the rebellion. Thirty thousand Soviet troops, mostly already garrisoned in Hungary, intervened the next day, but the fighting escalated and spread to other Hungarian cities.

The Soviet leadership now faced the choice of intervening in force to quell the revolt or seeking a peaceful political resolution along Polish lines. Its initial inclination was to give the new Hungarian government, headed by the reform communist Imre Nagy, a chance to stabilize the situation in the same way Gomulka had done in Poland. But Nagy soon made matters worse from Moscow's perspective by proposing to end the communist monopoly of political power in Hungary and to take the country out of the Warsaw Pact. Faced with the loss of communist power in Hungary and the potential destabilization of the whole Soviet bloc, Moscow decided to launch a massive military intervention. On

November 4, hundreds of Soviet tanks and tens of thousands of troops were sent into Budapest and other cities. The fighting was brief but bloody, resulting in twenty-five thousand civilian casualties, including five thousand dead. Nagy was arrested and replaced by Janos Kadar at the head of a new, pro-Soviet government. Nagy was deported to Romania, then returned to Hungary in 1957, and executed in 1958.

Molotov advocated a tough line throughout the Hungarian crisis. When it broke on October 23, he told the Presidium, "Hungary is falling apart under Nagy's leadership. I'm for the introduction of troops." On October 28 Molotov stated that "things are going badly. The situation has deteriorated, and it is gradually moving toward capitulation. . . . The question of friendship with the USSR, of help for our forces—this is the minimum. . . . It was right to introduce troops. . . . Regarding the government—support it. But regarding friendship with the USSR, they are talking about the withdrawal of troops. Act cautiously." At the Presidium meeting on November 4, Molotov had a sharp exchange with Khrushchev when he urged the Soviet leadership to "exert influence on Kadar so that Hungary does not go the route of Yugoslavia. . . . Reinforce the military victory through political means." Khrushchev commented, "I don't understand Comrade Molotov. He comes up with such harmful ideas." Molotov retorted that Khrushchev should keep quiet and not be so overbearing. Undeterred by Khrushchev's censure, Molotov referred again to the Yugoslavian analogy at the Presidium meeting on November 6, this time in the context of a proposal to change the name of the Hungarian Workers Party (i.e., the communists) to the Hungarian Socialist Workers Party: "We must not forget that a change of name is a change of character. What's going on is the creation of a new Yugoslavia."[10]

Molotov did not get his way on the name change, but his star rose after the Hungarian crisis had subsided. On November 21 he was given the job of minister of state control, with responsibility for ensuring that government decrees were enforced. As Taubman says, the post was not as important as foreign minister, but it was a sign that Molotov "was making a comeback."[11]

MOLOTOV VERSUS KHRUSHCHEV

Molotov used his new position to express himself freely on a range of domestic and foreign issues, and there was a sharp clash with Khrushchev over proposals to decentralize the economic system by abolishing national economic ministries and replacing them with regional economic councils. When Khrushchev's proposal came before the Presidium at the end of January 1957, Molotov demurred, saying the matter required further discussion and that any decisions should be implemented on a staged basis. Khrushchev's approach was endorsed by a plenum of the Central Committee in February, but when the matter came back to the Presidium in March, Molotov continued to raise objections. Khrushchev's proposals were unclear, he argued, and the need remained for a national economic council to coordinate the work of decentralized bodies. All the other Presidium members supported Khrushchev, pointing out to Molotov that the proposal was in accordance with the decisions of the February plenum. Molotov circulated a long note to the Presidium after the meeting that criticized Khrushchev's proposal as a one-sided interpretation of the policy adopted at the plenum and urged, once again, the necessity for strong central control over the economy. Khrushchev responded with his own note to the Presidium accusing Molotov of opposing party policy and of being against any reform of the functioning of economic institutions. The Presidium backed Khrushchev, and when the two notes were discussed on March 27, Molotov was accused of disloyalty and divisiveness. As usual Khrushchev was particularly scathing: "Molotov has completely lost touch with reality. About the Virgin [Lands policy] he does not agree, about foreign policy he does not agree, about this [issue] he does not agree. At the plenum he did not speak but most likely he was against it even then. Now he proposes a commission—in order to delay. Molotov was not always so unhurried. He hurried during collectivization, he hurried when the generals were repressed."[12]

The Presidium's lack of support for Molotov on this issue masked growing dissatisfaction with Khrushchev's leadership. An early sign of the coming revolt was a Presidium discussion in April 1957, conducted in Khrushchev's absence, about awarding him the title of Hero of Socialist Labor for his work on the Virgin Lands program—a pet project of his to expand Soviet agriculture by developing new farmlands in places like Kazakhstan and Siberia. At the Presidium meeting the majority spoke in favor of the award, but Molotov suggested they should think the matter over since Khrushchev had been given another award not so long ago. He was supported by Kaganovich, who suggested that giving an award to Khrushchev alone might give the impression that there was a cult of personality. Malenkov, the former prime minister ousted by Khrushchev in January 1955, also spoke up to say that further discussion was required.[13]

Molotov, Malenkov, and Kaganovich formed the core of a group opposed to Khrushchev. They were joined by other members of the Presidium following a speech Khrushchev made in Leningrad in May 1957 in which he pledged the USSR would overtake the United States in meat, butter, and milk production in a few short years. This unrealistic target was proclaimed by Khrushchev without consulting the Presidium and seemed to symbolize a self-centered style of decision making that was increasingly usurping the power and prerogatives of the rest of the leadership. In short, the post-Stalin collective leadership was being superseded by the emergence of a new "boss"—a development unwelcome to the majority of the Presidium, including Bulganin, Malenkov's successor as prime minister, and Shepilov, the new foreign minister.

With a majority of full (i.e., voting) members of the Presidium on their side, the Molotov group attempted a coup against Khrushchev. On June 18 they lured him to a meeting, supposedly of the Council of Ministers but which turned into an impromptu gathering of the Presidium. Khrushchev was not without his supporters, however, and he managed to fend off demands that he immediately resign as party leader. Among the senior members of the Presidium, his strongest supporters were Deputy Prime Minister (and former trade minister) Anastas Mikoyan and Defense Minister Marshal Georgii Zhukov. With Zhukov's help Khrushchev was able to arrange military transport for Central Committee members to fly to Moscow to demand the convening of a CC plenum. By day three of the Presidium meeting, the Molotov group— dubbed the "anti-party group" by their opponents—were forced to agree to call a Central Committee meeting to discuss and decide the leadership question. As Molotov later told Chuev, "We had no unity in our group, and we had no program. We merely agreed to have [Khrushchev] removed, but at the same time we were totally unprepared to assume power."[14]

THE JUNE PLENUM

The Central Committee—which had been elected at the twentieth party congress— was overwhelmingly pro-Khrushchev, and the CC plenum of June 22–29, 1957, was from the outset a forum to attack the so-called anti-party group. Much of the critical onslaught was directed at Molotov. The tone of the attack was set by Zhukov in the first speech to the plenum when he told the Central Committee that Stalin alone was not responsible for the repressions of the 1930s. He had been aided and abetted by other members of the leadership:

between February 1937 and November 1938, Stalin, Molotov, and Kaganovich had sanctioned the execution of 38,679 people caught up in the military purge of that period. On a single day–November 12, 1938–Stalin and Molotov had authorized the shooting of 3,167 people, recounted Zhukov.[15] The theme of Molotov's complicity in Stalin's prewar terror recurred throughout the plenum. Molotov responded that all the decisions had been taken collectively, not just by him and Stalin. When Khrushchev intervened to ask what positions Molotov had taken personally during Politburo discussions, he replied, "I objected to Stalin more than you or anyone else, Comrade Khrushchev, and as a result got into more trouble."[16]

Khrushchev's interruption–one of many from him and others–came during Molotov's speech to the plenum. Molotov argued for a balanced view of Stalin's mistakes and achievements. He criticized Khrushchev's foreign policy, citing the pursuit of agreements with the United States while at the same time neglecting relations with other capitalist states. This, said Molotov, infringed on the Leninist principle of exploiting the contradictions between imperialist states and had resulted in missed opportunities to strengthen the international position of the Soviet Union. In relation to Yugoslavia, Molotov pointed out that his view that Tito was a liberal and not a communist was shared by Mao Zedong and the Chinese communists. Molotov also criticized Khrushchev for his personal behavior, including acting in an undignified way by sharing a sauna with the president of Finland.[17]

Of all the speakers who subsequently laid into Molotov, the unkindest cut came from his old deputy, Andrei Gromyko, soon to be appointed foreign minister by Khrushchev. Gromyko praised Khrushchev's contribution to Soviet foreign policy and criticized Molotov's. One example he gave was the normalization of relations with West Germany in September 1955, which Gromyko attributed to Khrushchev. When Molotov intervened to say he had supported this policy, Gromyko responded that Molotov had been away at the United Nations when the proposal to establish diplomatic relations with the FRG had come before the Presidium and had objected to the proposal when he returned to Moscow. Molotov interjected that his objections had been a matter of form, not essence.[18]

Khrushchev took up the theme of Molotov's foreign policy errors in his concluding speech to the plenum on June 29. He accused Molotov of being a dogmatist whose actions as foreign minister had united the USSR's imperialist enemies and alienated its friends and neighbors. Khrushchev specifically cited Molotov's policy in relation to Iran and Turkey after the war, his position on the Austrian State Treaty, and his opposition to the normalization of relations with West Germany, Japan, and Yugoslavia. This critique was incorporated into the formal resolution passed by the plenum:

> In this sphere of foreign policy [the anti-party] group, especially Comrade Molotov, dragged their feet and tried in every way to hinder the implementation of new measures to reduce international tension and strengthen world peace. Not only did Comrade Molotov as foreign minister not take measures to improve relations between the USSR and Yugoslavia, he more than once came out against the measures that the Presidium wanted implemented to improve relations with Yugoslavia. . . . Comrade Molotov impeded the conclusion of the State Treaty with Austria and the improvement of relations with that state. . . . He was also against the normalization of relations with Japan, which played an important role in the reduction of international tensions in the Far East. He was against the development of the party's principled positions on the possibility of preventing war in contemporary conditions, on the possibility of different paths to socialism in different countries, and the necessity of strengthening the CPSU's contacts with progressive parties abroad. Comrade Molotov more than once opposed the Soviet government's new steps in defense of the peace and security of all peoples. In particular, he derided the establishment of personal contacts between the leaders of the USSR and the leaders of other countries for the purposes of achieving mutual understanding and the improvement of international relations.[19]

Molotov had no opportunity to comment on the resolution. Had he done so, he might have said that it was his policy of European collective security and a settlement of the German question—opposed by Khrushchev—that had presented the best hope of achieving a permanent détente after Stalin's death. Far from opposing the Austrian State Treaty, it had been he and his foreign ministry who had initiated the changes in Soviet policy that made that treaty possible. At the twentieth party congress Molotov had made the same argument as Khrushchev about the possibility of preventing war. The one grain of truth in the indictment concerned Molotov's attitude toward the rapprochement with

Yugoslavia. At the plenum he repeated his view that Tito's Yugoslavia was a bourgeois state and unsuitable for membership of the socialist camp.

At the end of the plenum Molotov, Malenkov, and Kaganovich all made statements confessing their sins against the party. While Malenkov and Kaganovich capitulated completely, Molotov remained somewhat defiant. He recognized the correctness of the party's policy and leadership but insisted it was Khrushchev's infringements of collective leadership that had provoked the present crisis. While he had been wrong to raise the question of Khrushchev's removal as party leader at the Presidium, he had been right to raise the problems that needed discussion.[20] When the vote on the plenum resolution was taken, Molotov abstained, but after the meeting he changed his vote and agreed to support the condemnation of the anti-party group, thus repeating the pattern of defiance followed by compliance that he had shown when his wife was expelled from the party in 1948.

AMBASSADOR TO MONGOLIA

Molotov, like Malenkov and Kaganovich, was stripped of his government posts and expelled from the Presidium and the Central Committee. He remained a party member, however, and on August 3 the Presidium decided to give him another job: ambassador to the People's Republic of Mongolia. This was not such a bad fate compared with that of Malenkov (sent to direct a power station in Kazakhstan) and Kaganovich (who became manager of a potash factory in the Urals). As Taubman notes, despite everything Khrushchev still respected Molotov. The feeling was not mutual. According to Chuev, Molotov told him, "Khrushchev reminded me of a livestock dealer. A small-time livestock dealer. A man of little culture." On another occasion he said, "As for Khrushchev, he is not worth one of Stalin's fingernails." On the other hand, Molotov did not think Khrushchev was stupid: "He was a real foe of Marxism-Leninism, a real enemy of communist revolution, a covert, cunning, skillfully camouflaged enemy. . . . No, he was no fool. Why would people follow a fool?"[21]

Molotov's sojourn in Mongolia lasted for three years. While there Molotov developed a good working relationship with the Mongolian leader, Yumjaagin Tsedenbal. Polina accompanied her husband to Mongolia, and she developed a close personal relationship with Tsedenbal's Russian wife, Anastasia Filatova. Molotov endeared himself to Filatova when he arranged for doctors to fly in from Moscow to treat her youngest child, who was very ill.[22]

As ambassador, Molotov continued to do what he had always done—give speeches on foreign policy. Some were of the formal, diplomatic kind expected of a second-tier ambassador, but others were wide-ranging commentaries on contemporary international affairs worthy of a foreign minister. Many of these latter speeches were delivered in the semipublic setting of the "Lenin Club" in the Mongolian capital of Ulan Bator. In these speeches Molotov was careful to toe the party line and to treat Khrushchev with respect, albeit without sub-scribing to the growing cult of the new leader's personality. But his audience would have been in no doubt that what Molotov had to say was the result of independent thinking, not merely the parroting of the party line.

One of his constant themes was the need to steer a middle course between the dangers of revisionism (the Khrushchevite position) and sectarianism and dogmatism, which the Khrushchevites accused him of. Another theme was the continuing centrality of the struggle for peace. "The essential question of to-day," he said in a speech in December 1957, "is the question of preserving and strengthening peace." Giving a report on the twenty-first congress of the CPSU of January–February 1959, Molotov warned his audience that it was important "not to underestimate the danger of war. It is necessary to remain vigilant and to strengthen the worldwide struggle for peace." In June 1960 he delivered a speech on the international situation in the aftermath of the failure of a Paris summit meeting between Khrushchev and Eisenhower. The summit failed when Khrushchev walked out in protest of American spy flights over the USSR after a U-2 reconnaissance aircraft was shot down. Molotov was as indignant as Khrushchev about this incident: "Today the imperialists don the mask of peace lovers; tomorrow we will see the true face of the beast. . . . The Soviet Union stands for negotiations with the imperialist states when ne-gotiations can help international détente, when they can strengthen peace. . . . However, conducting negotiations when under threat by the military aircraft of the imperialist powers is not acceptable because it will only encourage further imperialist aggression." Molotov concluded, "We must be able and prepared to conduct the struggle for peace to the very end."[23]

EXILE IN VIENNA

Shortly after this speech Molotov was transferred from Mongolia to Vienna to become head of the Soviet delegation to the International Atomic Energy Agency (IAEA). It may be that Molotov was moved from Mongolia because

Khrushchev was annoyed by his many private missives to Moscow during this period, which lacked the humility expected of a lowly ambassador. In May 1959 Molotov sent the Central Committee a memo proposing the establishment of a confederation of socialist states based, in the first instance, on a confederation of the USSR and Communist China.[24] During Richard Nixon's visit to the USSR in July and August 1959, Khrushchev told him that Molotov had opposed the Austrian State Treaty. Molotov read or heard about this and was moved to complain to the Party Control Commission: "I protest N. S. Khrushchev's attempt to depict me, a Communist, as a virtual advocate of war against the 'West' and I must declare that his statement constitutes slander similar to the sorts of poisonous attacks which the Mensheviks directed against the Bolsheviks."[25] Then, in October 1959, Molotov wrote to the Central Committee correcting the treatment of Lenin in a new official history of the CPSU.[26] In a similar vein, in early 1960 he sent an article to the party's theoretical journal *Kommunist* on the ninetieth anniversary of Lenin's birth, which was rejected because it did not discuss Molotov's own errors.[27]

Another explanation for Molotov's transfer to Vienna is that it was connected to the Sino-Soviet split, which had just come into public view with the publication in April 1960 of an editorial in *Red Flag*–the main Chinese communist newspaper. Entitled "Long Live Leninism," the editorial was ostensibly devoted to the ninetieth anniversary of Lenin's birth but was in fact a thinly disguised critique of Khrushchev's foreign policy.

The developing split between the Soviet Union and Communist China— and between Khrushchev and Chinese Communist Party leader Mao Zedong— dated back to the twentieth party congress. Like Molotov, Mao was opposed to the attack on Stalin and critical of Khrushchev's argument that war was no longer inevitable under capitalism and that the transition to socialism could be achieved by peaceful means. Mao's views and those of Molotov coincided in their emphasis on the threat of capitalist and imperialist aggression and the continuing danger of war.[28]

If Khrushchev thought that sending Molotov to Vienna would put some manners on him, he was mistaken. Molotov continued to make political speeches, albeit in private and less frequently. In January 1961 he spoke to the Soviet delegation to the IAEA about the outcome of a recent gathering of the World Communist Movement in Moscow. Molotov warned that "the danger of a new world war has still not passed." He also inveighed against the "revisionists" who forgot that competition between states with different social systems was a form of class struggle.[29]

One witness to Molotov's time in Vienna was the young Soviet diplomat Vladimir Sokolov, who was impressed by the former foreign minister's exceptional memory, self-control, and composure. Molotov's speeches to the Soviet group at the IAEA, recalled Sokolov, were always well received.[30]

In advance of the twenty-second party congress in October 1961, Molotov submitted two documents to the Central Committee.[31] First, in August 1961, was "On Leninism and the Possibility of Preventing War in the Contemporary Epoch," in which he criticized Khrushchev's argument that war was no longer inevitable under capitalism and imperialism. Molotov also accused the party leadership of fostering the pacifist illusion that disarmament was the way to end war. According to Molotov the only way to banish war was to abolish capitalism and imperialism.

The second document, dated October 12, 1961, was a critique of the new party program, which had announced that communism (i.e., a very advanced form of socialist economic and social development) would be built in the Soviet Union in twenty years or so. Molotov rejected this idea as unrealistic and as unrealizable in the absence of the global spread of the socialist project.

At the twenty-second congress the Khrushchevites launched a wide-ranging public attack on Molotov. In his opening report to the congress, Khrushchev said the members of the anti-party group were personally responsible for the mass repressions of the 1930s. Mikoyan accused Molotov of underestimating the forces of socialism and overestimating the forces of imperialism, and said this was the root of his erroneous denial of the possibility of preventing war. Petr Pospelov, the director of the party's Institute of Marxism-Leninism, went further, accusing Molotov of favoring war as a means to achieve communism. In his concluding speech to the congress, Khrushchev singled out Molotov as the leader of the anti-party group and implicated him in the murder of Kirov.[32]

These attacks on Molotov had a secondary target—Mao and the Chinese communists. Much like the Chinese used attacks on the "revisionist" Tito to indirectly criticize Khrushchev, the Soviets attacked the "dogmatist" Molotov as a means of targeting Mao.

Shortly after the congress Molotov was hauled before the party's control commission (i.e., the disciplinary committee) and asked to explain himself. Molotov protested his loyalty to the party and the leadership, but since he refused to withdraw specific criticisms of party policy, the commission considered his protestations of fidelity formalistic and insincere.

Molotov was expelled from the party in March 1962, and his appeal for readmission was rejected in July 1962. Recalled from his post in Vienna, Molotov was retired from the Foreign Ministry in September 1963.

STALINIST PENSIONER

By the standards of most Soviet citizens, Molotov's retirement was very comfortable. He was given a good pension, and he and his wife continued to live in a luxury apartment block reserved for members of the Soviet military and political elite. The apartments were not far from the Kremlin and just around the corner from the massive Lenin Library, where Molotov spent a lot of his time during retirement. Molotov also had use of a government dacha in Zhukovka, just outside Moscow.

In retirement Molotov devoted himself to writing numerous (unpublished) articles on party policy. Most of Molotov's writings dealt with domestic affairs—economic reform, the party program, the Soviet constitution, building socialism, and the early history of the CPSU.[33] His one sustained commentary on foreign policy was written just after his return from Vienna in early 1963. Entitled "On the War Danger and the Struggle for Communism," it was devoted to a critique of Khrushchev's repudiation of the doctrine of the inevitability of war. Molotov's critique was somewhat arcane, but it contained an important point of substance that helps to explain the foreign policy differences between him and Khrushchev.

At the twentieth party congress both he and Khrushchev had argued that while war was existentially inevitable as long as capitalism and imperialism existed, the peace movement could prevent the outbreak of actual wars. Khrushchev also said that in the contemporary epoch the forces favoring peace were so strong that the doctrine of the inevitability of war no longer applied in practice—a point he developed and strengthened in many subsequent speeches.[34] In opposition to Khrushchev, Molotov argued that the doctrine remained true irrespective of the strength of the peace movement, because the inherent tendency of imperialist states toward war still prevailed and would continue to do so until there was a world system of socialism. Importantly, in Molotov's view Khrushchev's revision of the doctrine of the inevitability of war led to an underestimation of the war danger, including the threat of a new world war.[35]

Molotov's criticism of Khrushchev's position was a little unfair. Khrushchev emphasized the importance of the continuing struggle for peace as much
as Molotov did and was frequently warning of the danger of war. The difference was that Molotov's doctrinal orthodoxy—his belief in the perpetual threat
of capitalist war—meant he was more prepared than Khrushchev to contemplate taking radical measures to avert what he saw as the very real danger of a
new world war. Paradoxically, it had been Molotov's ideological conservatism
that had prompted the innovative campaign for European collective security
and explained his flexibility and preparedness to enter into serious negotiations with the Western powers about the future of Germany. Khrushchev, on
the other hand, thought that the Soviet Union had sufficient political and military might to cope on its own with the capitalist war danger, including the
threat represented by a rearmed West Germany fully integrated into the Western bloc.

After Khrushchev lost power in October 1964, the Soviet ideological main-
stream became more congenial for Molotov. At the same time there remained
a gap between his views and those of the post-Khrushchev leadership. This
was particularly true in relation to the Stalin question. After Khrushchev's fall
the process of de-Stalinization ground to a halt, and a more sympathetic view
of Stalin was adopted by the regime, one that stressed his successes as well as
his failures. But this did not go far enough for Molotov. He wanted Khrushchev's attack on Stalin at the twentieth party congress repudiated, and he was
prepared to mount a vigorous defense of even the most extreme aspects of
the Stalinist regime. Serious mistakes had been made in the 1930s, admitted
Molotov in his private writings, but the mass repression of the era was justified
by the need to root out anti-Soviet elements that could have acted as a fifth
column when war came. Molotov also extolled Stalin's record as a war leader
and bemoaned the fact that his old boss's wartime speeches were no longer
on sale in the Soviet Union.[36] According to his grandson, on May 9 (Victory
Day in the USSR) Molotov always proposed a toast to Stalin—"our unknown
Supreme Commander."[37]

Molotov's critical attitude to the Soviet leadership was also evident in his
conversations with Chuev. When Leonid Brezhnev, Khrushchev's successor as
party leader, died in 1982, Molotov commented that the funeral showed "that
he had lost all sense of modesty and proportion. . . . He didn't spare himself
when it came to medals. This is disgraceful." Molotov was more impressed by

Molotov's gravestone (left) at the Novodevichy Cemetery in Moscow.
Below it is a smaller gravestone for Molotov's daughter, Svetlana, and her husband, Alexei,
who are buried in the same grave. The right-hand gravestone is that of Molotov's wife,
Polina Zhemchuzhina. Courtesy of the author

Brezhnev's successor, Yuri Andropov, but disappointed by the next leader, Konstantin Chernenko, "the type of person foisted on the people," he told Chuev. "We seem unable to nominate a real President."[38] It was Chernenko, however, who was responsible for Molotov's readmission to the Communist Party in 1984 along with Malenkov and Kaganovich.[39]

Molotov remained actively interested in politics until the very end of his life. His personal files contain his cuttings from *Pravda* on the April 1985 plenum of the Central Committee–the one that hailed Mikhail Gorbachev's assumption of power. Molotov's last conversation with Chuev was in April 1986, not long after his ninety-sixth birthday, and he was eager to discuss what had happened at the recent party congress.[40]

Molotov died on November 8, 1986–on the sixty-ninth anniversary of the Russian Revolution. Polina had predeceased him in 1970. She was buried in a quiet corner of the Novodevichy Cemetery in Moscow just behind a plot later occupied by Mikoyan, who had died in 1978, and not far from Kaganovich, who lived until 1991. In another part of the cemetery lay Khrushchev, who had died in 1971.

Molotov was buried in his wife's grave, his modest memorial stone made of white marble flecked with black. When I first visited the cemetery in 1995, the guide enthusiastically told visitors that the contrasting black-and-white design symbolized the good and bad sides of Molotov's life and character. (She said the same about Khrushchev's grave.) Fifteen years later the weathered stone looked more like shades of gray than black and white, especially when viewed from a distance.

7

CONCLUSION:
ASSESSING MOLOTOV

Everyone makes mistakes. Lenin made mistakes, and Stalin made mistakes.
Khrushchev was no exception. I had my own mistakes. Who is infallible?
                                                  — *V. M. Molotov (August 1974)*[1]

In January 1948 Molotov was nominated for the Nobel Peace Prize by a
group of Romanian academics. The nomination cited Molotov's role during
the war and his energetic defense of peace and democracy since 1945.[2]

The nomination came from within the communist bloc, but in light of the
evidence presented in this book Molotov's nomination was not as ridiculous
as it might once have seemed. Arguably, there have been far less worthy recipients of the prize. Certainly the Soviet public of the time would not have
thought it strange that Molotov was nominated. At home his image was that of
a peacemaker and a conciliator, a protector of popular hopes that another great
war could be avoided.[3]

As this book has shown, there is a wealth of evidence testifying to Molotov's abilities as a diplomat and foreign minister: his mastery of his brief, his
ability to negotiate successfully with friends and foes alike, and his legendary
persistence in pursuit of Soviet policy goals. However, for Molotov diplomacy
was less a profession and more a vocation in which he put realpolitik at the
service of building communism. Molotov was a true believer in Soviet ideology. When he compared the peace-loving policy of the Soviet Union to the
threats and aggression of capitalist and imperialist states, he really meant it. It
was Molotov's ideological worldview that was at the root of his fear of a Ger-

man revival in the 1950s. Paradoxically, it was this same ideology that led him to embrace the possibility of a pan-European system of collective security as a radical resolution of the Cold War. It is moot whether such a project could have succeeded, but Molotov deserves credit for the political risks he took when he returned as Soviet foreign minister after Stalin's death.

Molotov's effectiveness as a diplomat seems incontestable, but any claim to greatness as an international statesman is, to say the least, questionable. The cause he served was that of a brutal, authoritarian regime that must be held responsible for the deaths of millions of innocent people, albeit in the name of a utopian ideology that aspired to achieve human social perfection. That regime collapsed in ignominy in 1991. Had Molotov lived to see its demise, it is unlikely that he would have offered any apology for his role in its history. Rather, the USSR's disintegration would have reinforced his oft-repeated view that stern measures were needed to defend the socialist system from its enemies—both internal and external.

It is neither necessary to agree with Molotov's politics nor to accept the integrity of his ideology to recognize the positive as well as the negative aspects of his role as Soviet foreign minister, particularly during World War II. The overall outcome of the war was largely determined by the Soviet Union's capacity to survive Hitler's attack in June 1941 and then go on to win a resounding victory over Nazi Germany. As Molotov was fond of saying, European civilization was saved by the Red Army, by the sacrifices of the Soviet people, and by the resources generated by the communist system. However, the support of the USSR's American and British partners in the Grand Alliance was also crucial to Soviet survival and military success. The plaudits Molotov garnered during the war for his role in forging and maintaining the Grand Alliance were well deserved. But on the other side of the scale must be placed the USSR's collaboration with Germany during the period of the Nazi-Soviet Pact, in which Molotov also played a defining role.

After World War II came the Cold War. Molotov has long been viewed by orthodox history as a leading protagonist in that conflict. But new evidence from the Russian archives reveals him to be a resistor, not a proponent, of a cold war. Indeed, his finest hour was the sustained effort from 1953 to 1955 to achieve a lasting détente with the West.

In retirement Molotov acquiesced in the Khrushchevite caricature of him as an old-fashioned doctrinaire communist unable to come to terms with a post-Stalin world. It was a comfortable position for Molotov the Old Bolshevik to adopt and a convenient one from which to harass and berate Khrushchev as revisionist. But Molotov's stance did his reputation a disservice and gave credence to distorted perceptions of his broad role as Soviet foreign minister, which was positive in many respects.

After Khrushchev ousted Molotov the Cold War entered a new and dangerous phase of tension and confrontation culminating in the 1962 Cuban Missile Crisis, which brought the world perilously close to all-out nuclear war. In the aftermath, renewed efforts were made to secure a lasting détente, with eventual success achieved in the 1970s, in particular, the 1975 Helsinki Conference on Security and Cooperation in Europe. The post-Stalin détente Molotov worked so hard to achieve laid the groundwork for stabilizing the Cold War confrontation in Europe in the mid-1970s.

There was a relapse to the Cold War in the late 1970s and early 1980s. But when détente resumed under Gorbachev, one of its central tenets was the need for a common security system in Europe. After the fall of communism the Russian Federation continued to seek pan-European collective security, a project reanimated by the Vladimir Putin and Dmitry Medvedev regimes in the early twenty-first century. The full integration of Russia into Europe remains one of the big unresolved issues of the post–Cold War world. Often overlooked in the analysis of these developments is the founding role of Molotov's campaign for European collective security in the 1950s.

Molotov occupied the role of Soviet foreign minister for fifteen years during a prolonged period of constant crises and emergencies, beginning in 1939 with the international crisis that led to the outbreak of the World War II and ending with the disappointment and failure of the "spirit of the Geneva" in 1955. No simple epitaph could encompass Molotov's life and career. But, for both good and ill, he was a pivotal figure in shaping the diplomacy and politics of those extraordinary times.

NOTES

In these notes the reader will find numerous references to these Russian archives:

Arkhiv Vneshnei Politiki Rossiiskoi Federatsii (AVPRF): Foreign Policy Archive of the Russian Federation. This is the archive of the Russian (and Soviet) foreign ministry. It contains the files on Molotov's activities as foreign minister from 1939 to 1949 and from 1953 to 1956. The most-quoted files are from the collection Fond 6–the series of working files maintained by Molotov's secretariat.

Rossiiskii Gosudarstvennyi Arkhiv Noveishei Istorii (RGANI): Russian State Archive of Recent History. This archive contains the post-Stalin archives of the Soviet Communist Party. Important for the study of Molotov's foreign policy are the files of the party's International Department, which was responsible for links with foreign communist parties, including those in power in various countries.

Rossiiskii Gosudarstvennyi Arkhiv Sotsial'no-Politicheskoi Istorii (RGASPI): Russian State Archive of Social-Political History. This archive contains the Lenin- and Stalin-era files of the Soviet communist party, among them Molotov's *lichnyi fond*. While these files include some personal material, for the most part they are a record of Molotov's activities as a party official (as opposed to his role as prime minister or foreign minister). These files are important because they fill a gap in 1949–1953 when Molotov was no longer foreign minister but was the Politburo supremo in charge of foreign policy. Molotov's *lichnyi fond* also contains files on his political and diplomatic activities after his fall from power in 1957.

All Russian archives/organizations use a common filing system consisting of three or four main levels: the *fond* (a collection of files), the *opis'* (a thematic or organizational series of files within a collection), the *papka* (folder), and the *delo* (the individual file). In the notes these are abbreviated as f., op., pap., and d. When specific pages are quoted, they are abbreviated as l. (*list*) or ll. (*listy*), Russian for "page" and "pages."

Notes

Chapter 1. Introduction: "The Kremlin's Brilliant Mediocrity"

1. Albert Resis, ed., *Molotov Remembers* (Chicago: Ivan R. Dee, 1993), 198.
2. Ibid., 339; Feliks Chuev, *Sto Sorok Besed s Molotovym: Iz Dnevnika F. Chueva* (Moscow: Terra, 1991).
3. Cited by Oleg Troyanovskii, *Cherez Gody i Rasstoyaniya* (Moscow: Vagrius, 1997), 138. Troyanovskii, an aide and interpreter of Molotov's in the 1940s and 1950s, compared Molotov and Dulles as follows: "both were dogmatists to the core, both considered the systems they represented incompatible with each other, both were skeptical about the possibility of long-term agreements between the USSR and the USA, and both feared their leaders—Eisenhower and Khrushchev—would go for unjustified concessions and compromises. In short, both were made for the Cold War."
4. James F. Byrnes, *Speaking Frankly* (New York: HarperCollins, 1947), 278–79.
5. On Molotov's early political career, see Derek Watson, *Molotov: A Biography* (London: Palgrave, 2005) and the first volume of the biography written by his grandson Vyacheslav Nikonov, *Molotov: Molodost'* (Moscow: Vagrius, 2005).
6. Rachel Polonsky, *Molotov's Magic Lantern* (London: Faber and Faber, 2010).
7. According to Watson, *Molotov*, 40.
8. Nikonov, *Molotov*, 531.
9. I am grateful to Per Egil Hegge for explaining to me the chess origins of Molotov's nickname.
10. Resis, *Molotov Remembers*, 76.
11. See Lars T. Lih et al., eds., *Stalin's Letters to Molotov* (New Haven, CT, and London: Yale University Press, 1995). I am grateful to Shawn Borelli-Mear for drawing my attention to this amusing nickname of Stalin's.
12. On Molotov's role in industrialization, collectivization, and the Terror, see Watson, *Molotov*, chapters 7 and 8.
13. *Bol'shaya Sovetskaya Entsiklopediya*, vol. 39 (Moscow: Ogiz, 1938), 722–26.
14. *Rabotnitza*, no. 7 (March 1940), 2.
15. Cited by Watson, *Molotov*, 159.
16. *Na Priyome u Stalina: Tetradi (Zhurnaly) Zapisei Lits, Prinyatykh I. V. Stalinym (1924–1953gg)* (Moscow: Novyi Khroniograf, 2008).
17. "Pokhorony Iosifa Vissarionovicha Stalina: Rech' Tovarishcha V. M. Molotova," *Pravda*, March 10, 1953.
18. Resis, *Molotov Remembers*, 211, 369.
19. Konstantin Simonov, *Glazami Cheloveka Moego Pokoleniya* (Moscow: APN, 1989), 347.
20. *Politburo TsK VKP(b) i Sovet Ministrov SSSR, 1945–1953* (Moscow: Rosspen, 2002), doc. 255.
21. The documents on Polina's arrest may be found in *Gosudarstvennyi Antisemitizm v SSSR, 1938–1953* (Moscow: Materik, 2005).
22. Resis, *Molotov Remembers*, 324–25; Roy Medvedev, "V. M. Molotov: Muscovite Pensioner" in his *All Stalin's Men* (Oxford: Basil Blackwell, 1983), 99, 109.
23. See Larisa Vasilieva, *Kremlin Wives* (London: Weidenfeld & Nicolson, 1994), chapters 5 and 10.

24. C. D. Jackson Papers, Box 50, Eisenhower Correspondence 1954 (2), Eisenhower Presidential Library.
25. "*Zasedanie Politburo TsK KPSS, 12 Iulya 1984 goda,*" f. 89, op. 36, d. 15, Soviet Communist Party on Trial collection, Hoover Institution.

Chapter 2. Negotiating with the Nazis (1939–1941)

1. Vyacheslav Molotov, *Soviet Peace Policy* (London: Lawrence & Wishart, 1941), 19.
2. On Litvinov's dismissal see Geoffrey Roberts, "The Fall of Litvinov: A Revisionist View," *Journal of Contemporary History* 27 (1992), 639–57; Albert Resis, "The Fall of Litvinov: Harbinger of the German-Soviet Non-Aggression Pact," *Europe-Asia Studies* 52, no. 1 (2000); Zinovy Sheinis, *Maxim Litvinov* (Moscow: Progress Publishers, 1990), 292–97; and Watson, *Molotov,* 153–57
3. On the origins and course of the triple alliance negotiations, see Michael J. Carley, *1939: The Alliance That Never Was and the Coming of World War II* (Chicago: Ivan R. Dee, 1999) and Geoffrey Roberts, "The Alliance That Failed: Moscow and the Triple Alliance Negotiations, 1939," *European History Quarterly* 26, no. 3 (1996).
4. *Soviet Peace Efforts on the Eve of World War II,* hereafter SPE (Moscow: Novosti Press, 1971), doc. 267; *Dokumenty Vneshnei Politiki 1939 God,* hereafter DVP 1939 (Moscow: Mezhdunarodnye Otnosheniya, 1992), doc. 267.
5. William Strang, "The Moscow Negotiations 1939" in *Retreat from Power,* David Dilkes, ed. (London: Macmillan, 1981), 177.
6. SPE, docs. 278, 279, 280.
7. Ibid., docs. 291, 311, 312.
8. Ibid., doc. 314.
9. Ibid., docs. 315, 323.
10. Ibid., docs. 329, 330, 331.
11. Ibid., doc. 357.
12. *Documents on British Foreign Policy,* hereafter DBFP, second series, vol. 6 (London: HMSO, 1946), doc. 338; *Documents Diplomatiques Français,* hereafter DDF, second series, vol. 17 (Paris: Imprimerie Nationale, 1980), docs. 223–24.
13. SPE, doc. 376.
14. DBFP, vol. 7, 115–20; DDF, vol. 17, doc. 282.
15. The Soviet records of the military talks may be found in SPE docs. 411, 412, 413, 415, 417, 425, 429, 437.
16. *1941 God,* vol. 2 (Moscow: Mezhdunarodnyi Fond "Demokratiya," 1998), 557–71.
17. *God Krizisa, 1938–1939* (Moscow: Izdatelstvo Politicheskoi Literatury, 1990), doc. 362.
18. Ibid., doc. 442.
19. Cited by Sergei A. Gorlov, "Sovetsko-Germanskii Dialog Nakanune Pakta Molotova-Ribbentropa 1939g," *Novaya i Noveishaya Istoriya,* no. 4 (1993), 22.
20. *God Krizisa,* doc. 511.
21. Ibid., doc. 523.
22. *Nazi-Soviet Relations,* hereafter NSR (New York: Didier, 1948), 39–41.
23. Ibid., 52–57; DVP 1939, doc. 556.

24. *God Krizisa*, doc. 570; NSR, 59–61.
25. *God Krizisa*, doc. 572; NSR, 59–61.
26. *God Krizisa*, docs. 582, 583; NSR, 66–69.
27. NSR, 71–78.
28. Jane Degras, ed., *Soviet Documents on Foreign Policy*, vol. 3 (1933–1941) (London: Oxford University Press, 1953), 361–71.
29. NSR, 78.
30. Degras, *Soviet Documents*, 374–76.
31. Ibid., 108.
32. Molotov, *Soviet Peace Policy*, 28.
33. Degras, *Soviet Documents*, 388–92.
34. NSR, 78.
35. Ibid., 105–7.
36. *Ot Pakta Molotova-Ribbentropa do Dogovora o Bazakh* (Tallinn: Periodika, 1990), doc. 94.
37. *Polpredy Soobshchaut: Sbornik Dokumentov ob Otnosheniyakh SSSR c Latviei, Litvoi i Estoniei, Avgust 1939g–Avgust 1940g* (Moscow: Mezhdunarodnye Otnosheniya, 1990), docs. 57, 58.
38. *Report of the Select Committee to Investigate Communist Aggression and the Forced Incorporation of the Baltic States into the USSR* (Washington: U.S. Government Printing Office, 1954), 315.
39. Ivo Banac, ed., *The Diary of Georgi Dimitrov: 1933–1949* (New Haven, CT, and London: Yale University Press, 2003), 120.
40. *Polpredy Soobshchaut*, doc. 93.
41. Ibid., doc. 108.
42. Ibid., doc. 110.
43. Ibid., doc. 115.
44. Degras, *Soviet Documents*, 403–5.
45. Ibid., 436–49.
46. See Geoffrey Roberts, "Soviet Policy and the Baltic States, 1939–1940: A Reappraisal," *Diplomacy and Statecraft* 6, no. 3 (November 1995).
47. *Dokumenty Vneshnei Politiki*, vol. 23, book 1, hereafter DVP 1940 (Moscow: Mezhdunarodnye Otnosheniya, 1995), doc. 224.
48. Ibid., doc. 240.
49. Degras, *Soviet Documents*, 461–70.
50. *Dokumenty Vneshnei Politiki*, vol. 23, book 2, hereafter DVP 1940–1941 (Moscow: Mezhdunarodnye Otnosheniya, 1998), doc. 491.
51. Ibid., docs. 497, 498, 502; NSR, 217–34.
52. Cited by Watson, *Molotov*, 184.
53. DVP 1940–1941, docs. 506, 507, 510, 511; NSR, 234–47.
54. DVP 1940–1941, doc. 512; NSR, 247–54.
55. Valentin Berezhkov, *History in the Making: Memoirs of World War II Diplomacy* (Moscow: Progress Publishers, 1983), 38.
56. See the documents translated in "On the Eve: V. M. Molotov's Discussions in Berlin, November 1940," *International Affairs* (July 1991).

57. See Chadaev's interview with Georgy A. Kumanev in *Ryadom so Stalinym* (Moscow: Bylina, 1999), 401–6.
58. NSR, 258–59.
59. DVP 1940–1941, doc. 599.
60. Ibid., docs. 549, 564.
61. Degras, *Soviet Documents*, 482, 483; NSR, 278–79.
62. *Sovetsko-Yugoslavskie Otnosheniya, 1917–1941* (Moscow: Nauka, 1992), docs. 303, 304, 305, 307; DVP 1940–1941, doc. 745; NSR, 316–18.
63. NSR, 324.
64. Ibid., 335–34.
65. Evan Mawdsley, "Stalin's Secret Speeches of 5 May 1941" (unpublished paper).
66. NSR, 336–39.
67. DVP 1940–1941, docs. 814, 823, 828.
68. Gabriel Gorodetsky, *Grand Delusion: Stalin and the German Invasion of Russia* (New Haven, CT, and London: Yale University Press, 1999), 181–86.
69. Degras, *Soviet Documents*, 489.
70. DVP 1940–1941, docs. 875, 876; NSR, 355–56.
71. Resis, *Molotov Remembers*, 22–23.
72. Cited by Louis Rotundo, "Stalin and the Outbreak of War in 1941," *Journal of Contemporary History* 24 (1989), 291.

Chapter 3. Forging the Grand Alliance (1941–1945)

1. "'Nashe Delo Pravoe': Kak Gotovilos' Vystuplenie V. M. Molotova po Radio 22 Iunya 1941 Goda," *Istoricheskii Arkhiv*, no. 2 (1995), 32–39. Audio recordings of Molotov's radio broadcast are widely available on the Internet.
2. Resis, *Molotov Remembers*, 39.
3. Degras, *Soviet Documents*, 491–93.
4. Cited by Watson, *Molotov*, 193.
5. *Dokumenty Vneshnei Politiki*, vol. 24 (Moscow: Mezhdunarodnye Otnosheniya, 2000), doc. 228.
6. *Stalin's Correspondence with Churchill, Attlee, Roosevelt and Truman*, vol. 1 (London: Lawrence & Wishart, 1958), doc. 20.
7. The relevant documents may be found in Oleg A. Rzheshevsky, ed., *War and Diplomacy: The Making of the Grand Alliance* (Amsterdam: Harwood Academic Publishers, 1996).
8. Ibid., 54.
9. *Dokumenty Vneshnei Politiki*, vol. 24, doc. 26. This meeting between Cripps and Molotov took place on December 26, after Eden's departure from Moscow.
10. Georgy Kynin and Jochen Laufer, eds., *SSSR i Germanskii Vopros, 1941–1949*, vol. 1 (Moscow: Mezhdunarodnye Otnosheniya, 1996), docs. 15, 18, 38.
11. *Stalin's Correspondence*, vol. 2, doc. 17.
12. See Geoffrey Roberts, "Litvinov's Lost Peace, 1941–1946," *Journal of Cold War Studies* 4, no. 1 (spring 2002).
13. *Sovetsko-Amerikanskie Otnosheniya vo Vremya Velikoi Otechestvennoi Voiny, 1941–1945*, vol. 1 (Moscow: Politizdat, 1984), doc. 70.

14. Ibid., docs. 68, 70, 73, 77, 80. See further: Hugh Phillips, "Mission to America: Maksim M. Litvinov in the United States, 1941–1943," *Diplomatic History* 12, no. 3 (summer 1988).
15. *Stalin's Correspondence*, vol. 2, doc. 18.
16. Rzheshevsky, *War and Diplomacy*, doc. 28. This volume contains the Soviet documents on Molotov's trips to London and Washington.
17. Ibid., doc. 36.
18. Ibid., doc. 38.
19. Ibid., doc. 47.
20. Ibid., doc. 63.
21. Andrei Gromyko, *Memories* (London: Hutchinson, 1989), 312.
22. Rzheshevsky, *War and Diplomacy*, doc. 68.
23. Ibid., doc. 70.
24. Ibid., doc. 87.
25. AVPRF, f. 06, op. 4, pap. 22, d. 235.
26. Rzheshevsky, *War and Diplomacy*, doc. 126.
27. Ibid., doc. 112.
28. *Vneshnaya Politika Sovetskogo Soyuza v period Otechestvennoi Voiny*, vol. 1 (Moscow: Ogiz, 1944), 260.
29. *Stalin's Correspondence*, vol. 1, doc. 57.
30. Oleg A. Rzheshevsky, ed., *Stalin i Cherchil'* (Moscow: Nauka, 2004), doc. 147.
31. "New Documents about Winston Churchill from Russian Archives," *International Affairs* 47, no. 5 (2001), 137–38.
32. *Sovetsko-Angliiskie Otnosheniya vo Vremya Velikoi Otechestvennoi Voiny, 1941–1945*, vol.1 (Moscow: Politizdat, 1983), doc. 147.
33. Rzheshevsky, *Stalin i Cherchil'*, doc. 158.
34. The Soviet preparatory documents may be found in AVPRF, f. 6, op. 5b, pap. 39, dd. 1–6, and pap. 40, d. 11.
35. AVPRF, f. 6, op. 5b, pap. 39, d. 6, ll. 16–27.
36. "K Predstoyashchemu Soveshchaniu Trekh Ministrov," AVPRF, f. 6, op. 5b, pap. 39, d. 6, ll. 52–57. This document is printed in *SSSR i Germanskii Vopros*, doc. 59.
37. For the Soviet record of the conference proceedings: *Moskovskaya Konferentsiya Ministrov Inostrannykh Del SSSR, SShA i Velikobritanii* (Moscow: Politizdat, 1984).
38. AVPRF, f. 0511, op. 1, d. 1, l. 72.
39. Cited by D. Watson, "Molotov and the Moscow Conference, October 1943," BASEES conference paper, 2002 (in French: "Molotov et la Conférence de Moscou Octobre 1943," *Communisme*, no. 74/75, 2003).
40. Harriman Papers, Library of Congress Manuscript Division, container 170, chronological file 8-17/11/1943.
41. Cited by Watson, "Molotov and the Moscow Conference."
42. Letters of Kathleen Harriman dating from October 1943 to October 1944, in the author's possession. Ms. Harriman's letters may also be found interspersed in the wartime files of her father's archive in the Library of Congress and in Pamela Harriman's archive in the Library of Congress. (Pamela Churchill, at

the time married to Randolph Churchill, Winston's son, later married Averell Harriman.)

43. Cited by Watson, "Molotov and the Moscow Conference."

44. See Roberts, "Litvinov's Lost Peace."

45. The Soviet files on the EAC (known in Moscow as the European Consultative Commission) may be found in AVPRF, f. 0425, op. 1, dd. 1–5, 11–12.

46. The Soviet documents on these discussions may be found in *Konferentsiya Predstavitelei SSSR, SShA i Velikobritanii v Dumbarton-Okse* (Moscow: Politizdat, 1984).

47. AVPRF, f. 06, op. 6, pap. 13, d. 133, ll. 1–11; d. 134, ll. 1–35, 44–50, 70–79; d. 135, ll. 9–18. For further exploration of Litvinov's views, see Roberts, "Litvinov's Lost Peace," and T. U. Kochetskova, "Voprosy Sozdaniya OON i Sovetskaya Diplomatiya," *Otechestvennaya Istoriya*, no. 1 (1995).

48. See Roberts, "Litvinov's Lost Peace."

49. "Sovetskii Soyuz i OON: Direktivy Politburo TsK VKP(b) Sovetskoi Delegatsii na Konferentsii v Dumbarton-Okse 1944g," *Istoricheskii Arkhiv*, no. 4 (1995).

50. *Stalin's Correspondence*, vol. 2, doc. 227.

51. Antony Polonsky, ed., *The Great Powers and the Polish Question, 1941–1945* (London: Orbis Books, 1976), doc. 107.

52. Rzheshevsky, *Stalin i Cherchil'*, doc. 162. This volume also contains the Soviet records of the Stalin-Churchill conversations, including the percentages discussion.

53. For further discussion of the percentages agreement, see K. G. M. Ross, "The Moscow Conference of October 1944 (Tolstoy)" in William Deakin et al., eds., *British Political and Military Strategy in Central, Eastern and Southern Europe in 1944* (London: Macmillan, 1988); Albert Resis, "The Churchill-Stalin Secret 'Percentages' Agreement on the Balkans, Moscow, October 1944," *American Historical Review* (April 1978); P. Tsakaloyannis, "The Moscow Puzzle," *Journal of Contemporary History* 21 (1986); P. G. H. Holdich, "A Policy of Percentages?: British Policy and the Balkans after the Moscow Conference of October 1944," *International History Review* (February 1987); and Geoffrey Roberts, "Beware Greek Gifts: The Churchill-Stalin 'Percentages Agreement' of October 1944," *Mir Istorii*, www.historia.ru/2003/01/Roberts.htm.

54. *Stalin's Correspondence*, doc. 230.

55. AVPRF, f. 06, op. 7a, d. 5, ll. 7–28.

56. *SSSR i Germanskii Vopros*, doc. 79.

57. *Sovetsko-Amerikanskie Otnosheniya, 1939–1945* (Moscow: Materik, 2004), doc. 244.

58. Ibid., doc. 246.

59. I am relying on the summary and quotes from this document in Silvio Pons, "In the Aftermath of the Age of Wars: The Impact of World War II on Soviet Foreign Policy" in Silvio Pons and Andrea Romano, eds., *Russia in the Age of Wars, 1914–1945* (Milan: Feltrinelli, 2000); Alexei M. Filitov, "Problems of Post-War Construction in Soviet Foreign Policy Conceptions during World War II" in Francesca Gori and Silvio Pons, eds., *The Soviet Union and Europe*

in the Cold War, 1943–1953 (London: Macmillan, 1996); Vladimir O. Pechatnov, "The Big Three after World War II: New Documents on Soviet Thinking about Post-War Relations with the United States and Great Britain," Cold War International History Project working paper no. 13; and Alexei M. Filitov, "V Kommissiyakh Narkomindela" in O. A. Rzheshevsky, ed., *Vtoraya Mirovaya Voina* (Moscow: Nauka, 1995).

60. *SSSR i Germanskii Vopros*, doc. 140.
61. *Stalin and the Cold War, 1945–1953: A Cold War International History Project Documentary Reader* (n.d.), 130.
62. Banac, *Diary of Georgi Dimitrov*, 357–58.
63. *The Tehran, Yalta & Potsdam Conferences* (Moscow: Progress Publishers, 1969), 137.
64. Ibid., 136–37.
65. *SSSR i Germanskii Vopros*, doc. 144.
66. "Istoricheskie Resheniya Krymskoi Konferentsii," *Pravda*, February 13, 1945, and "Krymskaya Konferentsiya Rukovoditelei Trekh Soyuznykh Derzhav," *Izvestiya*, February 13, 1945. But note that the term "Grand Alliance" was not used. That was a later invention of Churchill's. The Soviets usually referred to the "anti-Hitler coalition," while the Americans' preferred term was the "United Nations"—hence the name of the organization when it was founded in 1945 at a conference of the victor states in San Francisco.
67. *SSSR i Germanskii Vopros*, doc. 154.
68. Harriman Papers, c. 178, cf. 10, April 13, 1945.
69. See further Geoffrey Roberts, "Sexing up the Cold War: New Evidence on the Molotov-Truman Talks of April 1945," *Cold War History* 4, no. 3 (April 2004).
70. *Sovetsko-Amerikanskie Otnosheniya* (1984), doc. 224.
71. AVPRF, f. 06, op. 7b, pap. 60, d. 1, ll. 6–8. The main text of this document is printed in ibid., doc. 226. A full English translation may be found in Roberts, "Sexing up the Cold War."
72. AVPRF, f. 06, op. 7b, pap. 60, d. 1, ll. 1–5. This document is printed in *Sovetsko-Amerikanskie Otnosheniya* (2004), doc. 295.
73. AVPRF, f. 06, op. 7b, pap. 60, d. 1, ll. 11–13. This document is printed in *Sovetsko-Amerikanskie Otnosheniya* (2004), doc. 296. A full English translation may be found in Roberts, "Sexing up the Cold War."
74. *Sovetsko-Amerikanskie Otnosheniya* (2004), doc. 298.
75. V. M. Molotov, *Problems of Foreign Policy* (Moscow: Foreign Languages Publishing House, 1948), 13–20.
76. Arthur. H. Birse, *Memoirs of an Interpreter* (London: Michael Joseph, 1967), 200. This practice of comparison probably explains why the British and Soviet records of meetings were so similar when Birse and Pavlov were the interpreters.
77. *Sovetsko-Amerikanskie Otnosheniya* (2004), doc. 303.
78. *The Tehran, Yalta and Potsdam Conferences*, 265.
79. For example, the editorials published in *Pravda* and *Izvestiya* on August 3, 1945, were both under the headline "Berlinskaya Konferentsiya Trekh Derzhav" (Berlin Conference of the Three Powers).

80. Cited by Ralph B. Levering, Vladimir O. Pechatnov, et al., *Debating the Origins of the Cold War: American and Russian Perspectives* (Lanham, MD: Rowman & Littlefield, 2002), 105.
81. Cited by Leonid Gibianskii, "Doneseniya Yugoslavskogo Posla v Moskve o Otsenkakh Rukovodstvom SSSR Potsdamskoi Konferentsii i Polozheniya v Vostochnoi Evrope," *Slavyanovedeniye,* no. 1 (1994).
82. Banac, *Diary of Georgi Dimitrov,* 377.

Chapter 4. Fighting the Cold War (1946–1952)

1. Molotov, *Problems of Foreign Policy,* 49.
2. "28-ya Godovshchina Velikoi Oktyabr'skoi Sotsialisticheskoi Revolutsii: Doklad V. M. Molotova na Torzhestvennom Zasedanii Moskovskogo Soveta 6-go Noyabrya 1945g.," *Pravda,* November 7, 1945. An English translation of this article was published in *Soviet News,* November 8, 1945.
3. AVPRF, f. 0431/1, op. 1, d. 1, ll. 1–16.
4. Cited by Vladimir Pechatnov, "'The Allies Are Pressing on You to Break Your Will': Foreign Policy Correspondence between Stalin and Molotov and Other Politburo Members, September 1945–December 1946," Cold War International History Project working paper no. 26, September 1999, 2.
5. AVPRF, f. 0431/1, op. 11, pap. 4, d. 18, l. 24. See also *Sovetsko-Amerikanskie Otnosheniya, 1945–1948* (Moscow: Materik, 2004), doc. 9.
6. *Documents on British Policy Overseas* (hereafter: DBPO), series 1, vol. 2 (London: HMSO, 1985), 177. On Soviet policy on the trusteeship question: S. Mazov, "The USSR and the Former Italian Colonies, 1945–1950," *Cold War History* 3, no. 3 (April 2003).
7. DBPO, 317. For the Soviet version of this conversation: AVPRF, f. 0431/1, op. 2, pap. 4, d. 18, ll. 39–47.
8. DBPO, 454. For the Soviet version of this conversation: AVPRF, f.0431/1, op. 2, pap. 4, d. 18, ll. 62–64.
9. AVPRF, ibid., ll. 5–16.
10. AVPRF, f. 0431/1, op. 2, pap. 4, d. 18, ll. 25–27; *Sovetsko-Amerikanskie Otnosheniya, 1945–1948,* doc. 10.
11. Pechatnov, "The Allies Are Pressing," 5.
12. Ibid.
13. Ibid., 4.
14. Ibid., 6–7.
15. "V. M. Molotov's Press Conference," *Soviet News,* October 5, 1945.
16. AVPRF, f. 0431/1, op. 1, d. 26, ll. 22–24.
17. Pechatnov, "The Allies Are Pressing," 8. A Soviet stenographic record of the conference was produced subsequently and may be found in AVPRF, f. 0431/1, op. 1, d. 5.
18. Pechatnov, "The Allies Are Pressing," 10.
19. Cited by Alexander O. Chubariyan and Vladimir O. Pechatnov, "Molotov 'the Liberal': Stalin's 1945 Criticism of His Deputy," *Cold War History* 1, no. 1 (August 2000), 131–32.

20. *Politburo TsK VKP(b) i Sovet Ministrov SSSR, 1945–1953* (Moscow: Rosspen, 2002), doc. 173.
21. Ibid., doc. 174.
22. Ibid., doc. 177.
23. Byrnes, *Speaking Frankly*, 118.
24. Kynin and Laufer, *SSSR i Germanskii Vopros*, doc. 71.
25. DBPO, 868.
26. *Stalin's Correspondence*, vol. 2, 280–81.
27. Pechatnov, "The Allies Are Pressing," 14. One observer of Molotov in action at the foreign ministers' conference was George Kennan, who recorded in his diary: "Molotov, conducting the meeting, sat leaning forward over the table, a Russian cigarette dangling from his mouth, his eyes flashing with satisfaction and confidence as he glanced from one to the other of the other foreign ministers, obviously keenly aware of their mutual differences and their common uncertainty in the face of the keen, ruthless, and incisive Russian diplomacy. He had the look of a passionate poker player who knows that he has a royal flush and is about to call the last of his opponents. He was the only one who was clearly enjoying every minute of the proceedings." George Kennan, *Memoirs* (London: Hutchinson, 1968), 287.
28. Kynin and Laufer, *SSSR i Germanskii Vopros*, doc. 112.
29. Pechatnov, "The Allies Are Pressing," 19–20.
30. Paris Peace Conference Box, Hoover Institution archives.
31. Pechatnov, "The Allies Are Pressing," 21.
32. Ibid., 23.
33. *Sovetsko-Amerikanskie Otnosheniya, 1945–1948*, doc. 138.
34. Molotov, *Problems of Foreign Policy*, 243–67.
35. Zhdanov's speech was published in *Izvestiya* on November 7, 1946. A translation may be found in *Soviet News*, November 8, 1946.
36. Churchill's Iron Curtain speech is widely available on the Internet.
37. Joseph Stalin, *Sochineniya*, vol.16 (Tver': Soyuz, 1997), 26–30. For an English translation: Walter Lafeber, ed., *The Origins of the Cold War, 1941–1947* (New York: John Wiley & Sons, 1971), doc. 37.
38. See further Geoffrey Roberts, "Moscow's Cold War on the Periphery: Soviet Policy in Greece, Iran and Turkey, 1943–1948," *Journal of Contemporary History* (January 2011).
39. *Berlinskaya (Potsdamskaya) Konferentsiya Rukovoditelei Trekh Soyuznykh Derzhav-SSSR, SShA, i Velikobritanii* (Moscow: Politizdat, 1984), doc. 47.
40. Banac, *Diary of Georgi Dimitrov*, 441.
41. RGASPI, f. 17, op. 166, d. 807, ll. 18–24.
42. Nataliya I. Yegorova, "The 'Iran Crisis' of 1945–1946: A View from the Russian Archives," Cold War International History Project working paper no. 15 (May 1996), 2–6.
43. Ibid., 8.
44. Fernande S. Raine, "Stalin and the Creation of the Azerbaijan Democratic Party in Iran, 1945," *Cold War History* 2, no. 1 (October 2001), 6.

45. Jamil Hasanli, *At the Dawn of the Cold War: The Soviet-American Crisis over Iranian Azerbaijan, 1941–1946* (Lanham, MD: Rowman & Littlefield), 64–66.

46. DBPO, docs. 289, 300, 337, 341, 343, 349, 352, 353.

47. Ibid., doc. 308.

48. Hasanli, *At the Dawn of the Cold War,* 267.

49. J. M. Siracusa, "The Meaning of Tolstoy: Churchill, Stalin and the Balkans, Moscow, October 1944," *Diplomatic History* (fall 1979), 449.

50. *Krymskaya Konferentsiya Rukovoditelei Trekh Soyuznykh Derzhav–SSSR, SShA i Velikobritanii* (Moscow: Politizdat, 1979), 201–2.

51. *Vneshnyaya Politika Sovetskogo Soyuza v Period Otechestvennoi Voiny* (Moscow: Ogiz, 1947), 146.

52. The content of the two conversations, as recorded by the Soviets, is recounted in detail by Jamil Hasanli, *SSSR-Turtsiya: Poligon Kholodnoi Voiny* (Baku: Adilogly, 2005), 162–74.

53. *Berlinskaya (Potsdamskaya) Konferentsiya Rukovoditelei Trekh Soyuznykh Derzhav–SSSR, SShA i Velikobritanii* (Moscow: Politizdat, 1984), doc. 63.

54. Ibid., 444.

55. DBPO, 317–18.

56. Ibid., 781.

57. Walter Bedell Smith, *Moscow Mission, 1946–1949* (London: Heinemann, 1950), 41–42.

58. See Eduard Mark, "The War Scare of 1946 and Its Consequences," *Diplomatic History* 21, no. 3 (summer 1997).

59. *Vneshnyaya Politika Sovetskogo Soyuza, 1946 god* (Moscow: Ogiz, 1952), 167–70.

60. A. R. De Luca, "Soviet-American Politics and the Turkish Straits," *Political Science Quarterly* 92, no. 3 (autumn 1977), 519.

61. *Vneshnyaya Politika Sovetskogo Soyuza, 1946 god,* 193–202.

62. See Hasanli, *SSSR-Turtsiya,* 370–73, and N. V. Kochkin, "SSSR, Angliya, SShA i 'Turetskii Krizis' 1945–1947gg.," *Novaya i Noveishaya Istoriya,* no. 3 (2002).

63. *Sovetsko-Amerikanskie Otnosheniya, 1945–1948,* doc. 185.

64. Ibid., 57–67.

65. Pechatnov, "The Allies Are Pressing," 18. Many of the documents submitted by Soviet officials are reproduced in Kynin and Laufer, *SSSR i Germanskii Vopros.*

66. Molotov, *Problems of Foreign Policy,* 55–69.

67. The Soviet public and private documents on the Moscow CFM may be found in Kynin and Laufer, *SSSR i Germanskii Vopros,* vol. 3. For Molotov's speeches at the conference, see his *Problems of Foreign Policy.*

68. *Vneshnyaya Politika Sovetskogo Soyuza 1947 god,* part 1 (Moscow: Ogiz, 1952), 377–83, 534; "K Itogam Soveshchaniya Ministrov Inostrannykh Del," *Pravda,* April 27, 1947.

69. "Novoe Izdanie 'Doktriny Truman,'" *Pravda,* June 16, 1947; K. Gofman, "Mr. Marshall's 'New Plan' for Relief to European Countries," *Novoe Vremya (New Times),* June 17, 1947.

70. Galina Takhnenko, "Anatomy of the Political Decision: Notes on the Marshall Plan," *International Affairs,* July 1992, 121.

71. *Sovetsko-Amerikanskie Otnosheniya, 1945–1948*, docs. 198, 200.
72. Directive to the Soviet delegation to the Paris conference, reproduced in Takhnenko, "Anatomy of the Political Decision."
73. Molotov, *Problems of Foreign Policy*, 465–68.
74. Giuliano Procacci et al., eds., *The Cominform: Minutes of the Three Conferences* (Milan: Feltrinelli, 2000), 225–27.
75. Molotov, *Problems of Foreign Policy*, 483–91.
76. The Soviet position was outlined publicly by Molotov in a series of speeches at the two CFMs. See Molotov, *Problems of Foreign Policy*, 343–456, 503–55. For the internal Soviet briefing documentation, see Kynin and Laufer, *SSSR i Germanskii Vopros*, vol. 3.
77. On the Stalin-Tito split, see in particular the writings of Leonid Gibianskii, including "The Soviet-Yugoslav Split and the Cominform" in Leonid Gibianskii and Norman Naimark, eds., *The Establishment of Communist Regimes in Eastern Europe, 1944–1949* (Boulder, CO: Westview, 1997).
78. See Vladimir Pechatnov, *Stalin, Ruzvel't, Trumen: SSSR i SShA v 1940-kh gg* (Moscow: Terra, 2006), 540–46.
79. *Sovetsko-Amerikanskie Otnosheniya, 1945–1948*, docs. 261, 263. Smith's reports on his two meetings with Molotov may be found in *Foreign Relations of the United States 1948*, vol. 4 (Washington: Government Printing Office, 1974), 845–57.
80. See J. Samuel Walker, "'No More Cold War': American Foreign Policy and the 1948 Soviet Peace Offensive," *Diplomatic History* (winter 1981), 75–91.
81. William Stivers, "The Incomplete Blockade: Soviet Zone Supply of West Berlin, 1948–1949," *Diplomatic History* 21, no. 4 (fall 1997). On Soviet policy in general: Mikhail M. Narinskii, "The Soviet Union and the Berlin Crisis" in Gori and Pons, *The Soviet Union and Europe in the Cold War*.
82. *Sovetsko-Amerikanskie Otnosheniya, 1945–1948*, docs. 281, 287.
83. RGASPI, f. 82, op. 2, d. 1164, ll. 15–86; *Sovetsko-Amerikanskie Otnosheniya, 1949–1952* (Moscow: Materik, 2006), doc. 14.
84. *Sovetsko-Amerikanskie Otnosheniya, 1949–1952*, doc. 90.
85. The stenographic records of the Prague conference may be found in RGASPI, f. 82, op. 2, d. 1335, ll. 57–96.
86. On Stalin and the Korean War, see the outstanding work of Katherine Weathersby posted on the website of the Cold War International History Project.
87. This summary of the January 1951 meeting is based on report of the Romanian defense minister, Emil Bodnaras, which can be found on the website of the National Security Archive at George Washington University.
88. See David Holloway, *Stalin and the Bomb* (New Haven, CT: Yale University Press, 1994).
89. The outstanding study of the early development of the communist peace movement remains Marshall D. Shulman, *Stalin's Foreign Policy Reappraised* (Cambridge, MA: Harvard University Press, 1963). For an important, archive-based study of the peace movement within the Soviet Union during this period, see Timothy Johnston, "Peace or Pacifism?: The Soviet 'Struggle for Peace in All the World,' 1948–1954," *Slavic and East European Review* 86, no. 7 (April 2008).

90. There are a series of files on the peace movement in Molotov's personal file series in RGASPI (f. 82, op. 2, dd. 1396–1403), which contain the reports, instructions, and data for the period 1949–1953.

91. Procacci, *The Cominform*, 697.

92. Detailed statistics on the three signature campaigns may be found in RGASPI, f. 82, op. 2, d. 1402.

93. RGASPI, f. 82, op. 2, d. 1397, ll. 27–29, 51–52, 72–74, 115–16, 147–48, 158–59, 190–92.

94. Joseph Stalin, *Economic Problems of Socialism in the USSR* (Moscow: Foreign Languages Publishing House, 1952), 37–41.

95. The various drafts of Malenkov's speech, together with the handwritten corrections of Stalin's secretary, may be found in RGASPI, f. 592, op. 1, dd. 6–9.

96. *Sovetsko-Amerikanskie Otnosheniya, 1949–1952,* doc. 109.

97. My summary is based on Stein Bjørnstad, *The Soviet Union and German Reunification during Stalin's Last Years* (Oslo: Norwegian Institute for Defence Studies, 1998); *Sovetsko-Amerikanskie Otnosheniya, 1949–1952,* docs. 148–49; and RGASPI, f. 82, op. 2, d. 1169, ll. 73–137 and d. 1170, ll. 1–95.

98. Alexei M. Filitov, *Germaniya v Sovetskom Vneshnepoliticheskom Planirovanii, 1941–1990* (Moscow: Nauka, 2010), chapter 3.

99. The exchange of notes can be followed in *The Efforts Made by the Federal Republic of Germany to Re-Establish the Unity of Germany by Means of All-German Elections* (Bonn: Federal Ministry for All-German Affairs, 1954), 84–110. The drafts of the Soviet replies to the various Western notes may be found in RGASPI, f. 82, op. 2, dd. 1170–71. A reply to the final Western note was drafted by the Soviet Foreign Ministry but never sent: AVPRF, f. 082, op. 41, pap. 271, d. 19, ll. 58–65.

100. RGASPI, f. 82, op. 2, d. 1171, ll. 104–6.

101. *Istochnik,* no. 3 (2003), 122–25. A translation of this document may be found on the Cold War International History Project website.

102. *Politburo TsK VKP(b) i Sovet Ministrov SSSR, 1945–1953,* doc. 91.

103. There is no definitive version of Stalin's comments at this plenum, but see Konstantin Simonov, *Glazami Cheloveka Moego Pokoleniya: Razmyshleniya o I. V. Staline* (Moscow: APN, 1989), 240–44; Anastas Mikoyan, *Tak Bylo* (Moscow: Vagrius, 1999), 574–75; Resis, *Molotov Remembers,* 313–16; and Joseph Stalin, *Sochineniya,* vol. 18 (Tver': Soyuz, 2006), 584–87.

104. Resis, *Molotov Remembers,* 315–16.

Chapter 5. Partisan of Peace (1953–1955)

1. "Press-Konferentsiya u V. M. Molotova v San-Frantsisko," *Pravda,* June 27, 1955.

2. "Pokhorony Iosifa Vissarionovicha Stalina: Rech' Tovarishcha V. M. Molotova," *Pravda,* March 10, 1953.

3. AVPRF, f. 082, op. 41, p. 271, d. 18, ll. 3–29. A number of the archive documents cited in this section may be found in English translation in Christian F. Ostermann, ed., *Uprising in East Germany 1953* (Budapest: Central European Press, 2001).

4. AVPRF, f. 082, op. 41, pap. 271, d. 19, ll. 13–19.
5. Ibid., d. 18, ll. 30–43; d. 19, ll. 1–12; and d. 19, ll. 20–30.
6. "O Nashikh Dal'neishikh Meropriyatiyakh po Germanskomu Voprosu," AVPRF, f. 082, op. 41, pap. 271, d. 18, ll. 44–48.
7. "Zapiska po Germanskomu Voprosu," AVPRF, f. 082, op. 41, pap. 271, d. 18, ll. 52–59.
8. AVPRF, f. 06, op. 12, pap. 16, d. 259, ll. 39–73.
9. Ostermann, *Uprising*, 133–36.
10. RGASPI, f. 83, op. 1, d. 3, ll. 131–32, 134–36, 141. For a full translation of and commentary on the Malenkov statement, see Geoffrey Roberts, "Malenkov on the German Question, 2 June 1953," Cold War International History Project e-dossier no. 15. Also see Alexei Filitov, "'Germany Will Be a Bourgeois-Democratic Republic': The New Evidence from the Personal File of Georgiy Malenkov," *Cold War History* 6, no. 4 (November 2006), 552–55.
11. AVPRF, f. 06, op. 12a, pap. 51, d. 301, ll. 1–49.
12. *Lavrentii Beria, 1953: Stenogramma Iul'skogo Plenuma TsK KPSS i Drugie Dokumenty* (Moscow: Mezhdunarodnyi Fond "Demokratiya," 1999), 223.
13. Ibid., 97.
14. Ibid., 102.
15. Ibid., 359.
16. "Krakh Avantury Inostrannykh Naimitov v Berline," *Pravda,* June 23, 1953.
17. AVPRF, f. 06, op. 12, pap. 16, d. 264, ll. 2–7; and op. 121, pap. 3, d. 36, ll. 37–39.
18. "Note of the Soviet Government, August 4, 1953," supplement, *New Times,* August 12, 1953, 2–4.
19. "Note of the Soviet Government to the Governments of France, Great Britain and the USA on the German Question," supplement, *New Times,* August 17, 1953, 2–6.
20. "Soviet-German Communiqué," supplement, *New Times,* no. 35 (1954), 2–4; "Speech by G. M. Malenkov", 5–7.
21. Supplement, *New Times,* November 14, 1953, 4; supplement, *New Times,* November 28, 1953, 4, 6.
22. AVPRF, f. 0129, op. 37, pap. 266, d. 24, ll. 135–43, 145–53; and pap. 265, d. 17, ll. 1–127 passim.
23. AVPRF, f. 06, op. 13g, pap. 65, d. 28, ll. 13–24, 25–51, 62–64, 83–85, 90–116.
24. AVPRF, f. 082, op. 42, pap. 287, d. 35, ll. 54–70.
25. AVPRF, f. 06, op. 13, pap. 6, d. 42, ll. 14–16.
26. Molotov's correspondence with Khrushchev, Malenkov, and the Presidium is contained in AVPRF, f. 06, op. 13, pap. 5, d. 41. The Gromyko/Pushkin drafts of January 12 and 17 can be found in AVPRF, f. 06, op. 13, pap. 6, d. 42.
27. AVPRF, f. 082, op. 42, pap. 287, d. 34, ll. 1–40, 41–52, 57–99; f. 06, op. 13a, pap. 35, d. 167, ll. 15–41.
28. AVPRF, f. 06, op. 13g, pap. 65, d. 25, ll. 1–5.
29. My summaries and citations from the conference proceedings are derived from the Soviet records: "Stenogrammy Zasedaniya Ministrov Inostrannykh Del Chetyrekh Derzhav," AVPRF, f. 06, op. 13g, pap. 63, d. 12. The proceedings of the conference were covered in detail by the Soviet press.

30. "Memorandum of Conversation, February 6, 1954," Eisenhower Papers, Dulles-Herter Series, box 2, file February 54 (1), Eisenhower Library.

31. "The Soviet Union and the Safeguarding of European Security," supplement, *New Times*, no. 8 (1954), 3–8.

32. "Letter from C. D. Jackson dated February 10, 1954," C. D. Jackson Papers, box 33, Berlin Basics (1).

33. AVPRF, f. 6, op. 13g, pap. 63, d. 12, ll. 250, 501, 504, 548–49.

34. "Soviet Union and Safeguarding of European Security," 6.

35. "Report on Berlin: Address by Secretary Dulles," Department of State Bulletin, March 8, 1954, 343–44.

36. "Memorandum of Discussion at the 186th Meeting of the National Security Council, Friday, 26 February 1954," *Foreign Relations of the United States, 1952–1954*, vol. 5, part 1 (Washington: Government Printing Office, 1983), 1221–31.

37. C. D. Jackson Papers, box 33, Berlin Miscellaneous, Eisenhower Library.

38. The published version of Molotov's plenum report may be found in the supplement to *New Times*, no. 10 (1954), 3–14. For the fuller archive version, see RGANI, f. 2, op. 1, d. 77, ll. 28–29. Drafts of Molotov's report may be found in AVPRF, f. 6, op. 13, pap. 6, d. 46.

39. AVPRF, f. 082, op. 42, pap. 287, d. 35, ll. 34–47.

40. Ibid., f. 06, op. 13, pap. 2, d. 9, ll. 1–15.

41. Ibid., ll. 56–59.

42. Khrushchev, Malenkov, and Molotov election speeches in the *Current Digest of the Soviet Press* 6, no. 11 (1954).

43. "Collective Security," *New Times*, no. 12 (1954), 3–7.

44. "Note of the Soviet Government . . . 31 March 1954," supplement, *New Times*, no. 14 (April 3, 1954); "US Rejects Soviet Proposals for European Security: Text of US Note," Department of State Bulletin, May 17, 1954, 756–57.

45. AVPRF, f. 06, op. 36, pap. 36, d. 169, ll. 1–3; "Statement of the Soviet Government on Relations Between the Soviet Union and the German Democratic Republics," *New Times*, March, 27, 1954, 1.

46. AVPRF, f. 06, op. 36, pap. 36, d. 169, ll. 6–9; f. 082, op. 42, pap. 284, d. 14, ll. 34–62.

47. On the Soviet Union and the Geneva Conference, see Ilya V. Gaiduk, *Confronting Vietnam: Soviet Policy toward the Indochina Conflict, 1954–1963* (Washington: Woodrow Wilson Center Press, 2003); and Marie Olsen, *Soviet-Vietnam Relations and the Role of China, 1949–1964* (London: Routledge, 2006).

48. "Statement of the Soviet Government on the Geneva Conference," *New Times*, July 24, 1952, 2.

49. "Note of the Soviet Government of July 24, 1954," supplement, *New Times*, no. 31 (1954), 4–8.

50. "Statement of the Ministry of Foreign Affairs of the USSR," supplement, *New Times*, no. 37 (1954), 2–5.

51. "Note of the Soviet Government to the Governments of France, Great Britain and the USA," *New Times*, no. 44 (1954), 3–8. This contains the text of both the Western and Soviet notes.

52. "Note of the Soviet Government to the Governments of Europe and the USA," *New Times*, no. 46 (1954), 2–4.
53. "Conference of European Countries on Safeguarding European Peace and Security, Moscow, November 29–December 2, 1954," *New Times*, no. 49, December 4, 1954, 15, 69.
·54. AVPRF, f. 06, op. 13a, pap. 27, d. 27, ll. 2–4.
55. AVPRF, f. 06, op. 14, pap. 13, d. 183; and pap. 4, d. 54, ll. 38–39, 68–74. I have profited from the reconstruction of the drafting process in Nina E. Bystrova, *SSSR i Formirovanie Voenno-Blokogo Protivostoyaniya v Evrope (1945–1955gg)*, vol. 2 (Moscow: Institut Rossiiskoi Istorii, 2005), 471–77.
56. "Statement of the Soviet Government on the German Question," *New Times*, no. 4 (1955), 5.
57. Vyacheslav M. Molotov, "The International Situation and the Foreign Policy of the Soviet Government," *New Times*, no. 7 (1955), 21.
58. The text of this speech can be found on the website of the Cold War International History Project.
59. For the Bulganin speech and the other documentation, see "Conference of European Countries on Safeguarding European Peace and Security, Warsaw, 11–14 May 1955," *New Times*, no. 21, May 21, 1955, 5–70.
60. The text of the Warsaw Pact is widely available on the Internet.
61. *New Times*, no. 7 (1955), 23.
62. Rolf Steininger, "1955: The Austrian State Treaty and the German Question," *Diplomacy and Statecraft* 3, no. 3 (1992), 500.
63. "Soviet-Austrian Communiqué," *New Times*, no. 17 (1955), 2.
64. "Statement by V. M. Molotov at the Signing of the Austrian State Treaty, May 15, 1955," *New Times*, no. 22 (1955), 4.
65. "*Plenum TsK KPSS, Iul' 1955 goda: Stenograficheskii Otchet: Vypusk Vtoroi*," RGANI, f. 2, op. 1, d. 143. The discussion on the Austrian question may be found in ll. 151, 161–62, 167, 175, 180–81, 196, 199–200.
66. Molotov's opposition within the Presidium on the Yugoslavian question is documented in Alexander A. Fursenko, ed., *Prezidium TsK KPSS, 1954–1964: Chernovye Protokol'nye Zapisi Zasedaniya Stenogrammy* (Moscow: Rosspen, 2004), 41–54.
67. *Plenum TsK KPSS, Iul' 1955 goda*, l. 196.
68. These documents can be found in AVPRF, f. 06, op. 14, pap. 9, d. 116.
69. *Plenum TsK KPSS, Iul' 1955 goda*, l. 141.
70. See F. I. Novik, *"Ottepel'" i Inertsiya Khlodnoi Voiny (Germanskaya Politika SSSR v 1953–1955gg.)* (Moscow: Institut Rossiiskoi Istorii, 2001).
71. The relevant documentation may be found in *Ustanovlenie Diplomaticheskikh Otnoshenii Mezhdu SSSR i FRG: Sbornik Dokumentov i Materialov* (Moscow: MGIMO, 2005).
72. For the text of the treaty and the other announcements, see *New Times*, no. 39 (1955), 8–12. On the process leading to the treaty, see Novik, *"Ottepel',"* 156–69.
73. Ibid.

74. "Proposal of the Soviet Government on the Reduction of Armaments, Prohibition of Atomic Weapons, and Elimination of the Threat of Another War," *New Times*, no. 20 (1955), 2–6.

75. Bulganin's opening and closing speeches: *New Times*, no. 30 (1955), 15–19, and no. 31 (1955), 20–23.

76. The Soviet records of the foreign ministers' discussions at Geneva can be found in "Stenogrammy Zasedaniya Ministrov Inostrannykh Del na Soveshchanii Glav Pravitel'stv Chetyrekh Derzhav v Zheneve," AVPRF, f. 448, op. 1, pap. 3, d. 8.

77. The Soviet record of the private exchanges between the four heads of government may be found in "Zhenevskoe Soveshchanie Glav Pravitel'stv 1955g: Stenogrammy Zasedanii Glav Pravitel'stv Chetyrekh Derzhav," AVPRF, f. 445, op. 1, pap. 1, d. 1, ll. 74–76, 92–97, 106–13, 156–69.

78. See Saki Dockrill, "The Eden Plan and European Security" in Gunter Bischof and Saki Dockrill, eds., *Cold War Respite: The Geneva Summit of 1955* (Baton Rouge: Louisiana State University Press, 2000).

79. "Directive of the Heads of Government of the Four Powers to the Foreign Ministers, Geneva, July 23, 1955," *Foreign Relations of the United States, 1955–1957*, vol. 5 (Washington: Government Printing Office, 1988), 527–28.

80. Fursenko, *Prezidium TsK KPSS, 1954–1964: Chernovye Protokol'nye Zapisi Zasedaniya Stenogrammy*, 14. The text of the draft statement may be found in Alexander A. Fursenko, ed., *Prezidium TsK KPSS, 1954–1964: Postanovleniya, 1954–1958* (Moscow: Rosspen, 2006), 97–100.

81. See "Molotov and the Importance of Political Theory," *Current Digest of the Soviet Press* 7, no. 38 (November 1955).

82. "Miting v Berline po Sluchau Prebyvaniya v Germanskoi Demokraticheskoi Respublike Sovetskoi Pravitel'stvennoi Delegatsii: Rech' Tovarishcha N.S. Khrushcheva," *Pravda*, July 27, 1955.

83. "Press-Konferentsiya u V. M. Molotova v San-Frantsisko," *Pravda*, June 27, 1955.

84. *New Times*, no. 33 (1955), 14.

85. "Proekt Informatsii Poslov Stran Narodnoi Demokratii ob Itogakh Zhenevskogo Soveshchaniya Glav Pravitel'stv Chetyrekh Derzhav," AVPRF, f. 06, op. 14, pap. 3, d. 44, ll. 29–47.

86. AVPRF, f. 06, op. 14, pap. 3, d. 46, l. 1.

87. "O Sozdanii Germanskoi Konfederatsii," AVPRF, f. 06, op. 14, pap. 3, d. 46, ll. 28–29.

88. Ibid., l. 82.

89. Ibid., ll. 73–108.

90. Eisenhower Papers, A. Whitman file, International Meetings series, box 2, Geneva Conference 1955 (4), Eisenhower Library.

91. Molotov's speeches at the conference can be found in *Soviet News*, October 28, 31, and November 1, 2, 3, 1955.

92. Department of State Bulletin, November 14, 1955, 780–81.

93. The resolution and the Presidium decision to reject it can be found in Fursenko, *Prezidium TsK KPSS, 1954–1964: Postanovleniya*, 104–7.

94. Fursenko, *Prezidium TsK KPSS, 1954–1964: Chernovye Protokol'nye Zapisi Zasedaniya Stenogrammy*, 58–60.
95. *Soviet News*, November 9, 1955, 2.
96. Harold Macmillan, *Tides of Fortune, 1945–1955* (London: Macmillan, 1969), 649.
97. Troyanovskii, *Cherez Gody i Rasstoyaniya*, 190.
98. Department of State Bulletin, November, 21, 1955, 825–27.
99. AVPRF, f. 06, op. 14, pap. 4, d. 51, ll. 2–10.
100. "Zasedaniya Verkhovnogo Soveta SSSR: Rech' Tovarishcha N.S. Khrushcheva," *Pravda*, December 30, 1955.
101. Resis, *Molotov Remembers*, 75.

Chapter 6. Defiant in Defeat (1956–1986)

1. Resis, *Molotov Remembers*, 215.
2. Fursenko, *Prezidium TsK KPSS, 1954–1964*, vol. 1 (Moscow: Rosspen, 2004), 89, 95–99.
3. "Molotov's Congress Speech on Foreign Policy," *Current Digest of the Soviet Press* 8, no. 9 (1956), 16–20.
4. Watson, *Molotov*, 256.
5. See Polly Jones, "From Stalinism to Post-Stalinism: De-Mythologising Stalin, 1953–1956" in Harold Shukman, ed., *Redefining Stalinism* (London: Frank Cass, 2003).
6. *Reabilitatsiya: Kak Eto Bylo*, vol. 1 (Moscow: Demokratiya, 2000), 296; vol. 2, (Moscow: Demokratiya, 2003), part 2, doc. 4; and part 3, doc. 27.
7. *Prezidium TsK KPSS, 1954–1964*, 135–39.
8. William Taubman, *Khrushchev: The Man and His Era* (New York: W. W. Norton, 2003), 293–94.
9. *Sovetskii Soyuz i Vengerskii Krizis, 1956 goda* (Moscow: Rosspen, 1998), doc. 83. This document is a report on the meeting by Antonin Novotny, the leader of the Communist Party of Czechoslovakia, who attended the Presidium along with other Eastern bloc leaders. An English translation of the document can be found on the website of the Cold War International History Project.
10. *Prezidium TsK KPSS, 1954–1964*, 176, 182, 185, 202, 205.
11. Taubman, *Khrushchev*, 301.
12. *Prezidium TsK KPSS, 1954–1964*, 221–22, 236–39, 245; *Prezidium TsK KPSS, 1954–1964*, vol. 2 (Moscow: Rosspen, 2006), 613–19.
13. Ibid., vol 1, 248–49.
14. Resis, *Molotov Remembers*, 347.
15. *Molotov, Malenkov, Kaganovich, 1957: Stenogramma Iun'skogo Plenuma TsK KPSS i Drugie Dokumenty* (Moscow: Mezhdunarodnyi Fond "Demokratiya," 1998), 38.
16. Ibid., 120.
17. Ibid., 122–32.
18. Ibid., 228–35. As Alexei Filitov has noted, Gromyko's criticism of Molotov in this regard raises more questions than it answers, since the Soviet note to the FRG proposing talks on the establishment of diplomatic relations was is-

sued on June 7, 1955, but the UN conference in San Francisco that Molotov attended took place in June 9–29. See Alexei Filitov, "Adenauers Moskaubesuch 1955: Vor-und Nachspiel im Spiegel der internen sowjetischen Berichte," *Rhondorfer Gesprache*, no. 22, 50–51.

19. Ibid., 565–66.
20. Ibid., 500.
21. Taubman, *Khrushchev*, 368; Resis, *Molotov Remembers*, 347, 364, 366.
22. Leonid Shinkarev, *Tsedenbal i Filatova* (Moscow: Sapronov, 2004), 183–85. I am grateful to Sergey Radchenko for sending me the relevant pages from this book.
23. "Deyatel'nost' V. M. Molotova v Kachestve Chrezvychainogo i Polnomochnogo Posla SSSR v MHR," RGASPI, f. 82, op. 2, dd. 1416a and 1416b passim.
24. Vladislav Zubok and Constantine Pleshakov, *Inside the Kremlin's Cold War* (Cambridge, MA: Harvard University Press, 1996), 90.
25. Taubman, *Khrushchev*, 368.
26. Vyacheslav Nikonov, *Molotov: Molodost'* (Moscow: Vagrius, 2005), 370–71.
27. Resis, *Molotov Remembers*, 318. Some extracts from the unpublished article are reproduced by Nikonov, ibid., 230–31, 520–52, 540.
28. Frederic S. Burin's classic exposition of Sino-Soviet differences on the inevitability of war has yet to be surpassed: "The Communist Doctrine of the Inevitability of War," *The American Political Science Review* 57, no. 2 (June 1963).
29. "Deyatel'nost' V. M. Molotova v Kachestve Predstavitelya SSSR pri Mezhdunarodnom Agenstve po Atomnoi Energii (MAGATE) v Avstrii," RGASPI, f. 82, op. 2, d. 1416v, ll. 23–24.
30. Vladimir Sokolov, "Narkomindel Vyacheslav Molotov," *Mezhdunarodnaya Zhizn'* no. 5 (May 1991), 99, 111.
31. The two documents are cited in *Reabilitatsiya: Kak Eto Bylo*, vol. 2, part 5, doc. 7. This is the report of the appeals committee on Molotov's (unsuccessful) request to have his expulsion from the party overturned.
32. The speeches may be found in Alexander Dallin, ed., *Diversity in International Communism: A Documentary Record, 1961–1963* (New York: Columbia University Press, 1963).
33. Molotov's retirement writings can be found in RGASPI, f. 82, op. 2, dd. 1659–69, 1684–1700. Other writings, including different versions of the texts in these files, are in his family's archive and cited in the Nikonov volume.
34. See Burin, "The Communist Doctrine of the Inevitability of War."
35. "Ob Opasnosti Voiny i Bor'be za Kommunizm" in A. Ryzhikov, *Khrushchevskaya "Ottepel'," 1953–1964* (Moscow: Olma-Press, 2002). This text is based on Molotov's handwritten notes in RGASPI, f. 82, op. 2, d. 1662.
36. "Otdel'nye Mashinnopisnye Listy s Popravkami k Zapiskam V. M. Molotova," RGASPI, f. 82, op. 2, d. 1700. Molotov's private musings in these notes correspond to what he said to Chuev.
37. Nikonov, *Molotov*, 586.
38. Resis, *Molotov Remembers*, 372, 407–8.
39. "Zasedanie Politburo TsK KPSS, 12 Iulya 1984 goda," Hoover Institute.
40. Resis, *Molotov Remembers*, 415.

Chapter 7. Conclusion: Assessing Molotov

1. Resis, *Molotov Remembers*, 353.
2. Archives of the Norwegian Nobel Committee, Oslo.
3. See Timothy Johnston, "Peace or Pacifism?: The Soviet 'Struggle for Peace in All the World,' 1948–54," *Slavic and East European Review* 86, no. 2 (April 2008).

SELECTED BIBLIOGRAPHY

The sources on which this book is based are cited in the notes. This bibliography is restricted to works by or substantially devoted to Molotov.

Bezymensky, Lev. "Vizit V. M. Molotova v Berlin v Noyabre 1940g v Svete Novykh Dokumentov." *Novaya i Noveishaya Istoriya,* no. 6, 1995.
———— and Sergei Gorlov. "On the Eve: V. M. Molotov's Discussions in Berlin, November 1940." *International Affairs* (July 1991).
Bromage, Bernard. *Molotov.* London: Peter Owen, 1956.
Chubariyan, Alexander O., and Vladimir O. Pechatnov. "Molotov 'the Liberal': Stalin's 1945 Criticism of His Deputy." *Cold War History* 1, no. 1 (August 2000).
Fedorenko, N. T. "Zapiski Diplomata: Rabota s Molotovym." *Novaya i Noveishaya Istoriya,* no. 4 (1991).
Haupt, Georges, and Jean-Jacques Marie, eds. *Makers of the Russian Revolution: Biographies of Bolshevik Leaders.* London: Allen & Unwin, 1974.
Kumanev, Georgy. *Govoryat Stalinskie Narkomy.* Smolensk: Rusich, 2005.
Lih, Lars T. et al., eds. *Stalin's Letters to Molotov, 1925–1936.* London and New Haven, CT: Yale University Press, 1995.
Medvedev, Roy. *All Stalin's Men.* Oxford: Basil Blackwell, 1983.
Miner, Steven Merritt. "His Master's Voice: Viacheslav Mikhailovich Molotov as Stalin's Foreign Commissar." In *The Diplomats, 1939–1979,* edited by Gordon A. Craig and Francis L. Loewenheim. Princeton, NJ: Princeton University Press, 1994.
Molotov, Malenkov, Kaganovich, 1957: Stenogramma Iun'skogo Plenuma TsK KPSS i Drugie Dokumenty. Moscow: Mezhdnarodnyi Fond "Demokratiya," 1998.
Molotov, Vyacheslav M. "Ob Opasnosti Voiny i Bor'be za Kommunizm." In A. Pyzhikov, *Khrushchevskaya "Ottepel'," 1953–1964.* Moscow: Olma-Press, 2002.
————. *Problems of Foreign Policy: Speeches and Statements, 1945–1948.* Moscow: Foreign Languages Publishing House, 1949.
————. *Soviet Peace Policy.* London: Lawrence & Wishart, 1941.

Nikonov, Vyacheslav E. *Molotov: Molodost'*. Moscow: Vagrius, 2005.

"On the Eve: V. M. Molotov's Discussions in Berlin, November 1940," *International Affairs* (July 1991).

Pechatnov, Vladimir. "'The Allies Are Pressing on You to Break Your Will': Foreign Policy Correspondence between Stalin and Molotov and Other Politburo Members, September 1945–December 1946." Cold War International History Project, working paper no. 26, September 1999.

———. "V. M. Molotov." In *Ocherki Istorii Ministerstva Inostrannykh Del Rossii*, vol. 3. Moscow: Olma-Press, 2002.

"Pis'mo V. M. Molotova v TsK KPSS (1964g)," *Voprosy Istorii*, nos. 1–6, 2001.

Polonsky, Rachel. *Molotov's Magic Lantern: A Journey in Russian History*. London: Faber and Faber, 2010.

Resis, Albert, ed. *Molotov Remembers*. Chicago: Ivan R. Dee, 1993. (In Russian, Chuev, F. *Sto Sorok Besed s Molotovym: Iz Dnevnika F. Chueva*. Moscow: Terra, 1991.)

Roberts, Geoffrey. "Molotov." In *Encyclopedia of the Cold War*, edited by R. van Dijk et al. London and New York: Routledge, 2008.

———. "Sexing Up the Cold War: New Evidence on the Molotov-Truman Talks of April 1945." *Cold War History* 14, no. 3 (April 2004).

Rzheshevsky, Oleg A., ed. *War and Diplomacy: The Making of the Grand Alliance*. Amsterdam: Harwood Academic Publishers, 1996.

Sokolov, Boris V. *Molotov: Ten' Vozhdya*. Moscow: Ast-Press, 2005.

Sokolov, Vladimir V. "Molotov Vyacheslav Mikhailovich." *Diplomaticheskii Vestnik*, no. 7 (2002).

———. "Narkomindel Vyacheslav Molotov." *Mezhdunarodnaya Zhizn'* (May 1991).

Vasilieva, Larisa. *Kremlin Wives*. London: Weidenfeld & Nicolson, 1994.

Watson, Derek. *Molotov: A Biography*. London: Palgrave, 2005.

———. "Molotov: The Making of the Grand Alliance and the Second Front, 1939–1942." *Europe-Asia Studies* 54, no. 1 (2002).

———. "Molotov and the Moscow Conference, October 1943," British Association for Slavonic and Eastern Studies conference paper (2002). (In French: "Molotov et la Conférence de Moscou Octobre 1943." *Communisme*, no. 74/75 [2003].)

———. *Molotov and Soviet Government: Sovnarkom, 1930–1941*. London: Macmillan, 1996.

———. "Molotov, the War and Soviet Government." Unpublished paper.

———. "Molotov's Apprenticeship in Foreign Policy: The Triple Alliance Negotiations in 1939." *Europe-Asia Studies* 54, no. 2 (2000).

Yerofeyev, Vladimir. "Desyat' Let v Sekretariate Narkomindela," *Mezhdunarodnaya Zhizn'*, nos. 8–9, 1991 (also published in English in *International Affairs*, August-September 1991).

Zubok, Vladislav, and Constantine Pleshakov. *Inside the Kremlin's Cold War*. Cambridge, MA: Harvard University Press, 1996.

INDEX

ABOUT THE AUTHOR

Geoffrey Roberts is a professor and head of the School of History at University College Cork. He is the author of several previously published books on Soviet history, most recently *Stalin's Wars: From World War to Cold War, 1939–1953* (Yale University Press, 2006). He lives in County Cork, Ireland.

CPSIA information can be obtained
at www.ICGtesting.com
Printed in the USA
BVOW06*1146221217
503451BV00005B/7/P